BASMITZVAH PRESENT FROM ROCHEL SEGEL MARCH 2000

TURNABOUT

THE MALBIM ON MEGILLAS ESTHER

TURNABOUT

The Malbim on Megillas Esther

by

Mendel Weinbach

TARGUM / FELDHEIM

First published 1971

Second revised edition

ISBN 0-944070-24-8

Phototypeset at Targum Press

Published by:
Targum Press Inc.
22700 W. Eleven Mile Rd., Southfield, Mich. 48034

Distributed by:
Philipp Feldheim Inc.
200 Airport Executive Park
Spring Valley, N.Y. 10977

Distributed in Israel by:
Nof Books Ltd.
POB 23646
Jerusalem 91235

Printed in Israel

Dedicated to

Reb Yitzchok Feldman
and
Reb Daniel Sukenik
and their families.

Their special friendship and inspiring partnership in Klal work have been responsible for a "turnabout" in my own dedication to Torah and Klal Yisrael.

Acknowledgments

Special thanks to the following:

- My wife, Sheindel, who has made her own significant contribution to the world of Torah literature in English, for her unique understanding and encouragement.

- Rav Nota Schiller and all of his colleagues at Ohr Somayach Institutions, especially Reb Yehoshua Bezalel Kaplan, Reb Michoel Schoen, and Reb Yirmiyahu Abramov, for creating a revolution in the Torah world and producing thousands of *talmidim* whose personal "turnabouts" could fill many a volume.

- My many *talmidim* throughout the world, who have taught me more than I was able to teach them.

- The staff of Targum Press for their talented and dedicated efforts in producing this book.

TABLE OF CONTENTS

Foreword

he heart of this effort is the adaptation of the Malbim's commentary on Megillas Esther to a novelette form of the Purim Story.

Megillas Esther is not only one of the sacred twenty-four *seforim* of *Tanach,* it is also the account of one of the best known chapters of Jewish history. The reading of this *sefer* is mandatory once each year for every Jewish man, woman and child. Its story has been the subject of the widest range of interpretations, from the *drashos* of scholars to the plays of Hebrew-school children, and its theme of miraculous heavenly intervention has been the inspiration of troubled Jews throughout the ages.

But the casual reader of Megillas Esther can, at best, appreciate only one dimension of the magnificent Purim Story. Character and motivation are difficult to discern from a simple reading of the text. We therefore owe a great debt of gratitude to the Malbim for opening our eyes to the hidden meanings lurking behind the apparent redundancies and superfluities which abound in Megillas Esther. This giant of Torah commentary has shown us a logical step by step development of the plot, and has endowed each character's action with both purpose and pattern.

For those who are accustomed to the Midrashic interpretation of Megillas Esther, the Malbim's version of the Purim Story may come as a surprise. But the distinction between equally sacred *pshat* and *drush* is stressed by such eminent commentaries as the Ramban and Ibn Ezra. Even Rashi, who included a great many *midrashim* in his commentary, sometimes goes to great lengths to stress the difference between these two dimensions of Torah interpretation. It might be said that *pshat* is the proper reading of the lines while *drush* is the reading between the lines, both approaches emanating from Sinai.

In the "reading of the lines" the Malbim is incomparable. We have translated the questions he posed on text and plot as a basis for his interpretation. This has also made it necessary to translate the Hebrew text according to the way the Malbim understood the meaning of the words. This reason, as well as considerations of accuracy and style, have necessitated a translation somewhat different from the standard one.

The Purim Story as we here present it is a faithful rendition of the Malbim's interpretation, and imaginary dialogue has been added only in rare instances where there was a need to flesh out the narrative. Historical background and a chronological table have been added in order to give the reader a broader perspective. Since the entire value of this effort rests on the reputation of the Malbim we have included a biographical sketch describing the man and his impact on his and future generations.

We offer thanks to G-d for enabling us to edit and publish this work, and we pray that its success will mark the beginning of a long overdue introduction of the Malbim's magnificent writings to the English-speaking public.

M.W.

Historical Background of Megillas Esther

The miracle described in Megillas Esther took place during the Babylonian exile, only four years before the beginning of the building of the Second Beis Hamikdash. Mordechai and the rest of the Jewish elite were exiled by Nevuchadnetzar along with King Yechonyah (Yehoyachin), in the year 3327. Eleven years later, in 3338, the Beis Hamikdash was destroyed and almost all of the remaining Jews were taken into captivity by the Babylonian Empire. The Babylonian dynasty of Nevuchadnetzar came to an end in 3389 with the assassination of Belshatzar, foreseen by Daniel in the "writing on the wall," and power was transferred to the Persians and Medes, with Darius the Mede ascending the throne. In 3390, seventy years after Babylon first extended its power over Israel, Koresh the Persian granted permission for Jews to return to their homeland and build a new Beis Hamikdash. Under pressure from the "enemies of Yehudah and Binyamin" in Eretz Yisrael, King Koresh ordered a halt to this construction. This ban was in effect during the entire reign of

Achashveirosh and provides the background for our Sages' explanation of his offer to do anything for Esther "up to half the kingdom." This, says the Gemara in *Masechta Megillah,* was intended to exclude "something which stands in the middle of the kingdom—the Beis Hamikdash, which is located in the center of the universe."

This ban was finally lifted by King Darius the Second, whom our Sages identify as the son of Queen Esther and heir to his father's throne, in the year 3408, seventy years after the destruction of the first Beis Hamikdash.

The feast described at the beginning of the Megillah took place in the year 3395, when Achashveirosh mistakenly calculated that the date for the prophesied redemption of exiled Jewry had already passed. He followed in the path of his predecessor Belshatzar and used the stolen vessels of the Beis Hamikdash, incurring the wrath of heaven and bringing about the death of Vashti.

The miracle of Purim occurred in the twelfth and thirteenth years of Achashveirosh's reign in the year 3404-3405.

Chronology of the Purim Miracle

3395 Feast of Achashveirosh in the third year of his reign; Queen Vashti, granddaughter of Nevuchadnetzar, slain for defying the king.

3399 Teves—Esther becomes queen in place of Vashti. Mordechai appointed to king's gate; Bigsan-Seresh plot; promotion of Haman.

3404 Nisan 13—Haman casts lots; sends out letters; Mordechai sends message to Esther; three day fast begins.

Nisan 15—On third day of fast Esther comes before king; Achashveirosh and Haman attend Esther's banquet.

Nisan 16—Haman leads Mordechai through Shushan streets; joins king at second banquet and is hanged after being exposed.

3405 Adar 13—Jews turn the tables by subduing their enemies; ten sons of Haman slain in Shushan the Capital.

Adar 14—Jews in Shushan destroy their enemies; bodies of Haman's sons hanged. Jews in other cities rest and celebrate.

Adar 15—Jews in Shushan rest and celebrate.

3406 Writing of the Megillah and its acceptance as part of *Tanach.*

THE PURIM STORY

Chapter I

The king looked down at his capital from a palace tower and sighed. Achashveirosh was a king with a problem. He had power and wealth, and ruled over the entire known world, all the one hundred and twenty-seven nations in it. But he did not like the limited monarchy which characterized his reign. He hated to hear foolish talk about the king's responsibility to his subjects. How he longed for the absolute power of a Sancheirev or Nevuchadnetzar, who treated their subjects as slaves and had the freedom of doing whatever they desired with them. And talk of wealth! His finance minister was always cutting down on his personal spending with the argument that the national treasury belonged to the people and that the king was only its guardian. How wonderful it would be to have the powers of a Pharaoh and to know that all of the nation's riches were his own to use as he wished. But it wasn't the finance minister alone who annoyed this king. Whatever he did he always had to ask some minister or other for advice or approval. Every time he planned some drastic move he was reminded of the laws of the land. So he dreamed of the day that he would no longer have to worry about ministers and laws, and he could exercise his royal judgment freely.

This Babylonian capital that stretched before him in all its royal grandeur had come to symbolize for him his limitations. Why did he have to hold court here in this city just because his kingly predecessors had done so? A great king such as he should surely have the right to establish a new beautiful capital of his own where he would build a splendid palace worthy of an absolute monarch.

But Achashveirosh was not one to let such obstacles stand in his way. After all, he had been born a commoner and had succeeded in reaching this mighty throne of the Persians and Medes. It had been no easy task. True, his great fortune had enabled him to hire great armies and buy influence everywhere. But merely conquering nations doesn't make one a king. There was always the danger of revolution if the people felt that they were being ruled by someone unqualified to wear a royal crown. His rise to power was so swift that too many people remembered his common origins. That is why he married Vashti, princess of Nevuchadnetzar's family. Her royal lineage had given his reign the legitimacy and recognition he sought, but it had also aggravated the problem now facing him. Forgotten was the fact that he was a self-made king who owed his throne to no one and was entitled to rule with a free hand. His queen was a constant reminder of the rules which bound royal courts owing their existence to the allegiance of their subjects.

If he had come this far Achashveirosh saw no reason not to realize all of his ambitions for ultimate power. He drew up a plan of action designated to remove these obstacles from his path. The royal capital was moved from its present location to the city of Shushan. Plenty of mumbling was heard and some even dared to whisper that this commoner turned king was a haughty fellow indeed to transfer his throne from the capital occupied by the great kings before him. The implications of this move were not lost on the people either. Well did they understand the significance of the fact that he had not inherited a Babylonian throne thanks to their approval, but that he had arrived at his power on his own and would henceforth rule them as slaves from his new Persian capital.

Two years had passed of Achashveirosh's reign, years filled with scheming towards his objective of achieving absolute power. In the third year of his reign he unfolded to his trusted ministers a master plan for reaching this goal.

"Proclaim a great feast for all the officers and servants of my realm. Let invitations go out at once to all the princes and ministers whom I have appointed, as well as to all my brave soldiers and faithful servants."

"But your majesty," asked one of his ministers, "what about the nobles and princes of all the provinces? Are they not to be invited?"

"Nobles and princes indeed! They are simply common servants as far as I am concerned, for I was not the one who raised them to their posts. Why, I would not trade the viceroy of my largest province for one of the ministers whom I have appointed since ascending the throne."

"But the subjects in the provinces will not understand this, your majesty, and they will be deeply insulted that they are not represented at this feast."

"Don't be a fool! Of course I intend to invite these noblemen. But only after the lowliest archer in my army and the simplest servant in my palace have received their invitations will the call go to these insolent foreigners who still dare to speak with reverence of the kings before me. Let them stew with their memories of previous rulers. They will now learn that only those who owe their positions to my grace have any importance in this kingdom."

Now that the invitations had been ordered the king turned to the problem of financing the feast.

"This shall be the most magnificent feast the world has ever known. No expense is to be spared in making it a great success!"

"If your majesty will allow me," haltingly interrupted the finance minister, "I will remind the king that we are already very close to exceeding the royal budget for celebrations."

"You and your cursed budget!" thundered the king. "You speak of it as if it was your own money, or the people's. If not for my mighty conquests the treasury would be empty today. It is my gold and silver which fill the royal coffers and I intend to use them as I wish. So much money will be spent on this feast that no one will ever forget that all of the realm's riches are mine, and mine alone."

Everyone expected this gala feast to last for a day or two, but Achashveirosh had other plans. He was determined to make an unforgettable impression on his subjects by exhibiting the riches of his kingdom and his mastery over this wealth. Only after one hundred and eighty days of displaying the majesty of his power did the feast finally come to a conclusion.

But no sooner had this feast ended than the king announced another feast for the citizens of the capital, Shushan. Everyone was invited, regardless of station and rank, for all were equally subservient to a king who was to wield absolute power.

"This feast shall last for only seven days," ordered the king, "but it shall take place in the court of the garden on my palace grounds."

"That will be a grave insult to Persian custom, your majesty!" ventured the king's legal advisor. "Persian rulers have never allowed anyone save nobles and princes to enter the king's courtyard."

"That is precisely why I am arranging the feast there. The citizens of Shushan, where I have established the capital for my reign of absolute power, are as deserving of entry as any nobleman. The time has come for the lords of the land to realize that they are servants no more important than the lowliest subject. Only then will they cease advising me to curb my powers and allow me to rule this kingdom as befits a mighty king."

Magnificent tents soon sprang up in the open palace courtyard. Their walls were made of white weaves, fine cottons and blue materials. Even the cords which bound these tents to the silver-based marble pillars were made of fine linen and purple strands. The guests were seated on couches of gold and silver whose beauty vied with the splendor of pavements formed from precious green and white stones, shell and onyx marble.

But the service exceeded everything in its uniqueness. A royal decree abolished the need for observing the elaborate rules of etiquette which attended drinking at Persian banquets, so that there was no longer any need to wait for the more respectable guests to first partake. Fine wine flowed incessantly and no one had to hurry his drinking because a neighbor awaited the use of his cup. Each guest received a clever golden bottle which included both the wine and the golden cup.

Just as the preparations were completed for this great feast, Queen Vashti announced that she too was making a feast. The king's reaction was another link in his intricate strategy and he confided his thoughts to his closest advisors.

"Let Vashti make her party. But our royal consent is based on two conditions. She must invite only women and hold the party in my royal house, not her queenly palace chambers. I have suffered enough from the general impression that I owe my throne to her royal ancestry. True, the fact that she was a Babylonian princess helped me calm the people's fears about my common background. But I have long outgrown the need for such crutches. Total power is at stake now and Vashti must be reduced in importance. To allow her to make a feast for the nobles and princes just as I did and to let her entertain in her part of the palace would only serve to strengthen the impression that she is a queen by her own right and I a mere consort. She shall therefore be permitted to arrange only such a feast which will make it clear that she is queen by grace of my majesty."

Vashti, as a stumbling block to his bold designs for power, had been preying on the king's mind throughout the week of festivities and on the seventh day he decided to settle this problem once and for all. Seven chamberlains sat before the king to cater to his every wish—Mehuman, Bizzesa, Charvona, Bigsa, Avagsa, Zeisar and Charkas. To these chamberlains he now turned with a wine-happy smile on his face.

"Bring Vashti to this feast immediately so that I may show all the nations and princes her splendid beauty. Those foolish princes of India and Ethiopia who whisper that I married Vashti in order to gain a claim to the throne have never seen how attractive the queen is. Now they will realize that a mighty king such as I need no such claims and that I took her as a wife only because of her extraordinary beauty.

"But," he whispered to the one nearest him, "make certain that she does not come here wearing her crown. She will be permitted to don her crown only after she is in my presence because she is a queen thanks only to me."

Vashti, however, had ideas of her own.

"Out, you insolent rascals," she shouted at the chamberlains who came to abruptly fetch her away from her noble guests. "Am I a common concubine that the king sends his servants to fetch me unto him! Has Achashveirosh forgotten how he became such an important king? The royal blood of Nevuchadnetzar pulsing through my veins is the foundation of his throne and I shall not allow him to insult me like this.

Tell your king that Queen Vashti refuses to appear for him and his guests."

As the shocked guests began buzzing with excitement over the queen's show of independence the chamberlains beat a hasty retreat to report their failure to the king.

"Insolent woman, how dare she refuse to obey my command! She shall pay with her life."

Just as their womenfolk moments before, the king's guests were electrified by this amazing turn of events. Here and there a voice was heard in defense of Vashti but the overwhelming feeling was one of sympathy for the hospitable ruler who had been so insulted by a disobedient wife. Domestic disobedience, however, worried Achashveirosh much less than anyone imagined, despite his outraged cry. His real anger was saved for the way in which the queen had wrecked all of his well laid plans for power, and he confided his frustration in one of his trusted chamberlains.

"I spent a fortune on these feasts in order to project to my subjects the image of an absolute ruler. Success was just within my reach when that vicious woman made her terrible scene and publicly refuted the claims I had so carefully prepared. No punishment could be too great for such treachery."

Word of Vashti's deed quickly spread through the palace and everyone anxiously waited for the trial at which she would be judged for her rebellion against the king.

By the time the king had begun arranging the trial for Vashti, his love for her had overcome his anger and he sought to have her acquitted of any guilt. The special royal court which judged all offenses against the crown had already been called into session, but the king quickly ordered its adjournment.

"Queen Vashti need not be tried before the royal court," he explained, "because she is not accused of a crime committed by a subject against his ruler. As a queen of royal blood she can be tried only as a wife who has disobeyed her husband. For such a trial, domestic judges will suffice."

After carefully studying a list of all prospective judges, the king called together seven princes of Persia and Media. Karshena, Sheisar, Admassa, Sarshish, Meres, Marsena and Memuchan were princes who constantly sat before the king and could discern from his facial expressions how he wished them to judge Vashti.

"Princes of Persia and Media," he charged them, "you have been appointed to judge the queen because of several reasons. A queen should, first of all, be judged only by men of such noble rank as you all possess. You also have been responsible for justice in the realm for many years and have the experience necessary for judging such an important case. Finally, the crown is determined to keep this entire affair as quiet as possible and there is no need to involve judges who were not present at the feast and are unaware of what transpired."

At this point, the king took a long, hard look at each of his seven judges and concluded his charge.

"I must insist that you judge not only the legal aspect of the case but the moral one as well. The queen disobeyed her husband, a grave offense in our society, but you must consider the mitigating circumstances in this matter. You know how modest our Persian women are. Rarely is one of them seen outside of her home, and even then she is dressed most modestly. Asking a Persian woman to appear immodestly before a large gathering of men is inviting an inevitable refusal. Please keep all this in mind in reaching your decision as to what should be done with Queen Vashti."

The judges conferred together for a moment and one of them, Memuchan, requested permission to address the king.

"If your majesty will allow me to question one of his statements, I believe that we can arrive at true justice in this trial. We have been told that a factor guiding our selection as judges is the crown's desire for secrecy. But I ask, can there still be any secrecy left? Vashti flaunted her defiance of the king in front of all the princesses of Persia and Media and her rebellion will have repercussions throughout the realm!

"Of course the princesses who were there will not necessarily learn from Vashti to disobey their husbands since they heard her explain that her entire role as queen was at stake. But my wife already told me today what Vashti said about the king owing his very throne to her royal lineage. This same report has already reached all the princes of the kingdom and will completely upset his majesty's claim to absolute power. We all know that a king such as his majesty is entitled to such power by virtue of his conquests. No, your majesty, Vashti's crime is not a private affair between a Persian and his disobedient wife. It is a rebellion which affects the role of the king and is therefore of grave concern to the entire realm.

"But were we even to judge this as a domestic issue, Vashti's crime is beyond forgiveness. The women of the realm will not hear the details of her refusal. They will simply conclude that Vashti refused a simple request made by her royal husband. When their own husbands will request something, they will inevitably refuse them as well, arguing that Vashti refused a much smaller request of a much greater husband.

"In conclusion, if we allow Vashti's crime to go unpunished, we shall be guilty of shaming the men of the realm in the eyes of their wives and in incurring the wrath of the princes and nobles against the king's claim to greater power."

Taken aback by this sudden challenge to his plans for rescuing his beloved Vashti from death, the king paused for a while to weigh his love for his wife against his ambitions for power. No sooner had the crafty Memuchan discerned that the king had made peace with the fact that Vashti must be condemned than he continued his address.

"If it pleases your majesty, I would like to suggest how he

can still achieve the goal of absolute power despite this setback with Vashti. The parliament of ministers must be stripped of its power to issue and approve legislation. Henceforth the king must rule by ukase. His royal decree will automatically become the law of the land, without the approval of any ministers, and it will be recorded in the permanent statutes of the kingdom. This bold move will establish absolute power for the crown, as befits such a mighty king."

"You counsel wisely, Memuchan," said the king, "but you have not yet told us how this plan involves Vashti and how we shall salvage the honor of husbands throughout the realm."

"In order to firmly introduce this new manner of ruling," continued Memuchan, "the king must choose a crucial, popular issue as the subject for his first royal decree. May I therefore suggest that this be an order that Vashti be denied permission to come before the king for the purpose of appeasing him. This move will gain wide approval for the king's power of independent judgment and will also accomplish the restoration of manly honor throughout the realm. Should Vashti be executed without such a prior decree, feminine insubordination may yet rear its ugly head. Women will say that the king could not induce her to come before him and therefore had her put to death. Vashti will thus be a martyr for feminine equality and a dangerous inspiration to all wives of spirit. Now that it shall be heard throughout the lands of the kingdom that the king has decreed a ban on Vashti's appearance before him this will all be corrected. Everyone will conclude from this decree that Vashti realized her error and sought to come before the king and beg his forgiveness. It will be clear that she was prevented from doing so by the king's decree and her death will be a powerful lesson for all wives on the danger of defying their husbands."

"But what will happen after Vashti is gone?" asked the king. "Shall I not have the same problems with my next queen?"

"The next queen, your majesty," smiled Memuchan, "must be chosen for her own qualities, not her ancestry. Furthermore, she will not dare to defy the king because the fate of Vashti will deter her."

Memuchan's plan was laid before the princes and nobles of the realm and they agreed to abdicate their legislative powers in favor of an absolute monarchy. With his new power the king turned his attention to further improving the two situations aggravated by the late Vashti's deed. The first was in the area of politics. The official tongue of the realm had always been Persian, for that was the language of the dominant land. All correspondence to and from the government had to be conducted in Persian and schools in every land taught this language as a required subject. But with Achashveirosh's new dimension of power it was no longer Persia dominating but the king himself. Persians were the same subjects as all other nations and their language no longer had any supremacy. A royal decree therefore was issued to this effect.

"King Achashveirosh, mighty ruler of one hundred and twenty-seven nations, has this day decreed that henceforth each nation may address the king in its own tongue and write to him in its own script."

But the king's initial use of his new power was not limited to political activity. He was intent on further enhancing the dignity and power of the man in his home in order to undo the impression caused by Vashti's disobedience. To this end he added the following to the first royal decree.

"The king furthermore decrees that henceforth it shall not be sufficient for a woman to simply honor and obey her husband. She shall be considered his property and he has the right to punish her according to his judgment. The man shall be the absolute master in his home."

Chapter II

"Ah, that Vashti was a queen who honored the crown she wore," sighed the king. "How shall I ever find a woman of her beauty and heredity to take as my queen?"

Enough time had passed for the king's anger to subside, and his memories of the dead queen were fond ones. He turned to the young servants attending him and spelled out his other fears concerning his new queen.

"Even if I do succeed in finding someone as noble and attractive as Vashti, how can I be sure that she will not incite me to decree the same fate upon her and gain notoriety throughout the world as a wife-slayer? Will not this fear also dissuade any likely young lady from consenting to be my queen?"

The king's servants were equal to the challenges presented by their worried master.

"The king need have no doubts about finding a worthy replacement for Vashti as queen. If a search is conducted throughout the realm a virgin shall certainly be found whose beauty is equal to that of Vashti's. No attention need be paid to her family since a mighty king such as his majesty requires no royal lineage to bolster his claim to the throne.

"It is needless for the king to be concerned lest such a lovely woman refuses to be queen. If no one qualifies from the maidens who voluntarily come forth the king must order the conscription of all beautiful maidens throughout his kingdom. Special care must be taken to appoint new officers in charge of this project so that the wealthy will find it difficult to bribe them in order to overlook their daughters.

"Finally, the king need not fear that the new queen will be a haughty woman who will defy him in the manner of her predecessor. Let all candidates be put in the custody of the king's chamberlain, Heigai, keeper of the women. Let none of them bring cosmetics from their homes so that they will be dependent on the ointments supplied by the chamberlains. Thus will the future queen be trained to be subservient to the king's servants and will not dare to show such indignation as that exhibited by Vashti at being called for by the king's chamberlains."

The idea proposed by Mehuman and his fellow chamberlains appealed to the king and he immediately utilized his new power to issue the necessary decree. Machinery was soon set into motion for the finding of a new queen.

In another part of Shushan there lived a Jew by the name of Mordechai. He was a Benjaminite and a descendant of King Shaul. He had arrived years ago in the Persian capital together with the nobles of Yehudah who had been carried into exile from Jerusalem by the Babylonian king, Nevuchadnetzar, along with their ruler, Yechonyah, King of Yehudah. With Mordechai lived his young and beautiful cousin, Hadassah, otherwise known as Esther. Her parents had died while she was yet very young and Mordechai had adopted her as his ward.

When Mordechai heard the king's decree regarding the

gathering of young maidens he was determined to protect his ward from being defiled by the heathen king. He concealed her from the king's agents although he realized that discovery might well mean his life. He was in Shushan too long to claim ignorance of the decree and the activities going on in the capital. As her sole guardian he alone would surely be held responsible for withholding such a gem from the king, especially since he was descended from royalty and worthy of offering his ward as a bride to the king. His crime would certainly be magnified in its intensity by the fact that he was a stranger in this land who owed a debt of gratitude to the king's hospitality.

All of these considerations did not faze Mordechai. Not tempted by the promise of glory when the announcement was first made about a search for a queen, and not intimidated by the threat of death mentioned in the ensuing decree of conscription, Mordechai persisted in hiding Esther. But his efforts were to no avail. Esther was finally discovered and dragged off to the palace. There she was put in the custody of Heigai, keeper of the women, along with all the other candidates.

Esther, however, was not treated like the other candidates. Her fear that she and Mordechai would be severely punished for their defiance of the king's decree turned out to be unfounded. To her surprise, she found herself instead being favored with special attention. Her charms had so captivated Heigai, and so convinced him that she would be the chosen one, that he began treating her as a future queen.

"Have the new girl begin applying the winter ointments of myrrh oil immediately," Heigai ordered one of the attendants.

"But it is already well into winter, my lord," replied the startled attendant, "and we never start a maiden on her ointments in the middle of a season. My lord himself explained to us that each maiden's beauty and health must be tested against the effects of the year's four complete seasons before she is permitted to meet the king. We have been providing each young lady with myrrh oil to massage warmth into her body during the six cold months and perfumes for banishing the discomforts of the six warm ones. We have never before allowed this twelve-month period of preparation to begin after a season is already under way."

"This particular young lady is an exception to the rule," replied Heigai. "Furthermore, I want her to receive special gifts and to be provided with the seven maids who customarily attend a queen. She and her maids are to receive the finest rooms in the women's house and the best food available. Some day you will see that I have not guessed wrong."

Esther was indeed a mysterious young lady. Despite all the favors showered upon her, she refused to divulge to Heigai the identity of her family and her people. Well did she recall the instructions Mordechai had given her while she was hiding from the king's agents.

"My dear Esther," Mordechai had said, "if they ever do take you away to the palace, you must do everything short of sacrificing your life to avoid becoming the wife of this heathen king. Never tell them who you are so that they will suspect you of being some unwanted child, abandoned by its mother and brought up in my home. The king's dignity will not allow him to make someone of such a questionable background his queen, and you will be sent away."

But what was even more mysterious about Esther was her reaction to Heigai's treatment of her as a future queen. She continued to behave as a prisoner waiting for sentence to be passed upon her crime of originally avoiding the king's agents. Each day Mordechai would visit the courtyard below the women's quarters and inquire about Esther's fate.

"Why does he come each day?" angrily asked Heigai of Esther. "He always asks what has been decided, as though I were holding you as some condemned prisoner. Here I am treating you like a queen but you both behave as if we plan to punish you or send you away from the palace in disgrace. This is all part of the silent rebellion you began by refusing to tell me about your family. You had better start thinking about becoming more cooperative if you are concerned for your safety."

Esther ignored the mounting danger created by her silence and anxiously watched the days go by with no change in her situation. All of her hopes of being discredited as a candidate began to fade as the time approached for her scheduled appearance before the king. Each day she saw another one of the maidens from the house of the women leave for her appointment with the king. She noticed that they all went with smiles upon their faces despite the fact that many of them had been brought to the palace by force and that all but one would hereafter spend the rest of their lives as royal concubines. The king had cleverly arranged that each maiden be given, on that particular evening, any gift she requested so that she would look forward happily to her rendezvous.

When Esther's turn finally arrived she refused to request any gifts in addition to those which Heigai forced upon her. Deep in her heart she knew that she was offering the king much more than the health and beauty demanded of all candidates. She was the daughter of a tzaddik and her exceptional virtues had been so developed by her wise guardian that she was truly fit to be a queen. But not the wife of this heathen! No threat had intimidated her until now and no gifts could now sway her from her refusal to be defiled by the king. This stubbornness so riled Heigai that he was momentarily tempted to put her to death for insubordination. But Esther's charm once again overcame his anger and he ordered that she be dragged to the king's chambers.

So it was, that in the month of Teves, in the seventh year

of Achashveirosh's reign, Esther found such favor in the eyes of the king that he loved her more than all of his wives and concubines and chose her from among all the candidates. He personally placed the crown upon her head, proclaimed her queen, and set her upon the throne vacated by Vashti.

The king was extremely proud of his new queen and found in her every virtue he had dreamed of. He was disturbed only by her refusal to divulge her origins and was determined to break her silence.

"My dear Esther," he said, "I am proclaiming a great feast to be known as Esther's Feast. All of my princes and servants shall be invited to participate and you will be greatly honored. It's a shame, though, that the princes keep whispering that you are nothing more than some abandoned foundling with no legitimate family. Perhaps you will use this opportunity to quash this rumor by divulging the secret of your background."

But when he saw that pride and honor could not influence her to disclose her secret, the king attempted a different strategy.

"Let there be a reduction in taxes for all the lands of the realm," Esther heard him announce, "and have magnificent royal gifts sent to them. How sad that we know not the land of our new queen for we should surely have showered its people with the most wonderful presents."

Frustrated by his inability to move Esther with the lures of honor for her and her people, the king turned to his trusted advisors for help.

"Perhaps the queen is too insecure to reveal her family," ventured one of these counsellors. "She may be afraid to admit coming from a lowly family and risk losing her throne to one of the other candidates."

"Then I shall dismiss all the maidens who have not yet been introduced to me so that Esther will have no more reason to fear competition. Furthermore, I shall appoint Mordechai, in whose home she was found, to a position of judge at the palace gates. Perhaps this will inspire Esther to admit that he is her relative in the hope of gaining even greater glory for him."

The feast was celebrated and the nations were enriched, the maidens were sent home and Mordechai was appointed a judge—but Esther remained silent. Just as she had been faithful to Mordechai's commands while still his ward she continued to maintain the silence he had ordained even as she sat upon the throne as a queen.

* * *

"Blast it, Seresh," said Bigsan to his fellow sentry, "I'm sick and tired of standing here all day guarding the palace. There must be more pleasant ways of serving the king, so why did we get stuck with this?"

"Don't forget what the captain said when he chose us," replied Seresh. "He made such a moving speech about the great honor of receiving such positions of trust and of being so close to his majesty and responsible for his safety."

"Sure, sure," countered Bigsan, "but take a look at that new fellow over there, Mordechai. Out of the clear blue sky the king appoints him a judge here at the palace gates. He sits there so comfortably while we have to pace back and forth all day long. What kind of royal justice is that?"

Day after day, Bigsan and Seresh discussed their grievance towards the king and grew more and more bitter. Their bitterness finally turned their minds to thoughts of vengeance.

"I have the poison at last!" whispered Seresh to his accomplice. "They say there is no way of assassinating such a powerful and well-protected ruler. We shall see about that. A drop of this into his wine and we will have our sweet revenge."

While the conspirators were carefully planning the right

moment for their bold act of regicide, Mordechai was rushing to give Esther an important message for the king.

"Tell Achashveirosh that his life is in danger. Those two traitors, Bigsan and Seresh, are planning to poison him!"

"But how did you learn their secret?"

"My dear, when G-d wishes one to know, He has ways of revealing everything to him."

The king was shocked when Esther rushed in with an announcement that she had information vital to his very life.

"Mordechai, who sits in the king's gates, has uncovered a plot to assassinate his majesty. Bigsan and Seresh, two of the king's trusted sentries, have secured some deadly poison and are now conspiring to put it into the king's wine."

"It is most difficult for me to believe such a charge against men who have always served me so faithfully. I shall order an investigation immediately."

Minutes later the king's special security agents were searching the quarters of Bigsan and Seresh. The poison was found and the would-be assassins were hanged.

"Mordechai has performed a great service to the crown," the king declared to his scribe. "But such an act deserves a better place than the historical records of the realm because I wish to have a reminder of my personal debt to him for saving my life. I wish to have you record this entire affair, right now and in my presence, in my personal book of chronicles."

Mordechai's life-saving role in this affair was duly recorded and, with the passing of time, duly forgotten. By the time the king got around to granting a long overdue reward to his rescuer he could only recall that Esther was the one who had given him the crucial information. But rewarding her was no easy task since she already enjoyed every imaginable pleasure as queen of the realm. It then occurred to him that Esther would appreciate a gesture shown by the king towards those responsible for her ascension to the throne.

After all, it had been the king's chamberlains who had urged him to gather the maidens and had thus afforded Esther the opportunity to be chosen as Vashti's successor. He would show his gratitude to Esther by elevating the senior chamberlain, Mehuman, otherwise known as Haman.

Chapter III

Thus it came to pass that Haman, the son of Hamdasa, descendant of Agog, king of the Amalekites, was summoned before the king to hear the news of his promotion.

"You are today being raised to a very high position because your advice made possible the selection of the queen who saved my life from the assassination attempt of those two scoundrels."

"I shall be most pleased to serve his majesty," said Haman with a low bow, "in my new position as faithfully as I did in my former one. It is a tribute to the prophetic wisdom of his majesty that he has chosen to honor me in connection with this particular Bigsan-Seresh affair. After all, I did have a modest part in the rescue, for it was I who revealed the plot to the queen."

The king was so impressed with Haman that he decided to grant him every possible honor. He raised him from one post to another as fast as royal custom allowed. Soon Haman had risen in rank above all the king's ministers and enjoyed all the power and glory of being prime minister of the kingdom.

Haman's rise to power was as complete as it was swift. Only the king himself stood above him, and it was he who constantly sought ways of honoring his favorite minister. A royal decree had been issued that all the king's servants must bow to Haman. Now it was extended to include even those on the palace grounds. Achashveirosh's legal advisors had warned him that it was an insult to the crown to honor someone besides the king in the palace area, but he insisted on sharing his glory with Haman.

On the day this decree went into effect, Mordechai was approached by a group of the king's servants.

"I noticed that you didn't bow to Haman just now, as he entered the palace," said one of them. "Why do you refuse to obey the king's decree?"

"Do you not see," explained another of Mordechai's challengers, "that he has achieved such wealth and power? This is surely a sign that he is favored by the stars and that the gods wish us to respect him and treat him as a god."

"Now you understand why I cannot prostrate myself before him. I am a Jew and I believe only in the invisible G-d who created heaven and earth. My religion forbids me to bow down to a mere creature of flesh and blood, regardless of how important he is. But I am surprised that you even ask me about this. You all know that Persian custom denies a Jew the privilege of being considered a servant of the king. I never even thought that a decree issued to the king's servants would include me as well."

Mordechai's religious objection made sense to most of the servants but some suspected other motives for his refusal. As their daily pleas to Mordechai brought no results they began to be concerned about the fact that they would be held responsible for his violation of the king's command. They therefore approached Haman with a suggestion.

"Mordechai tells us that he cannot bow when he sees you

because his religion forbids him to do so. But he might be hiding his real motives, personal jealousy and hatred. Let him then be put to the test. The next time you pass through the palace courtyard, walk directly towards Mordechai. Common courtesy requires him to bow in such a situation and what religious objection can there be to a show of elementary respect. If he refuses to bow even then it is a sure sign that he is purposely trying to insult you and he deserves to be severely punished."

No sooner had he heard this counsel than Haman was headed for his confrontation with Mordechai. He walked directly towards him, but Mordechai did not stir. Furious at Mordechai's defiance, and convinced that it was inspired by envy rather than religion, Haman began plotting his vengeance.

"I see that Mordechai is a personal enemy," he thought to himself, "but he has convinced most of the king's servants that his religion is responsible for his defiance. I shall therefore settle my accounts not with Mordechai alone but with all of his people."

All the way home his mind was busily working out the details of his plans to destroy all the Jews. By the time he reached his mansion, everything had been decided and all that remained was to choose an auspicious date for this genocide. He knew exactly how to choose the date, for this was not the first time he had to decide on the ideal time for performing a crucial act. Unlocking a drawer in his office desk he pulled out some device for casting lots and set himself to the task of selecting a date in his customary manner.

"Let's see," he said to himself. "Today is the thirteenth day of Nisan. I will first cast lots to see which day of the month is best suited to my plans in regard to the Jews. If I'm lucky the lots will indicate tomorrow and give me the signal to go ahead with my plans immediately."

But the lots rejected the fourteenth of Nisan. He took a

deep breath and tried again. Fifteenth... sixteenth... seventeenth—no luck! Eighteenth... nineteenth... twentieth—rejected again!

He began muttering angrily as the lots kept rejecting day after day, until all of Nisan had been tried without success. He swallowed hard and began casting lots for the next month, Iyar. First... second... third... never had he encountered such stubborn luck. Fourth... fifth... sixth... this month was beginning to be as unproductive as the last. He consoled himself that the lots must indicate at least one day in the month but he fumed at the thought that each unsuccessful try would delay his vengeance another day. Tenth... eleventh... twelfth... Haman's patience began to reach the breaking point. When the lots finally indicated the thirteenth of the month Haman was concerned about the fact that he had been pushed off till the very last day possible.

"Perhaps the month is not a lucky one," he concluded. "I shall cast lots to see if Iyar is truly the best time, or if another month is more favorable."

When the lots rejected Iyar, Haman's relief that his suspicions had been justified clashed with his frustration that his plans would have to wait yet another month.

Beads of sweat began forming on his forehead as he cast lots for the next month. But Sivan too was rejected and Haman began to wonder if some force was mocking him. Tammuz... Av... Elul... again he drew blanks. Tishrei... Cheshvan... Kislev... Haman began recalling something he had once heard about heavenly protection of the Jews. But he quickly banished such disturbing thoughts from his mind and continued with his lottery. Teves... Shevat... it now dawned on Haman that he had arrived at the last possible month. When the lots finally indicated Adar he combined the results of his two lotteries and designated the thirteenth of Adar as the day for destroying Jewry. The lots had given the Jews an eleven month reprieve, but Haman was determined that when the fateful day arrived his vengeance would be complete.

"The lots have decreed a day at last," he announced to his wife, Zeresh. "Now all I have to do is gain royal permission to destroy the Jews on the thirteenth of Adar."

"But the king will never agree to such a thing," protested Zeresh. "The Jews are respected as a wise people and he is not anxious to lose them. Besides, no king will allow an entire people to be slaughtered, no matter who they are."

"Do you take me for a fool? I will explain to his majesty that my followers wish to engage in a religious crusade against some obscure tribe. Once I get the royal seal I'll write the death sentence for the Jews without the king even being aware."

Haman did not have to wait very long before he was ushered into the king's presence. Achashveirosh's curiosity had been aroused by his request for an audience in regard to what Haman had termed a most urgent matter affecting the crown.

"What is all this urgency about?" he asked his prime minister.

"There is a certain people," he began, "scattered abroad and dispersed among the people in all the provinces of your majesty's kingdom. It is a race so obscure that their name is not even familiar to the king. Their laws are diverse from those of every people because their religion insists not only on other beliefs but on other practices, and on different foods and clothes. Neither do they keep the king's laws, even in financial matters where their religion is not affected. They set a terrible example for all the nations since they are to be found everywhere. It does not behoove his majesty to allow this people to thus continue because the damage they do far exceeds any possible benefit derived from them.

"Only one solution remains. We must eliminate the religion which corrupts these people. They must be forced to abandon the faith which separates them from all nations. There are loyal patriots in the kingdom who are so anxious to serve his majesty in such a religious crusade that they are willing to pay a large sum of money for the privilege. The kingdom will thus be rid of a great danger at no cost to the crown and the king's coffers will even be enriched by the ten thousand talents of silver contributed by those privileged to perform this great deed."

"Let these loyal subjects keep their silver," cried the king joyously. "The royal treasury will even be proud to pay all their expenses in doing such a great service for their king."

Removing the signet ring from his hand, Achashveirosh continued his remarks to Haman.

"Here is the royal ring which you are authorized to use in signing any documents necessary for accomplishing your important mission of converting this scattered people."

As Haman reached out to receive the valuable ring he thought of his family's tradition of hatred for the Jews. His Amalekite ancestors had long ago tried to destroy the Jews when they first became a nation and they had been sworn enemies ever since. Once, the Jewish king, Shaul, almost destroyed all of his people, but his ancestor, Agog, was spared long enough to sow the seed for the perpetuation of Amalek. Now it was his turn to destroy the Jews and the ring he was about to receive would seal their doom.

As soon as he had bowed his way out of the king's chambers with ring in hand, Haman summoned the royal scribes to appear before him. Flanked by two of his most trusted patriots he began his charge.

"You are about to write two historic letters which his majesty, in his great wisdom, deems necessary for the security of his subjects throughout the kingdom. But I must first warn you that one of these letters is so secret that to divulge its contents to anyone is to invite certain death by the king's executioner."

The scribes were soon busily copying the text of the first letter. There was an air of nervous excitement in the great hall where they had gathered as each writer speculated with his neighbor as to the purpose of the letters. Most of them were new at their posts, for up until that trouble with Vashti, all communication with foreign lands had been conducted in Persian, and only a few scribes were needed. Now the letters to the king's satraps, the governors of the provinces and the princes of every people had to be written in their particular language and script. Experts in the Ethiopian and Macedonian tongues now sat together with scribes who could write in the Indian and Greek languages, and all about them were scribes for each nation and people in the king's vast realm.

When they had finished recording the first letter, the new Macedonian scribe turned to the Persian veteran and checked the correctness of his text by reading it to him.

"To the Governor of Macedonia, greetings and peace from His Royal Highness, Achashveirosh, King of Persia and Media and master of one hundred and twenty-seven provinces. Let it be known unto all the subjects of your province that on the thirteenth day of the month of Adar they must all be prepared for a military action whose nature will then be revealed."

"Perhaps it is because I am new here," said the Macedonian, "but I don't understand what is so secret about this letter and why its message is so mysterious."

"Sh!" whispered the Ethiopian sitting behind him. "The prime minister is calling for our attention."

"Now that you have all finished recording the first letter," resumed Haman, "I shall explain my instructions regarding the second letter. As you have all noticed, the first letter, which will be made public, fails to mention the purpose of the miliary preparedness. The one you are about to write will spell out clearly that the purpose is to destroy all the Jews throughout the kingdom, young and old, women and children, in one day."

A hush fell upon the stunned assembly of scribes as they looked at one another, hardly believing that they were about to write the death warrant of an entire people. Smiles sprouted on many faces and some cheers were even heard, but from a few seats there came a faint murmur of protest.

"There are some Jew-lovers in this room," whispered one of Haman's henchmen to him.

"I am well aware that the Jews have good friends in high places," Haman assured him, "and if they were to know of this decree they would come crying to the king that he rescind it. That is precisely why I have chosen to keep this second letter sealed until the 13th day of Adar so that no one will know in advance that doom is to befall the Jews. The only threat to this plan is that some of these scribes may reveal our secret, but they will be too afraid to thus defy me."

"Annihilation of the Jews," he announced with anger in his voice, "is the decision of his majesty, the king, in order to eliminate them as a threat to the security and morals of all our subjects. Your second letter will contain specific instructions regarding this final solution to the Jewish problem. When you have completed it you are to write on an accompanying envelope 'Not to be opened, upon orders of his majesty, until the thirteenth of Adar.' "

He then turned to his chief lieutenant and handed him the king's ring.

"Every one of these letters is to be signed with this ring and the second letters to be sealed in envelopes. Speed and secrecy are of the utmost importance to the success of our plan. Messengers must be dispatched immediately to all the lands so that the letters will arrive before there is even a chance of the king learning their contents. Once they are in the hands of the satraps and governors even his majesty cannot recall them, for a document signed with the royal ring is irrevocable. But just to be sure that the king doesn't find out too soon, hold up the letters to be delivered to the local governor of Shushan until all the messengers have departed."

"But can we rely on all the rulers of the provinces to go along with our plan to exterminate an entire people?" wondered the lieutenant.

"I have taken care of that problem," Haman assured him. "Each messenger has been given instructions to inform his particular governor or satrap that such letters were sent only to him. He will naturally assume that the crown is focusing all of its attention on the Jews in his particular province and will be very careful to obey these orders in regard to handling his local problem. Without any advance knowledge the Jews will have no chance to plead their cause before the king, to prepare their defenses, or even to flee to safety. They will be an easy target for our allies throughout the provinces who will lead the king's subjects in fulfilling his orders. After all, these carefully sealed orders clearly require his subjects 'to destroy, to slay, and to cause to perish, all Jews, both young and old, little children and women, in one day, the thirteenth day of Adar, and to take their possessions as spoils.' "

Soon after the last messenger had been dispatched, Haman went to see the king in order to check whether some information had leaked out about the manner in which he had duped him.

"I have just received word," the king began, "that a letter bearing the royal signature has been posted in the main square by the governor of Shushan. My agents report that there is much confusion among the local citizens for no one is aware of the purpose for being militarily prepared on the thirteenth of Adar. Perhaps you will explain this mystery to me."

"Surely, your majesty," replied Haman with a reassuring tone. "Today the king has allowed his signature to be placed on a document which will gain for him a glorious place in the history of mankind. Those dangerous people which the crown has decided to liberate from their corrupting faith must be taken by surprise if we are to succeed in converting them. Letters have therefore been dispatched to signal our loyal patriots to prepare for a certain day. When the great moment arrives they will be put into action for swiftly accomplishing their mission of forcing this rebellious race to live and believe as all the other peoples in the kingdom."

The king smiled with relief and raised his goblet of wine in a toast to the wisdom of Haman and the success of his patriotic mission.

Chapter IV

"What has happened?"

"Why did Mordechai call a mass meeting of all Jews in the city square?"

"Why has he been acting so strange of late?"

As the crowd in the square grew larger the waves of curiosity continued to break upon a shore of mystery. Then there was a hush as an old, dignified man wearing sackcloth and ashes walked towards the center of the square.

"My brothers," began Mordechai, "Heaven has revealed to me some dreadful tidings which I must share with you. We are to be punished for the sins we committed in bowing to the image of Nevuchadnetzar and in partaking of the forbidden foods at the feast of King Achashveirosh. Heaven has therefore already caused a decree to be issued in this kingdom which calls for the death of every single Jew."

Although no one yet understood the danger of which Mordechai spoke, his words paralyzed his audience with fearful anticipation. The older Jews who had accompanied Mordechai into exile from the land of Yehudah wept at the thought that for the second time in their lives they were being faced with disaster. The others had been looking forward impatiently to the day a few years hence when the seventy years of Babylonian exile would be over and they could return to Jerusalem and rebuild the Beis Hamikdash, as the prophets had promised. Now they began to worry that their dream would never come true. They all gasped with nervous anxiety as Mordechai continued.

"I have rent my garments and donned sackcloth and ashes. My every hour is filled with repentance and prayer to G-d in whose hands are the hearts of kings."

"The king! What does the king have to do with this?"

"Tell us, O Mordechai, what danger you speak of."

Mordechai calmed the crowd with a gesture of his hand and raised his voice to make the fateful announcement.

"In eleven months our enemies are planning to kill every Jew throughout the kingdom, men and women, young and old."

Cries of disbelief mingled with sighs of agony, subsiding only when his listeners saw that Mordechai wished to continue.

"The letter bearing the king's signature which you see posted in this square tells only half the story. The governor of Shushan, as well as the governors, satraps and princes of the provinces throughout the realm, have received a second letter from the king which is sealed with instructions that it is not to be opened until the thirteenth of Adar. That letter, my dear brothers, pronounces a death sentence upon all of us and our families."

"But how could the king do such a thing?"

"Whatever are we to do?"

"It is not the king who is to blame," explained Mordechai. "He has been fooled by the anti-Semitic Amalekite, Haman. Still, all is not lost. If we repent our sins and pray to G-d, He will save us as He always saved our ancestors. But let us not rely on a miracle alone, and do whatever is humanly possible. The only way we can do something with our own powers is to spread the word to all of our neighbors and acquaintances that the purpose of military preparedness mentioned in the letters is the destruction of Jewry. This information will eventually reach the king and perhaps he will find a way to abolish this terrible decree."

Word spread quickly enough throughout all the provinces of Mordechai's revelation, and great sorrow descended upon the Jewish communities when the messengers arrived with the king's decree. Fasting, weeping and wailing echoed Jewish repentance while the mass application of sackcloth and ashes mirrored it.

Although the most distant Jew had heard the news, the palace walls seemed impregnable against its reaching the king's ears. Haman's agents had seen to it that no one approached the king with such information. But Mordechai knew that his only hope was in reaching the king, or at least getting through to the queen. He therefore decided on a bold gamble. Up to the palace gates he marched, wearing his sackcloth. There he stood, waiting for the reaction of the palace guards.

The reaction was not long in coming. Mordechai was a familiar fixture on the palace grounds and he startled the palace retainers with his refusal to now enter. Sackcloth was, after all, not permitted as attire within the king's gates. Several of her excited maids and chamberlains came running to Queen Esther to report Mordechai's strange conduct.

"Have some raiment brought to Mordechai immediately," she ordered in a trembling voice that betrayed her shock. "Let him don these garments over his sackcloth so that he may enter the palace grounds at once."

But Mordechai waved aside the proffered clothes as he turned his eyes to Heaven.

"O merciful G-d. I shall not pause for a moment in my sackcloth repentance and prayer for I know that only Thou are my salvation and that it is vain to trust in flesh and blood."

When Esther heard of Mordechai's refusal she summoned her most trusted confidant, Hasach, whom the king had appointed as one of her special chamberlains.

"Mordechai must certainly have some vital information to relay to me," she told him. "You are to go out to him and probe the reasons for his mysterious appearance until you learn what has happened."

Out on the street Hasach found Mordechai most anxious to reveal everything. He told him how Haman's hatred had begun with his refusal to bow to him. Then he detailed Haman's deception in offering a large sum of money to the king as the gift of his patriots for the privilege of converting some obscure race. He then handed him a letter and said:

"Where that scoundrel actually intended getting the money was from the spoils his murderers would take, and he was merely offering the crown the share due to it from such booty. For Haman has placed the king's signature on a document which spells death for all Jewry. Show this letter to Queen Esther, for it is a copy of the letter sent to the rulers of all the provinces. Tell her that a second, sealed letter has also been sent containing instructions to kill every Jew on the thirteenth of Adar. There is no time to lose so she must immediately come before the king and plead for her people."

When Queen Esther recovered from her shock at hearing Hasach's report she asked him to see to it that her reply was brought to Mordechai.

"But don't go yourself, Hasach," warned the queen, "for Haman's agents will certainly become suspicious. Send another messenger to tell Mordechai that I cannot approach the king now. All the king's servants and the people of the king's provinces know that any man or woman who shall come uninvited unto the king, into the inner court, shall be put to death. This law makes no exception as to who it is that comes uninvited and for what vital purpose. There is an automatic penalty of death. Should the king extend his golden scepter, however, then, and only then, is the doomed person spared his life. Even if I should be fortunate enough to have my life spared after my uninvited appearance, how can I then dare to plead for the life of my people as well?

"Tell Mordechai that if there would be no other way to save our people, I would readily consent to this move despite its personal dangers. But there is a much more secure and practical way for me to approach the king. Thirty days have already passed since I have been called to the king and it is certain that I will be called again any day. If we wait a few days I will have the opportunity of making an invited appearance when I can more easily plead our people's cause."

Mordechai was furious with Esther's reply and he sent her back a sharp challenge.

"Your rise to the throne was an unnatural event and obviously dictated by heaven for some particular purpose. The present danger to Jewry clearly indicates that this purpose was to grant you an opportunity to influence the king. But this opportunity cannot be delayed. When the appointed hour of salvation arrives for Jews in trouble nothing can prevent it. Should you fail to play your destined role in this salvation, our merciful G-d will rescue His people through other means. He shall surely not allow His people's fate to hang upon the whim of one woman. But you and your father's house shall be lost, for once the purpose of your glory has passed, there is no longer any reason for you to remain a queen. Do not delude yourself that you can achieve this salvation in a few days, for you have been elevated to the throne by Heaven just for this very moment."

Esther received Mordechai's message not as a rebuke, but as an assurance, and smilingly sent back her final message.

"Now that I am confident of my people's salvation regardless of what happens to me I am ready to face almost certain death in order to play my Heaven-ordained part in this rescue. But I beg of you to gather all the Jews in Shushan and fast three days for the success of my mission. For three days and three nights shall they not partake of food and drink. My maidens and I shall likewise fast. With such repentance and prayer behind me I shall boldly come before the king with nothing more to lose than my own life."

Mordechai fulfilled Esther's request and a three-day fast was proclaimed for all of Jewry in the capital.

Chapter V

On the third day of the fast Esther donned her royal robes and prepared for her fateful visit to the king. Heaven had ordained that Achashveirosh forsake his usual seat in the private chambers of the king's house, where he was always to be found at this particular hour. He sat instead on the royal throne in the Royal House which he occupied only when judging his subjects. This throne had today been turned to face in the direction of the inner court towards which Esther was now heading. Despite her weakened condition after fasting for three days, Esther's dignity aroused in all who beheld her at this moment a sense of awe at her natural majesty. As she entered the inner courtyard and stood facing the king's house, where she believed him to be, she immediately came into his view. The moment of decision had arrived.

Achashveirosh was overwhelmed by her present appearance as she stood facing the vacant chambers of the king's house humbly waiting for him to extend his scepter. Surpassing his love for her was his admiration of her humility. Never had he intended the ban on uninvited entrances to include his beloved queen and he was deeply impressed that Esther so modestly felt that she needed his permission. He glanced at his own hand and was surprised to see the golden scepter which he never held while seated here. This scepter he extended to Esther and bade her come forward to explain the nature of her unexpected visit. Certain that she had come to either prevent some harm or gain some reward, the king waited until she touched the tip of the scepter and then asked her.

"What is it that troubles you, Queen Esther, or the request you wish granted? I am prepared to grant you even half of my kingdom."

"If it pleases the king," replied a relieved Esther, "let the king and Haman come this day to the banquet I have prepared for them."

As the king issued orders that Haman be immediately brought to fulfill the queen's request, Esther swiftly reviewed in her mind the strategy she had chosen for postponing the ultimate confrontation with her people's enemy. Aware that she might be suspected by the king of a personal hatred towards Haman, Esther wished to demonstrate that she honored him greatly and acted against him purely to save her people. She also feared that the wily Haman might yet convince the king of his innocence and loyalty. By setting the stage for this confrontation at an unexpected moment during a banquet, she hoped to catch Haman unprepared in his defense, and the king in a wine-inebriated mood when he could be easily spurred to pronounce harsh and swift judgment.

At the banquet, the king repeated his offer to Esther.

"What is your petition and what is your request? Even unto half of the kingdom shall be granted to you."

"All I desire, your majesty, is to please the king," Esther graciously replied. "Only if both I and my request are deserving of the king's favor would I dare to ask for anything. But since your majesty insists on receiving a request from me, I shall oblige him tomorrow at a banquet which I beg him to attend together with Haman."

Haman left this banquet flushed with triumph and truly happy for the first time since he began his dizzy rise to power. Each previous success had disturbed him with ambitions for greater glory. But now that the queen had equated him with the king himself he was finally content that he had reached the peak of his power.

This smugness of her people's oppressor was not lost on Esther. She was hoping that by raising him to the apex of his fortune she would precipitate his crashing descent.

Haman's joy was short-lived. When he reached the palace gates he saw that his archenemy, Mordechai, persisted in completely ignoring him. Not only did he fail to rise in respect but he betrayed not even the slightest sign of fear that he might pay with his life for this insubordination. It was no longer the religion or people of Mordechai which angered Haman but the man himself. In his fury he began to turn back to the palace to ask the king for Mordechai's head. But he restrained himself. He decided instead to confer with his family and friends before taking such a major step.

Home at last in the company of his wife, Zeresh, and his trusted friends, Haman unfolded his problem.

"Here I am, a powerful and wealthy man, with many sons, being defied by a lowly Jew. Not only has the king elevated me above his servants and princes but the queen too has shown how important I am by inviting me alone to join the king at her banquet. This is surely a sign that she considers me as important as all of the other ministers combined. She has invited me again tomorrow to join her and the king at the banquet, where she will make a major personal request. The queen undoubtedly feels that I have more influence with the king than even she and wishes me to intercede with his majesty on her behalf.

"But all of this glory is meaningless in comparison to the shame I suffer from Mordechai's defiance. That stubborn Jew is deserving of the greatest penalty for shaming so mighty a prince as I. But how dare I admit to the world that the actions of such an insignificant person upset me enough to demand his death?"

Haman's frustration intensified his anger, but his wife and friends soon brought him relief with a plan for solving his dilemma. They proposed a way of executing Mordechai without harming Haman's reputation.

"Build a gallows fifty cubits high right here on your estate. Early in the morning secure permission from the king to immediately hang the rebellious Mordechai upon these gallows. Everyone realizes that when the king wishes to teach his subjects a lesson in discipline he chooses a lowly rebel and hangs him in a highly visible place, early in the morning, so that everyone will see him and take his example to heart. It will therefore be obvious to all that Mordechai has not been executed because of his crime towards you, since convicted criminals are hung later in the day, after the court adjourns, and on a lower gallows. You will thus be rid of your hated enemy at no cost to your prestige. Then you can join the king and queen at the banquet with a happy heart."

Haman was so enthusiastic about this plan that he immediately had the gallows constructed and waited impatiently for the following morning when he would at last gain his vengeance against Mordechai.

Chapter VI

That night was a sleepless one for the king. Over and over he repeated the words of his beloved queen and tried to fathom her strange behavior.

"Esther's elaborate efforts," he thought to himself, "obviously indicate that she has a most vital request to make. Her insistence that this request will be something which I should grant for its own sake is a sign that I have an obligation to one of my subjects. But I owe no one anything, unless perhaps an unpaid debt of gratitude for some forgotten favor."

Unable to fall asleep and troubled by his conscience that he owed a reward, the king ordered his private book of records to be brought before him. The official book of records which chronicled the nation's history for future generations was under the jurisdiction of the prime minister, and Haman had long ago rewritten the history of the Bigsan-Seresh affair to conform with his own version. But this private book of records was the king's personal diary and securely kept in his possession. When the king's attendant reached the story of the Bigsan-Seresh plot, the king suddenly interrupted him.

"Who does the diary mention as the one who told the

queen of the conspiracy by these two assassins to poison me?"

"Mordechai," replied the reader.

"That thieving scoundrel, Haman!" fumed the king. "He fooled me into believing that he had years before saved my life, relying on the fact that I had forgotten the entire affair. All the power and glory I bestowed upon him because of this really belonged to Mordechai. But perhaps Mordechai did receive some fitting recognition or promotion at the time of his revelation."

"No, your majesty," his servant assured him. "There is no record of any such reward and we do not recall that any recognition was ever granted to Mordechai for saving the king's life."

Just then the king heard the sound of someone entering the courtyard and he cried out in surprise. "What is someone doing out there so early in the morning? Go see who it is."

The visitor was making a last minute rehearsal of how he would ask the king for the right to hang Mordechai that very morning when his reverie was interrupted by the king's sentry.

"His majesty requests that you enter."

Achashveirosh took a long, distrustful look at the man standing before him. He was most disturbed at the thought that Haman had duped him into raising him to such greatness and he was determined to now trap him in an embarrassing situation. The prime minister would be asked to suggest honors which he would certainly assume were intended for himself and then...

But the king saw that Haman was about to speak so he quickly cut him short.

"We'll get to your request later. At present we are faced with a problem which only you can solve for us with your great wisdom. There is someone to whom I wish to pay a great tribute so I call upon you to suggest the proper manner for treating the man whom the king desires to honor."

Haman was so excited with this opportunity to outline the honors he inferred were intended for him that he momentarily forgot the original purpose of his visit and gave his imagination free rein.

"There is no greater honor for any man, your majesty," Haman began in his most diplomatic manner, "than the public knowledge that the king delights in his honor. But great care should be taken to publicize this fact in the most dramatic manner. The public will be properly impressed only if royal trappings are used and many princes are involved. Let the princes therefore dress this man in royal robes and mount him upon the horse which the king himself rode on his coronation day. Then he must be led out into the main thoroughfare of the capital by the noble princes who will proclaim, 'Thus shall be done to the man whom the king wishes to honor.' "

In his fancy, Haman already envisioned himself resplendent in the royal robes and proudly riding upon the king's steed, with princes all about him and streets filled with admirers cheering him. But he was rudely brought back to reality by the king's snapping order.

"Make haste and take the apparel and the horse as you suggested, and perform all the honors you have so wonderfully outlined on behalf of Mordechai the Jew, who sits at the king's gate."

The king's anger at Haman for deceiving him had turned into fury at now observing his ambitions for the crown itself and he refused to hear a word of protest.

"You are to personally dress him, mount him on the horse, and lead him through the streets with a proclamation that he is the man whom the king wishes to honor. For it was he who discovered the plot against me and saved my life. I warn you not to neglect one detail of all the honors you suggested, for Mordechai deserves them all. Now off with you!"

Stunned by the sudden turn of events, Haman spent the next few hours in a daze. Here he was, the prime minister of the land and second in importance to the king, forced to lead, like a slave, the horse upon which sat his worst enemy. He could hardly believe that it was his voice proclaiming, "Thus shall be done to the man whom the king wishes to honor" about the very same Mordechai whom he had expected to see dangling this morning from the lofty gallows.

When the parade was finally ended with Mordechai's return to the king's gate, Haman trudged homeward mournful and covered with shame. Once again he convened a council of his wife and friends, whom he hoped to convince that all was not yet lost.

"You probably think," he told them, "that your advice boomeranged and that the king not only refused to let me hang Mordechai but even insisted on my honoring him as a demonstration of his innocence. Well, it was not that bad. I just suffered a stroke of bad luck in setting Mordechai's execution on the very day when the king decided to pay him some old debt of gratitude. Now that this debt has been paid I am confident that I can convince the king that the Jew deserves to hang for disobeying the royal decree to bow down before me."

But Haman's wife and counselors did not share his confidence. "You are mistaken in assuming that your setback was coincidental," they warned him. "The Jews have a special Providence which guides their destiny and if you press your attack on Mordechai you will continue to fall before him. You see how your defeat, brought about by your own action in approaching the king this morning, has come even before Mordechai has suffered any damage from you. This should make it abundantly clear to you that Mordechai's prayers have triumphed for him. Your only hope is to wait until the Jew relaxes his guard and slackens in his prayers and repentance. Then you will have an opportunity to once more gain the upper hand."

Just as Haman was about to offer a reply, a group of the king's chamberlains entered.

"Just a moment," Haman waved them aside and turned to offer a final argument against the counsel of his advisors. "I still believe that the sooner I am rid of that irksome Jew, Mordechai, the more secure I will be. I won't be able to rest until I see him hanging from the gallows in our courtyard. I must try as soon as possible to get the king's permission for his execution."

Zeresh and the other advisors never got a chance to finish their warnings. The chamberlains, under orders to bring Haman without delay, saw that this discussion would take much more than the requested moment. They therefore insisted on terminating it and hustled Haman off to Esther's party.

Chapter VII

"What is your petition, Queen Esther?" asked the king at the second day's banquet. "You are my beloved queen and may ask the most precious thing for yourself. Should you wish to request something for someone else, that too shall be granted. Even half of my kingdom shall be given to satisfy your petition or request."

"If I have found favor in the king's eyes," replied Esther, "and if it please the king, let my life be given me at my petition and my people at my request. We have been sold to an evil man to be destroyed, to be slain, and to perish. This vile enemy has a deep personal hatred for me and wishes to dispose of me through the genocide of my people. Your majesty has been deceived into believing that some obscure race was involved, but in truth it is my own people. This wicked murderer has presented his entire plot to the king as a patriotic campaign to convert an unbelieving people while he has actually laid plans for their total annihilation.

"Had he duped the king into selling me and my people into slavery I would have held my peace rather than ask the king to rescind a decree signed in his name, without his knowledge of its victims. But now that he has so thoroughly misled his majesty in every aspect of his plot I feel that I must reveal his true intentions. It is not my people who endanger the kingdom, as he reported to the king, but this evil plotter who is a grave threat to the realm."

The king was completely taken aback by Esther's charges and turned to his household for an explanation.

"Who is the man that dares plot such a thing and what reason could have motivated him?"

"This adversary and enemy is none other than Haman!" cried Esther. "His deep personal hatred for me and my people has moved him to plot our destruction."

Haman felt the trap tighten about him and he desperately sought a way to save himself. If only he were alone with the king he would yet be able to convince him that his condemnation of the Jews was based, not on personal hatred, but on his patriotic interests in eliminating a danger to the kingdom. But to offer such a defense before the queen would be further inviting her wrath. He could handle even the furious queen alone by assuring her that this plot would never have begun if her Jewish identity were known and that the damage could be undone by recalling the letters. But to say this in the king's presence would be an admission that personal, not national, interests had motivated him all the while.

A gleam of hope appeared for him as the king furiously stormed from the room to refresh himself with a stroll in the palace garden. Haman quickly dashed over to Esther's couch to plead with her for his life. Just then the king returned and, seeing him fallen upon the couch of the queen, suspected the worst.

"It is not sufficient that you planned to kill the queen along with her people that you now stoop to such a dastardly act of murder, right here in the traditional refuge of the king's palace?"

Haman covered his face with his hands in a last desperate attempt to ward off the king's anger. But before he could attempt a last straw-clutching plea he heard the voice of Charvona, one of the king's chamberlains.

"This is not the only treason Haman is guilty of. When we went to fetch him today to this banquet we overheard him telling family and friends about his plans to hang Mordechai. What reason could he have for slaying Mordechai other than that he saved the king's life from the assassination attempt of Bigsan and Seresh, with whom he was probably in league? At the very moment that Mordechai was being paraded through the streets in the king's robes and heralded as the man whom the king honors, Haman was publicly displaying a gallows fifty cubits high on which he had boasted he would hang the king's savior."

This was the coup de grâce in the attack on Haman. The king's wrath did not subside until his execution order had been fulfilled and Haman was hung upon the gallows he had prepared for Mordechai.

Chapter VIII

Upon Haman's execution the king gave his estate to Esther as a demonstration that he was not slain as a rebel against the king, whose assets revert to the crown, but because of his designs against the queen and her people. Mordechai now became very powerful in the kingdom since Esther had revealed her relationship to him. He was now entitled to come before the king at any time without an invitation. The signet ring which Haman had worn was now put in the hands of Mordechai, and Esther placed him in charge of Haman's estate. Thus the power and riches in which Haman had so gloried had miraculously transferred to Mordechai in a moment.

Esther was worried, however, by the king's attention to the estate of Haman and the position of Mordechai. He had yet not answered her regarding her request for undoing Haman's plot against her people.

His attention to these other favors raised apprehensions that he was trying to appease her with mere gestures. She therefore spoke with the king and pleaded with him, putting forth the justice of her request and its benefits for the king, along with the importance of this request to her as his favored queen. Turning to the practical problem of nullifying the danger of Haman's letters without compromising the law that a decree signed by the king was irrevocable, she rejected the idea of a new letter from the king. Sending a second sealed letter in contradiction to the first would be impractical because of two reasons. First of all, word had already leaked out that the Jews were the target of the military preparedness. The anti-Semites had already begun troubling them, creating a need for immediate action. Secondly, on the day both letters would be opened, there was no guarantee that the local rulers would not choose to obey the original letter. She therefore proposed immediately recalling the sealed letters and clearly demonstrating that the Jews had been restored to favor. There was no need to worry about violating the sacred irrevocability of the king's decree because he himself was aware that he had been duped in regard to the letter's contents. Recall of a mistaken decree would hardly constitute a compromise of irrevocability.

But the king did not accept her logic regarding the revocability of these letters. He proposed instead to send a second letter which would serve as an explanation of the first letters. The sealed letter, to be opened on the same day as the first sealed one, would define the 'destruction of Jews' mentioned in the first one as 'destruction by Jews of their enemies.' The reader of both letters would, at worst, gain the impression that both the Jews and their enemies had been given a day to militarily square accounts, with no interference from the authorities. Along with this second sealed letter would go a second open letter defining the preparedness mentioned in the first. It was the Jews who were to be prepared for action against their foes on Adar 13. This plan would eliminate both the present and future dangers to Jewry. The arrival of the open letter would nullify the rumors that the preparedness mentioned in the first was a signal for anti-Semitic acts. Should the original sealed letter, arriving on Adar 13, encourage officials backing the anti-Jewish forces they would recall that Haman's execution was publicly attributed to his designs against the Jews and they would fear to meet with his fate. They would therefore conceal these documents and no one would ever know their true contents.

The king gave Mordechai and Esther permission to write these second letters in the manner most favorable to the Jews. But Mordechai waited until the messengers who had delivered the first letters had returned from their missions, because he wanted to establish the credibility of the second letters by sending them with the same agents. On the twenty-third day of Sivan, the royal scribes were summoned to write these letters according to the various scripts and tongues of the realm. Mordechai ordered that letters be sent not only to the satraps, governors and princes, but to Jewish leaders throughout the one hundred and twenty-seven lands of the realm as well. This was to demonstrate that the second letters superseded the first, since there were officials receiving them who had not received the earlier ones. Mordechai entered some subtle changes into the second letters which did not change their substance but provided important hints for the readers. Haman had written that the destruction of the Jews was to take place on the thirteenth day of Adar and that there would afterwards be an opportunity for spoils, in order to assure his murderous followers that they need not take time from their official day of slaughter to gather spoils. Mordechai wished, however, that the Jews avoid taking spoils, in order to show that only self-defense was their motivation. He therefore rearranged the wording of the order to read that the slaughter and spoils must be accomplished on the same day, making it clear to the Jews that they would have no time for such an ungainly activity. Haman had also tried to dupe each local ruler into believing that only in his land was there such a decree, lest the prospect of genocide dissuade them. But Mordechai made it clear in his letters that all of Jewry was at stake. The messengers, confused at suddenly being sent once again with letters, were quickly dispatched on horses before word got out in the capital, lest the anti-Semites there try to influence the king.

Now that the machinery for Jewish salvation had been set up, Mordechai finally permitted himself the luxury of exhibiting G-d's miraculous elevation of Jewry by walking out into public in his royal attire. With apparel of blue and white, a great crown of gold and a robe of fine linen and purple, he aroused respect and joy. All of Shushan rejoiced in the triumph of this saintly man, but for Jews it was a particular cause for light and gladness, joy and honor. Wherever the new letters arrived Jews rejoiced and feasted. Many of the non-Jews even converted out of fear of the Jews.

Chapter IX

The Jews were safe until Adar 13 because of the second open letter. When that day arrived the two sealed letters were opened and the hopes of the anti-Semites to destroy Jewry were upset by heavenly intervention. In the large walled cities, where the king's officers and armies provided official protection of their rights, the Jews gathered for battle but met no opposition. The citizenry feared the Jews because they knew only of the letters granting them official permission to destroy their enemies. The princes, satraps and governors knew of Haman's letter and its permit to wage war against the Jews as well. But their fear of Mordechai, whose power and prestige continued to grow, caused them to do away with this letter and to side with the Jews. The notoriously outspoken anti-Semites were slain while those with hatred in their hearts were merely subjected to humiliation. Nevertheless, five hundred such rabid anti-Semites, besides the ten mighty sons of Haman, were slain in the capital of Shushan alone.

Despite their triumph the Jews did not touch any spoils, in accordance with Mordechai's hint.

When this report of the battle in his capital was brought

before him, the king expressed his surprise to Esther.

"The Jews have slain five hundred men in Shushan along with the ten sons of Haman. I never realized that there were so many violent anti-Semites right here in the capital. Now I can imagine how many there must have been in other parts of the kingdom and what danger your people were faced with. Tell me what else you request for it shall be granted."

"If it please the king," replied Esther, "a powerful example must be set in Shushan to frighten the enemies of Jewry throughout the realm. Today my people have subdued their antagonists in the capital, including Haman's sons. Let tomorrow be given to them to eliminate their enemies in the residential city of Shushan adjoining the capital and let permission be granted to hang the bodies of Haman's ten sons."

Royal permission for further action was granted and Haman's sons were hanged. On the fourteenth of Adar the Jews in Shushan succeeded in destroying three hundred foes, and again they abstained from taking spoils.

In the unwalled cities and villages, where there were no officers or armies of the king to aid them, the Jews were forced to battle for their lives. They not only triumphed over their foes, but also destroyed all the known descendants of Amalek in the process. They thus succeeded in eliminating seventy-five thousand enemies. As in Shushan, they did not defile their victory with the taking of spoils.

There were great celebrations among the triumphant Jews the day after their victory. In the unwalled cities this holiday was on the fourteenth and in Shushan, where they battled for two days, on the fifteenth. But in the walled cities throughout the realm the Jews found no reason for rejoicing since they had been protected by the king's officers and armies and had not been forced to engage in real battle. Since the satraps and governors had hidden the letters out of fear of Mordechai these Jews were not aware that they had been miraculously saved from disaster. They believed that the early rumors regarding such anti-Semitic letters were unfounded reports circulated by Haman or that the king had soon recalled them, eliminating any danger before the arrival of the thirteenth. Since a large portion of Jewry did not yet celebrate this miracle, no problem in Jewish law yet arose regarding those who did make it a holiday, for it was a private, and not a national affair.

Mordechai wished, however, to point out the truth to the Jews in the walled cities and to show them how they had been miraculously saved. He therefore wrote letters to all the Jews throughout the realm detailing the entire story as it had happened. The first letters, he pointed out, were still in effect on the thirteenth and only the miracle of his meteoric rise to power had caused the king's officers to conceal them. The Jews in the walled cities were therefore also obliged to celebrate their miraculous rescue. But their celebration was to be on the fifteenth, in contrast to the celebration in the unwalled cities on the fourteenth. Mordechai's reasoning ran as follows: Haman's letter did not limit the enemies of Jewry to one day of slaughter. Should a Jew escape that day, he was fair game afterwards. But the second letter's grant of self-defense privileges for Jews was strictly limited to the thirteenth, and Esther had to have special royal permission for action in Shushan on the fourteenth. It was obvious then that Jews were in great danger on the fourteenth as well since the king's officers could not legally aid them on that day should their enemies be aware of their freedom to act and utilize it. In the unwalled cities the danger was over on the fourteenth, because they had subdued their foes on the thirteenth. Mordechai therefore asked that in those cities this day—the fourteenth—be ordained as a day of celebration. But in the walled cities the danger was at its peak on the fourteenth and only when that day was over did it become clear that the officers had hidden the first letter out of fear of Mordechai and that the anti-Semitic masses were unaware of their contents. The fifteenth day was therefore the day of rest for them and Mordechai asked that it be designated as the day of celebration.

The nature of this celebration was to be feasting, presents to friends and gifts to the poor. Since the month of Adar had been miraculously converted from tragedy to joy it was fitting to celebrate with feasting. Because of its transformation from mourning to a holiday a spiritual celebration was in order. Unwilling to create a new holiday for Jewry, Mordechai ordered the giving of charity as the exercise of a holiday whose essence was rising above worldly matters.

Mordechai's letter detailed the motivations of Haman. It was not hatred towards him personally that sparked him but the ancient hatred of his Amalekite forebears for Jewry. The miracle of his failure was even greater because the particular time was terribly unfavorable to Jewry. Although his very first idea was to merely destroy them spiritually, the lots he cast indicated such an opportune period that he decided on physical genocide. The miracle of G-d upsetting the dictates of the stars was enhanced by the miracle which happened on the very day scheduled for destruction. The king's refusal to recall the letters and to counteract them with a second sealed letter had necessitated the public execution of Haman to intimidate the officers into choosing to ignore the first letter over the second. These days of celebration were to be called Purim in memory of the lots and as a reminder that the bad fortune which the stars had dictated for Jewry on those days had turned into good fortune. Jews everywhere accepted Mordechai's suggestions as an obligation upon themselves and future generations. They agreed to observe the two separate days of Purim and to read the Megillah, and even laid down a condition that no future generation could abolish these days of festivity.

Then came the effort of Esther to have this Megillah included among the Holy Scriptures. Many of the Sages opposed this move as well as the establishment of Purim as a permanent holiday. Esther used all of her influence to have the Megillah accepted and urged the Sages to rule on the justice of her contention that it had a place in the Scriptures. To the argument against establishing a new holiday she pointed out that this was forbidden only if the intention was to create one on a par with the Torah holidays. Since she was only asking that it be established like a vow accepted by Jewry, it was no different from the four fast days which Jewry had accepted in addition to the Torah. Her arguments were eventually accepted by the Sages. The Megillah became part of the Scriptures and Purim became an official holiday.

Chapter X

Mordechai enjoyed great success as the king's prime minister. His military triumphs brought so much dominion to the king that he was able to levy taxes not only on the neighboring lands but on distant islands as well. All of his exploits and his glory are detailed in the history of the kings of Persia and Media. Although he was prime minister of the entire realm he handled his special post of minister in charge of Jewish affairs with such concern for his people that he continued to enjoy their affection.

Mordechai's triumph over Haman and his rise to such great power was a fulfillment of the promise in Psalm 37 that "the righteous shall inherit the earth and rest therein for ever."

MEGILLAS ESTHER

The Translation
The Challenges

A Note About This Translation

The deviations in this translation from the familiar version have been motivated by several considerations. The transliterations have been made in accordance with the vocalization used by the traditional reader of the Megillah (Achashveirosh instead of Ahasueros). To make the text more readable we have scrapped some of the antiquated expressions and stilted phrasing in favor of more fluid prose. Sometimes an adjustment has been made in recognition of a point made by the commentaries. We have, for instance, not translated Kush (in 1:1) as Ethiopia because one Talmudic opinion is that Hodu and Kush were adjoining lands, leading Rabbi Yaakov of Emdin to conclude that Kush here cannot mean Ethiopia but another land by that name bordering on India.

But the principal guideline of this translation was the Malbim's understanding of the text as reflected by both his questions and his commentary. These questions have been translated as well and are presented here in footnote form.

Chapter 1

[1] It happened in the days of Achashveirosh, the Achashveirosh reigning from India to Kush, over a hundred and twenty-seven provinces. [2] It was in those days when King Achashveirosh sat on the throne of his kingdom which was in the capital of Shushan. [3] In the third year of his reign he made a banquet for

---

I 1-2 ACHASHVEIROSH'S POLITICAL SITUATION

1) Why are we introduced to Achashveirosh with the phrase "In the days of," usually reserved for preparing unknown events in the life of an already familiar character?
   The Achashveirosh seems superfluous.
   Why is this the only place in the Megillah where he is not called King Achashveirosh?
   Why is the present tense used in referring to his reign?
2) **In those days** and **King Achashveirosh** seem superfluous.
   Why are we told that Achashveirosh's capital was Shushan?

I 3-8 THE BANQUET

3) Why are the princes, servants and soldiers mentioned before the nobles and princes of the provinces?
   What is the meaning of **before him?**

all of his princes and servants, the army of Persia and Media, the nobles and princes of the provinces before him. [4] It was then that he exhibited the riches of his glorious kingdom and the honor of his splendid majesty for many days, one hundred and eighty days. [5] When these days had been completed the king made a banquet for seven days in the court of the garden of the king's palace on behalf of all the people that were present in the capital of Shushan, from the greatest to the smallest. [6] There were white, green and blue silks, held by cords of fine linen and purple wool upon rods of silver and pillars of marble; couches of gold and silver upon a pavement of crystal, marble, pearls and jewels. [7] They served drink in vessels of gold, the vessels differing from one another, and royal wine was in abundance according to a king's means. [8] The drinking was regulated, with no pressure, for the king had thus established for all the stewards of his house that they must do according to every man's wish.

Why do we here find the term **third year of his reign** and in 2:16 **seventh year of his kingdom?**

4) What does **the riches of his glorious kingdom** add to the **honor of his splendid majesty?**
Why is the term **many days** included along with the exact number of days?

5) Why are people of Shushan referred to as those **present in Shushan?**
Why is the expression here **from the greatest to the smallest** rather than the traditional **from the smallest to the greatest?**
Why did he make the feast and why does the Megillah devote so much attention to its details?
Why did he exhibit his riches to all the nations?
What was the purpose of his second feast for the people of Shushan?

5-8) Why are we told that the feast took place in the king's courtyard and informed of all its details?

[9] Vashti, the queen, too made a banquet for the women in the royal house which belonged to King Achashveirosh. [10] On the seventh day, when the king's heart was merry with wine, he commanded Mehuman, Bizzesa, Charvona, Bigsa, and Avagsa, Zeisar, and Charkas, the seven chamberlains that served in the presence of King Achashveirosh—[11] to bring Vashti the queen before the king with her royal crown, to show the people and the princes her beauty, for she was a woman of fair appearance. [12] But Queen Vashti refused to come at the king's command through the chamberlains, and the king became incensed, and his anger burned within him.

I 9-12 VASHTI'S REBELLION

9) Why did Vashti make a separate party called **a banquet for the women?**
   Why are we told about this and informed that it took place in the king's royal house?
   Which belonged to King Achashveirosh seems superfluous.
10) Why are the king's chamberlains mentioned by name and described as ones that **served in the presence of the king?**
11) What logic was there in such a mighty king exhibiting the beauty of his wife before the masses, especially since our Sages say she was summoned in the nude; and why the undignified manner of calling her to immediately appear?
   Why is she referred to in passages 9, 11, and 16 as **Vashti the queen** while in passages 12 and 15 she is **Queen Vashti?**
   Before the king seems superfluous.
   Why is the wording so arranged as to imply that Vashti should not wear the crown until she was before the king?
12) **The king's command through the chamberlains** seems to be the reason for her refusal. Why? There is an apparent redundancy in **the king became incensed** and **his anger burned within him.**

[13] Then the king spoke to the wise men, who knew the times, for so was the king's custom towards all that knew law and judgment—[14] and those next to him were Karshana, Sheisar, Admassa, Sarshish, Meres, Marsna, Memuchan, the seven princes of Persia and Media, who saw the king's face, and sat first in the kingdom—[15] about what should be done according to the law to Queen Vashti for not doing the bidding of King Achashveirosh through the chamberlains.

[16] Memuchan replied before the king and the princes: "Vashti the queen has not wronged the king alone but also all the princes and the peoples in all the provinces of King Achashveirosh. [17] For this matter of the queen will go forth unto all the women to show contempt for their husbands by saying that King Achashveirosh commanded Vashti the queen to be brought before him and she did not come. [18] This very day will the princesses of Persia and Media, who have heard the matter of the queen, thus say to all the king's princes, and there is enough contempt and wrath. [19] If it please the king, let a

---

I 13-18 VASHTI'S TRIAL

13) Who are those **who knew the times** and **those who knew the law and judgment?** What is the difference between **law** and **judgment?**
14) Why is yet another description, **those next to him,** added to the judges?
15) Why are the words **through the chamberlains** added?
17) What is the meaning of **the matter of the queen will go forth?**
18) What is meant by **this very day?**
What will the princes say?
There is an apparent redundancy in **contempt** and **wrath.**

royal decree go forth from him, and let it be recorded in the laws of the Persians and the Medes, never to be revoked, that Vashti come no more before King Achashveirosh, and that the king give her royal position to another who is better than she. [20] When the king's decree, which he shall make, shall be heard throughout all of his kingdom, for it is a great one, all the wives will give honor to their husbands, from the greatest to the smallest." [21] This matter pleased the king and the princes and the king acted according to the word of Memuchan. [22] He sent letters to all of the king's provinces, to each province according to its script and to each people in its language—that every man should dominate in his home and speak according to the language of his people.

I 19-22 VASHTI'S SENTENCE

19) What sort of **royal decree** should be issued?
Why was the order to execute Vashti to be recorded in the law books as a permanent statute if it was only an action necessitated by the particular circumstances?
Why should Vashti be executed for fear of feminine insubordination when the same goal could be achieved by decreeing the superiority of husbands?

20) Why is this decree considered **a great one** when all it amounts to is a slaying of his defenseless wife?

21) Why was the royal decree regarding Vashti sent to each nation in its own language; and what was accomplished by the decrees that every man be master in his own home and free to speak the tongue of his people?
Does Achashveirosh not seem ridiculous in slaying his wife for the sake of protecting male superiority?
Why is the expression **great and small** used instead of vice versa?

Chapter 2

[1] After these events, when the wrath of King Achash-veirosh had calmed down, he remembered Vashti, what she had done and what was decreed upon her. [2] Then said the king's servants that ministered to him: "Let there be sought for the king young virgins of fair appearance. [3] Let the king appoint officers in all the provinces of his kingdom who will gather all the fair young virgins to the capital of Shushan, to the house of the women, to the custody of Heigai, the king's

---

II 1-4 SEARCH FOR A QUEEN

1) What three aspects are referred to in remembering [1] Vashti; [2] what she had done; and [3] what was decreed upon her?
2) What sort of suggestion was this that such a mighty king seek a new queen from the streets?
   Here the suggestion was **let there be sought,** implying voluntary candidates, while in the next passage they speak of appointing and **gathering,** which smack of coercion?
3) Why did the plan for finding a new queen call for putting all candidates in the custody of Heigai; and why did it even include details of their cosmetics?

chamberlain, keeper of the women, and let their ointments be given them. [4] The maiden that pleases the king will reign in place of Vashti." The matter pleased the king and he did so.

[5] There was a Jew in the capital of Shushan whose name was Mordechai, the son of Yair, the son of Shimmie, the son of Kish, a Benjaminite, [6] who had been exiled from Jerusalem with the captivity, taken into exile along with Yechonyah, king of Yehudah, whom Nevuchadnetzar, the king of Babylon, had carried away. [7] He raised Hadassah, that is, Esther, his cousin, for she had neither father nor mother, and the maiden was of beautiful form and fair appearance; and upon the death of her father and mother Mordechai adopted her as his daughter. [8] When the king's orders and his decree were heard and many maidens were gathered to the capital of Shushan, to the custody of Heigai, Esther was taken to the king's house, to the custody of Heigai, keeper of the women. [9] The maiden pleased him and she gained his kindness. He rushed to give her the ointments and portions due her and the seven maidens befitting her from the king's house; and he singled out her and her maids for the

---

II 5-8 ESTHER'S CONCEALMENT

5) Why is Mordechai's ancestry detailed?
6) Why is his exile from Jerusalem mentioned?
7) There is an apparent redundancy in the description of Mordechai as having raised Esther and the statement that **upon the death of her father and mother he adopted her for his daughter;** and an unexplained interruption between these two phrases to describe her beauty.
8) Why is it necessary to detail that the king's decree was heard and that many maidens were gathered when all that interests us is Esther's fate?

II 9-15 ESTHER IN THE PALACE

9) There is an apparent redundancy in **the maiden pleased him** and **she gained his kindness.**

best treatment in the house of the women. [10] Esther did not reveal her people nor her homeland, for Mordechai ordered her not to tell. [11] Mordechai walked each day before the court of the house of women to know Esther's condition and what would become of her. [12] The turn of each maiden arrived to come to King Achashveirosh after she had spent twelve months according to the rule for the women—for so were the days of their treatment spent: six months with oil of myrrh and six months with scents and feminine ointments. [13] With this the maiden came before the king; whatever she requested was granted her, to accompany her out of the house of the women to the king's house. [14] In the evening she came and the next morning she returned to the second house of the women, to the custody of Shashgaz, the king's chamberlain, keeper of the concubines; she came no more to the king unless the king desired her and she was called by name. [15] When there arrived the turn of Esther, the daughter of Avichail, the uncle of Mordechai, who had adopted her as his daughter, to come to the king, she requested nothing save what was said by Heigai, the king's chamberlain, the keeper of the women, and Esther

---

Why did he rush to give her ointments?
Why is there no mention made of gifts and maids provided for the other candidates? The phrase **maids befitting her** indicates that only she merited this attention. Why?

10) Why did Esther not reveal her origins?
11) Why did Mordechai daily inquire about her welfare when he knew that Esther would not meet the king until twelve months had passed?
12) Why did the preparations take exactly twelve months?
13) Why was each candidate granted whatever she wished?
What does **and with this the maiden came** refer to?
15) Why is Esther's **gaining favor in the eyes of all who beheld her** again repeated?
Why is Esther's ancestry repeated and why did she ask for nothing?

gained favor in the eyes of all who beheld her. [16] Esther was taken to King Achashveirosh, to the royal house, in the tenth month, the month of Teves, in the seventh year of his kingdom. [17] The king loved Esther more than all the women, and she gained grace and favor before him more than all the virgins. He set the royal crown upon her head and made her queen in place of Vashti. [18] Then the king made a great banquet for all of his princes and servants—the Banquet of Esther—and he decreed a tax reduction for the provinces and gave gifts according to the bounty of the king. [19] When the virgins were gathered a second time and Mordechai sat within the king's gate—[20] Esther had not yet revealed her homeland nor her people as Mordechai had ordered her; for Esther continued to do Mordechai's bidding just as when she was raised by him.

[21] In those days, while Mordechai sat within the king's gate, two of the king's chamberlains, Bigsan and Seresh, sentries of the threshold, became angry and sought to assassinate

---

II 16-20 ESTHER AND THE KING

17) Who are the **women** and who the **virgins?**
What is the difference between **love, grace,** and **favor?**

18) Why did he have to call the feast **Esther's Banquet** when it was obviously in celebration of the new queen: and why did he grant a tax-reduction and gifts?

19) What is the **second gathering of virgins** mentioned here after Esther's coronation; and what significance is there in Mordechai's sitting within the king's gate?

20) Why is there a repetition of Esther's refusal to divulge her origins?
Why is Esther's secret here described as **her homeland and her people** in contrast to passage 10 where it is characterized as **her people and her homeland?**

II 21-25 BIGSAN-SERESH PLOT

21) Why is there a repetition of passage 19's description of Mordechai as sitting within the king's gate?

King Achashveirosh. [22] The matter became known to Mordechai and he related it to Esther the queen, and Esther told the king in Mordechai's name. [23] The matter was investigated and discovered, and both were hanged on a tree. It was then recorded in the book of chronicles before the king.

---

23) **Before the king** seems superfluous.

Chapter 3

[1] After these events, King Achashveirosh promoted Haman, the son of Hamdasa, the Agagite, and elevated him, and set his position above all his princes. [2] All the king's servants that were within the king's gate bowed down and prostrated themselves before Haman, for so had the king commanded him. But Mordechai neither bowed nor prostrated himself. [3] The king's servants within the king's gate said to Mordechai, "Why do you violate the king's commandment?" [4] It came to pass that as they spoke daily to him and he did not listen to them, that they told Haman, to see whether Mordechai's words would stand, for

---

III 1-2 HAMAN'S RISE TO POWER

1) Why did the king elevate Haman to such heights?
   What connection did his elevation have with the preceding events?
   Promoted and **elevated** seem redundant.
2) What is the stress on **the servants that were within the king's gates?**
   Why does it say **commanded him** when it was the servants who were commanded?

he had told them that he was a Jew. [5] Haman saw that Mordechai neither bowed nor prostrated himself before him and he became full of wrath. [6] It was below his dignity to attack Mordechai alone for they had revealed to him the people of Mordechai. Haman sought to destroy all the Jews, Mordechai's people, who were throughout the whole kingdom of Achashveirosh. [7] In the first month, the month of Nisan, in the twelfth year of King Achashveirosh, he cast Pur, the lots before Haman, from day to day and from month to the twelfth month, the month of Adar.

[8] Haman said to King Achashveirosh: "There is a certain people scattered abroad and dispersed among the peoples in all the provinces of your kingdom. Their laws are different from

---

III 3-5 CONFRONTATION WITH MORDECHAI

4) Why did Mordechai refuse to bow to Haman?
   What is meant by **whether Mordechai's words would stand for he had told them that he was a Jew?** (There was no question about Mordechai's Jewishness, only about his resolve not to bow.)
5) Why did Haman not become angered from the reports of the servants, only when he personally saw Mordechai's refusal?

III 6-7 THE LOTS

6) Why did Haman decide to destroy all of Jewry because of one man's crime?
7) Why did the lots fall on the 13th of Adar?
   Before Haman seems superfluous and there is no apparent meaning in **from day to day** and **from month to the twelfth month.**

III 8-11 HAMAN AND THE KING

8) Why did Haman omit the name of the people he slandered; refer to his goal as **destroyed** rather than **slain;** make the redundant description of **scattered abroad** and **dispersed;** refer to their faith as **laws;** and claim that their laws were different from all **nations** rather than from all **laws?**

those of every people, and they obey not the king's laws; it is not worthwhile for the king to tolerate them. [9] If it please the king, let it be written that they be destroyed and I will pay ten thousand talents of silver, through those who do the work, into the king's treasuries. [10] The king removed the ring from his hand and gave it to Haman, the son of Hamdasa, the Agagite, enemy of the Jews. [11] The king said to Haman: "The silver is given to you as well as the people, to do with them as you see fit." [12] The king's scribes were summoned in the first month, on the thirteenth day thereof, and letters were written, according to all that Haman commanded, to the king's satraps and to the governors of each province, and to the princes of each people, to each province in its script and each people in its language; it was written in the name of King Achashveirosh and sealed with the king's ring. [13] The letters were sent by couriers to all the king's provinces to destroy, to slay and to cause to perish, all Jews, both young and old, little children and women,

---

9) How did a great ruler like Achashveirosh agree to the destruction of an entire innocent people?
If he was a guilty accomplice how did he later wonder at the identity and motive of the culprit; why did he pour out his wrath on Haman; and why did he allow them to write the Megillah in which he would achieve eternal notoriety?
How could Haman expect the king to sell a people for slaughter?
Why should Haman's money go to those **who do the work** rather than to the logical recipients, the king's treasurers?

10) Why is Haman referred to here as the **enemy of the Jews?**
Why are we told of the king's transfer of his ring to Haman?

11) If he meant to reject his offer of money why did he say it **is given to you** rather than the more appropriate **let it remain yours?**

III 12-15 THE DEADLY LETTERS

12) Why did Haman rush to have the letters written that very day, even though they could not take effect for another eleven months?

in one day, the thirteenth day of the twelfth month, the month of Adar, and to take their possessions as spoils. [14] The text of the writing was to issue a decree in each province, publicized to all the peoples, that they be prepared for this day. [15] The couriers left in haste on the king's matter and the decree was issued in the capital of Shushan. The king and Haman sat down to drink and the city of Shushan was perplexed.

---

14) What is meant by the **text of the writing** and the inference that it was openly publicized, in contrast to the documents mentioned in the previous passage?
What were the nations to be ready for on that day?
Why was the decree held up in Shushan until the messengers had departed?

15) How do we explain the callousness of a king on the verge of genocide casually enjoying his drinking; and how do we understand the reason for Shushan being **perplexed?**

Chapter 4

[1] Mordechai knew all that had been done. Mordechai tore his garments and donned sackcloth and ashes, and went out into the midst of the city and cried with a loud and bitter cry. [2] He came as far as just before the king's gate for it was improper to come to the king's gate clothed in sackcloth. [3] In every province that the king's commandment and his decree reached there was great mourning among the Jews, and fasting and weeping and lamenting: sackcloth and ashes were laid out for many. [4] Esther's maidens and her chamberlains came and

---

IV 1-6 MORDECHAI ACTS

1) What was the significance of Mordechai's knowledge of what had transpired since the decree was common knowledge?
   Why did Mordechai go out into the streets shouting his discovery rather than use strategical steps?
2) Why did he come in sackcloth to the king's gates?
3) Why are we suddenly told of Jewish reaction in foreign lands here rather than before, when the messengers are mentioned?
   Why is there no mention here of **every city** as in 8:17?
   The king's commandment and **his decree** seem redundant.

told it to her; and the queen was extremely pained; she sent garments to clothe Mordechai and to remove his sackcloth from him, but he did not accept. [5] Esther called to Hasach, one of the king's chamberlains, whom he had placed before her, and she charged him concerning Mordechai to know what this was and why it was. [6] Hasach went out to Mordechai in the city street in front of the king's gate. [7] Mordechai told him all that had happened to him and the meaning of the money that Haman had promised to pay to the king's treasuries for the destruction of the Jews. [8] He gave him the text of the written decrees that had been issued in Shushan to destroy them, to show it to Esther and to tell her about it, and to charge her that she should come to the king to beg him and to make a request before him on behalf of her people. [9] Hasach came and told Esther the words of Mordechai; [10] Esther spoke to Hasach and gave him a message for Mordechai: [11] "All the king's servants and the people of the king's provinces know that there

---

4) If he dons the garments she sent it is obvious that he will remove his sackcloth, so why mention it?
5) Why did she choose Hasach as her messenger?
6) **She charged him to go to Mordechai** would seem more appropriate than **charged him concerning Mordechai.**

IV 7-16 MORDECHAI-ESTHER DIALOGUE

7) Why did Mordechai relate **what had happened to him** when it was a general situation?
   What is meant by the **meaning of the money?**
8) What did Mordechai show Esther? (The open letters mentioned no slaughter of Jews and Mordechai had no access to the letters received by the ministers.)
   What is left **to tell her about it** after she has been shown the decree?
10) **Esther spoke** and **gave him a message** seem redundant.
11) Why are both the **king's servants** and the **people in the king's provinces** mentioned?

is a standard rule of death for any man or woman entering the inner court uninvited, except for the one to whom the king extends the golden scepter that he may live; and I have not been called to come to the king these thirty days." [12] They told Mordechai the words of Esther. [13] Mordechai said to return this reply to Esther: "Imagine not to yourself that you can escape, more than all Jews, into the house of the king. [14] For if you keep your silence at this time, relief and deliverance shall arise for the Jews from another place, but you and your father's house will perish, and who knows if you did not rise to royalty for just such a time." [15] Esther said to return this reply to Mordechai: [16] "Go, assemble all the Jews to be found in Shushan and fast for me, and neither eat nor drink for three days, night and day. I and my maidens shall likewise fast and so will I come to the king unlawfully and as I have perished so shall I perish." [17] Mordechai went his way and did all that Esther had commanded him.

Shall die would seem to be more appropriate than **there is a standard rule of death.**
Why did she add the apparently meaningless fact that she hadn't been called for 30 days?

12) Who are **they** of **they told Mordechai the words of Esther?**
13) **To yourself** seems superfluous.
14) What is meant by **this time** and **for just such a time?**
Why did Mordechai rush Esther to meet the king since there was still plenty of time for action and during the interlude she might be normally invited by the king?
16) Why did she say **fast for me** when their fasting was for all of Jewry?
Where did she **perish** the first time that she now cried **as I have perished so shall I perish?**

Chapter 5

[1] It came to pass on the third day that Esther donned royalty and stood in the inner court of the king's house facing the king's house; and the king sat upon his royal throne in the royal house, facing the entrance to the house. [2] As the king saw Esther the queen standing in the courtyard she gained favor in his eyes and the king extended to Esther the golden scepter which was in his hand. Esther drew near and touched the tip of the scepter. [3] The king said to her: "What is your will, Queen Esther, and what is your request, for even up to half the kingdom shall be granted to you." [4] Esther said: "If the

---

V 1-8 ESTHER ACTS

1) **Royal apparel** would seem more appropriate than just **royalty.**
   What is the difference between **the king's house** and **the royal house?**
3) **What is your will** and **what is your request** seem redundant.
   A request is usually granted by performing and here the expression is **it shall be granted to you.**

king considers it good let the king and Haman come today to the banquet I have arranged for him." [5] Then the king said: "Rush Haman to do what Esther has said." The king and Haman came to the banquet which Esther had prepared. [6] The king said to Esther at the banquet of wine: "What is your petition, for it shall be granted you; and what is your request, for even up to half a kingdom it shall be performed." [7] Esther replied and said: "My petition and my request—[8] If I have found favor in the king's eyes and if it pleases the king to grant my petition and to perform my request—let the king and Haman come to the banquet that I shall prepare for them: and tomorrow I will do as the king has said." [9] Haman went forth that day joyful and glad of heart; but when Haman saw Mordechai at the king's gate and he neither rose nor stirred because of him, Haman became filled with wrath towards Mordechai. [10] But Haman restrained himself and went home. He sent for and fetched his friends and his wife Zeresh. [11] Haman recounted

---

4) Here she said **if the king considers it good** and in 5:8 and 7:3 **if I have found favor.**
5) What is stressed by **to do what Esther has said?**
6) What is the difference between **petition** and **request** and why is the former **granted** and the latter **performed?**
8) **I have found favor** and **if it please the king** seem redundant.
   Why did Esther invite Haman along with the king?
   Why did she again repeat **my petition and my request?**
   What did Esther promise to do for the king tomorrow?

V 9-14 HAMAN BUILDS A GALLOWS

9) **That day** seems superfluous.
   Neither rose and **nor stirred** seem redundant.
   Here it says **Haman was filled with wrath towards Mordechai** and in 3:5 only, **Haman was full of wrath.**
10) From what action did he restrain himself in order to go home?
11) Why did Haman suddenly decide to tell family and friends of his glory?

to them the glory of his riches, of his many children and all that the king had promoted him and how he had elevated him above the princes and servants of the king. [12] Haman said: "Moreover, Queen Esther did not bring anyone but me along with the king to the banquet she had arranged; tomorrow, too, I am invited by her together with the king. [13] But all of this means nothing to me each time I see the Jew Mordechai sitting at the king's gate." [14] His wife, Zeresh, and his friends said to him: "Let a gallows fifty cubits high be made and in the morning speak to the king that Mordechai be hanged upon it. Then you can joyfully come together with the king to the banquet." This matter pleased Haman and he made the gallows.

---

12) **She brought me as well** would seem more appropriate than **she did not bring anyone but me.** Since there was no reason for inviting any ministers along with the king why is the stress not placed on the fact that he had deserved an invitation?

14) Why did they counsel Haman to build a gallows; to insist on a high one; and on an early morning request of the king for permission to hang Mordechai?

Chapter 6

[1] That night the king could not sleep and he said to bring the book of records of the chronicles, and they were read before the king. [2] It was found recorded that Mordechai had told of Bigsan and Seresh, two of the king's chamberlains, sentries of the threshold, who had sought to assassinate King Achashveirosh. [3] The king said: "What honor and position have been conferred upon Mordechai for this?" The king's servants that ministered to him said, "Nothing has been done for him." [4] The king said: "Who is in the court?" Haman had just come to the court of the king's house to speak to the king about hanging Mordechai on the gallows that he had prepared for him. [5] The king's servants said to him: "Behold, Haman is

---

VI 1-6 A SLEEPLESS NIGHT

1) Why was the king unable to sleep?
   Book of records and **chronicles** seem redundant.
2) Why is it stressed that **it was found recorded** as if to imply the likelihood of erasure?
3) **Honor** and **position** seem redundant.
   For this seems superfluous.

standing in the court." The king said: "Let him enter." [6] Haman entered and the king said to him: "What shall be done with the man whom the king wishes to honor?" Haman thought to himself: "Who could the king wish to honor more than myself?" [7] Haman said to the king: "The man whom the king wishes to honor! Let royal apparel be brought which the king is accustomed to wearing and the horse that the king rode upon when the crown was placed upon his head. [9] Let the apparel and the horse be put in the charge of one of the king's most noble princes so that they may array the man whom the king wishes to honor, and lead him on horseback through the streets of the city and proclaim before him: 'Thus shall be done to the man whom the king wishes to honor.' " [10] The king said to Haman: "Hurry and take the apparel and the horse as you have spoken, and do all this to Mordechai the Jew who sits at the king's gate: let nothing fail from all you have spoken." [11] Haman took the apparel and the horse and arrayed Mordechai and led him on horseback through the streets of the city, proclaiming before him: "Thus shall be done to the man whom the king wishes to honor." [12] Mordechai returned to the king's gate and Haman mournfully hurried home, his head covered with shame. [13] He recounted to his wife, Zeresh, and all his friends all that had befallen him. His wise men and his wife, Zeresh, said to him: "If

---

6) Why did the king omit **position** in his question to Haman?

VI 7-14 MORDECHAI'S TRIUMPH

7) Why did Haman repeat **the man whom the king wishes to honor?**

10) Why did the king order Mordechai to be rewarded so early in the morning?
Why did the king order Haman to personally handle everything in contrast to Haman's own suggestion that noble princes handle the details?

13) Why did Haman relate the bad news of his setback to family and friends?

Mordechai, before whom you have begun to fall, is of Jewish descent, you shall not prevail against him but shall surely fall before him." [14] While they were still speaking the king's chamberlains arrived and rushed to bring Haman to the banquet which Esther had arranged.

What did Haman mean by **all that had befallen him,** which implies that it was only a coincidence?

Why did Haman's wise men demoralize him by telling him that he would continue to fall before Mordechai?

14) Why are we told that the king's servants arrived while they were still talking?

Chapter 7

[1] The king and Haman came to drink with Queen Esther. [2] The king said again to Esther on the second day at the banquet of wine: "What is your petition, Queen Esther, and it shall be performed." [3] Queen Esther replied and said: "If I have found favor in the king's eyes and if it please the king let my life be given me at my petition and my people at my request. [4] For we have been sold, I and my people, to be destroyed, to be slain, and to perish. Had we been sold for slaves I would have held my peace. But the adversary is not worth the damage he causes the king." [5] King Achashveirosh

---

VII 1-9 THE SECOND BANQUET

2) Why did he here address her as **Queen Esther?**
   Why does the petition refer to herself and the request to her people?
4) Why did Esther say she would have been silent had her people been sold into slavery; and what did she mean by **the adversary is not worth the damage he causes the king?**
   Why did Achashveirosh suddenly ask who was responsible if he was a knowing accomplice?

spoke and then said to Queen Esther: "Who is he and which is he that dares to do so?" [6] Esther said: "An adversary and an enemy, this wicked Haman!"—and Haman was terrified in the presence of the king and queen. [7] The king rose in his wrath from the banquet of wine and went into the palace garden. Haman arose to plead for his life before Queen Esther for he saw that there was evil determined against him by the king. [8] The king returned from the palace garden to the place of the banquet of wine and Haman was fallen upon the couch which Esther occupied. The king said: "Will he even force the queen before me in the palace?" The statement left the king's mouth and Haman's face was covered. [9] Charvona, one of the king's chamberlains before the king, said: "Behold also the gallows fifty cubits high which Haman made for Mordechai, who spoke good for the king, standing in Haman's house." The king said: "Hang him on the gallows." [10] They hanged Haman on the gallows he had prepared for Mordechai and the king's wrath was calmed.

---

5) **King Achashveirosh spoke—and then said** seem redundant, as do **who is he** and **which is he.**
6) **Adversary** and **enemy** seem redundant.
7) Why did Haman not plead for his life before both the king and queen?
9) How did Charvona know about Haman's plans to hang Mordechai and what difference is it that it is fifty cubits high and now stands in Haman's home?

Chapter 8

[1] On that day King Achashveirosh gave the House of Haman, enemy of the Jews, to Queen Esther: and Mordechai came before the king, for Esther had revealed his relationship to her. [2] The king took off his ring, which he had removed from Haman, and gave it to Mordechai. Esther placed Mordechai in charge of the House of Haman. [3] Esther spoke once again to the king and fell before his feet and wept, begging him to remove the evil of Haman the Agagite and the plans he had made against the Jews. [4] The

---

VIII 1-2 MORDECHAI'S RISE

1) Why was Haman's estate given to Esther?
   What is so special about Mordechai's ability to come before the king since any subject can approach the ruler when he needs to?
   Why is Haman here referred to as **the enemy of the Jews?**
2) **Which he had removed from Haman** seems superfluous.
   What is the significance of Esther placing Mordechai in charge of Haman's estate?

VIII 3-8 UNDOING HAMAN'S TROUBLE

3) Why did Esther beg more intensely now than before?

king held out to Esther the golden scepter. Esther arose and stood before the king. [5] She said: "If it pleases the king and if I have found favor before him, and the thing seems proper before the king, and I am good in his eyes, let it be written to revoke the letters devised by Haman, the son of Hamdasa, the Agagite, which he wrote to destroy the Jews in all of the king's provinces. [6] For how can I bear to see the evil which will befall my people and how can I bear to see the destruction of my kindred?"

[7] King Achashveirosh said to Queen Esther and to Mordechai the Jew: "Behold, I have given the House of Haman to Esther and him have I hanged upon the gallows for laying hands on the Jews. [8] As you see fit concerning the Jews you shall write in the king's name and seal it with the king's ring, for the document which is written in the king's name and sealed with the king's ring cannot be revoked." [9] The king's scribes were summoned at that time, in the third month, the month of Sivan, in the twenty-third day thereof, and it was written according to all that Mordechai commanded, to the Jews, to the satraps and governors and princes of the provinces from India to Kush, one hundred and twenty-seven provinces, each province according to its script and each people according to its language, and to the Jews accord-

---

5) Several redundancies seem to exist here in regard to her pleas and in the description of Haman's evil intentions.
   Esther's words seem redundant and **devised by Haman** superfluous.
6) Again an apparent redundancy.
7) How did the king hope to comfort her fears for her people by recalling the execution of Haman and the giving of his estate to Esther?
8) How did the king's plan eliminate the problem of the irrevocability of the first letters signed by the king and how could Jewry be saved if they were not revoked?

VIII 9-17 MORDECHAI'S LETTERS

9) Why did Mordechai wait until Sivan 23 to write the second letters?

ing to their script and their language. [10] They wrote in the name of King Achashveirosh and sealed it with the king's ring and sent letters with mounted couriers, riders of the king's swift steeds, the mules born from mares—[11] that the king had permitted the Jews in every city to gather and defend their lives, to destroy and slay and cause to perish all the forces of the people and provinces threatening them, their little children and women, and to take their possessions for spoils; [12] in one day, in all the provinces of King Achashveirosh, the thirteenth day of the twelfth month, the month of Adar. [13] The text of the writing was to issue a decree in each province, made public to all the peoples, that the Jews should be prepared for this day to avenge themselves against all their enemies. [14] The couriers riding upon the king's swift steeds, the mules, went forth confused and hurried on the king's matter, and the decree was issued in the capital of Shushan.

[15] And Mordechai went forth from the king's presence in royal apparel of blue and white, with a great crown of gold and with a robe of fine linen and purple; and the city of Shushan sparkled and was glad. [16] The Jews had light and gladness, and joy and honor. [17] In every province and in every city, wherever the king's commandment and decree arrived, there was gladness and joy, a feast and a festival, and many of the peoples of the land became Jews, for the fear of the Jews had fallen upon them.

---

12) Haman's letter implied slaughter on the thirteenth and spoils afterwards while Mordechai implied that both would take place on the same day.
13) Mordechai mentioned that the decree was in effect in all lands but Haman omitted this fact.
14) Why is the word **hurried** added here?
Why did Mordechai send his messengers on horseback while Haman sent them by foot?
15) **The city of Shushan** implies non-Jews as well.
17) When Mordechai's letters arrived, **every city** is mentioned but by Haman's letters we find only a mention of lands.

Chapter 9

[1] In the twelfth month, the month of Adar, on the thirteenth day thereof, when the time had arrived for the king's commandment and his decree to be executed, on the day that the enemies of the Jews hoped to have control over them, it was turned about, that the Jews had control, they over their foes. [2] The Jews gathered together in their cities in all the provinces of King Achashveirosh, to lay their hands on those who sought to hurt them. No man stood before them for their dread had fallen upon all the peoples. [3] All the princes of the provinces, the satraps and the governors, and those who did the king's work, deferred to the Jews because the dread of Mordechai had fallen upon them. [4] For Mordechai was great

---

IX 1-18 TABLES ARE TURNED

1) **They** seems superfluous.
   Here **the fear of them was fallen upon all the peoples** and in the next verse **the fear of Mordechai was fallen upon them.**
2) What is the difference between this verse and 9:16?

in the king's house and his fame spread throughout all the provinces; for the man Mordechai grew greater and greater. [5] The Jews struck all their enemies with the stroke of the sword and with slaughter and destruction; and did as they wished to their foes. [6] In the capital of Shushan the Jews killed and destroyed five hundred men, [7] and slew Parshandossa, and Dalphon, and Asfassa, [8] and Porassa and Adalyah and Aridasa, [9] and Parmashta and Arisai and Aridai and Vaizasa; [10] the ten sons of Haman, the son of Hamdasa, the enemy of the Jews; but laid not a hand on the spoils. [11] On that day the number of those slain in the capital of Shushan came before the king. [12] Said the king to Queen Esther: "The Jews have killed and destroyed five hundred men in the capital of Shushan as well as the ten sons of Haman; what have they done in the rest of the king's provinces? What is your petition for it will be granted and what more do you request for it shall be performed." [13] Queen Esther said: "If it please the king let tomorrow also be granted to the Jews in Shushan to do according to today's decree and let Haman's ten sons be hanged upon the gallows." [14] The king ordered this to be done. The decree was issued in the capital of Shushan and they hanged the ten sons of Haman. [15] The Jews in Shushan gathered together again on the fourteenth day of Adar and they killed three hundred

---

4) What is meant by **the man Mordechai grew greater and greater?**
5) What is the difference between **enemies** and **foes?**
12) If the king was upset about the death toll in Shushan why did he invite Esther to request further security measures?
Why did he allow the Jews such a free hand in slaughtering the citizens of his own land?
13) How did Esther, after hearing the king's reaction to the report of the death toll in Shushan, dare ask for an extension?
15) Why is the city steadily referred to as **Shushan the capital** and here simply as **Shushan?**

men in Shushan but laid not a hand on the spoils. [16] The other Jews, in the king's provinces, gathered together to defend their lives. They gained relief from their enemies and killed seventy-five thousand of their foes, but laid not a hand on the spoils. [17] This was on the thirteenth day of the month of Adar and they gained relief on the fourteenth, which they made a day of feasting and gladness. [18] The Jews in Shushan gathered together on the thirteenth and fourteenth, gaining relief on the fifteenth and making it a day of feasting and gladness. [19] Therefore the Jewish townsmen who dwell in the unwalled towns celebrate the fourteenth of Adar as a day of gladness and feasting and a festival, and of sending portions to one another.

[20] Mordechai recorded these things and sent letters to all the Jews in the provinces of King Achashveirosh, both near and far—[21] to ordain for them that they observe the fourteenth of Adar and the fifteenth each year [22] like the days in which the Jews had gained relief from their enemies and the month which was transformed from sorrow to gladness and from mourning

---

16) How does this description of military defense mesh with 9:2, where no opposition existed, and how does its description of **killing** mesh with 9:5, where they only **did as they wished to their foes?**

IX 19-32 MAKING OF A HOLIDAY

19) The impression given here is that only the unwalled cities accepted the holiday and that only the 14th day of Adar was celebrated until Mordechai insisted on universal acceptance of the 14th and 15th.
Why did Mordechai not decree a holiday while they did accept it as such?

20) What were **these things** which Mordechai wrote in his letters? Why did Mordechai decree that all of the walled cities celebrate the 15th simply because the Jews of Shushan did not rest until then? If this dubious tribute was in honor of Shushan everyone's Purim should have been on that day?

to a festival; to make them days of feasting and gladness and of sending portions to one another and gifts to the poor. [23] The Jews accepted upon themselves what they had already begun and Mordechai had written them. [24] For Haman, the son of Hamdasa, the Agagite, the enemy of all the Jews, plotted against the Jews, to destroy them, and cast the lots of Pur, to terrify them and destroy them. [25] When it came before the king he said that with the letter his evil plot which he plotted against the Jews would return upon his own head; and they hanged him and his sons on the gallows. [26] They therefore called these days Purim, after the name of the Pur. Therefore, because of all the words of this letter, and what they saw concerning this and what had resulted for them, [27] the Jews ordained and accepted upon themselves and their posterity and all who joined them, to irrevocably observe these two days according to their writing and their time each year, [28] and that these days should be remembered and observed in each generation, every family, every province, and every city, and these days of Purim should never pass from among the Jews nor their remembrance from their posterity.

[29] Queen Esther, the daughter of Avichail, and Mordechai the Jew, wrote, with all their power, to confirm this second letter

---

23) **What they had already begun** and **what Mordechai had written them** are apparently one and the same—the celebration.

24) Why is there a repetition of Haman's plot and why is the word **terrify** added and the lots mentioned?

25) What is the subject of **it came before the king** and what is meant by **with the letter?**

26) What is the significance of calling the days **Purim?**
What is meant by **therefore, because of all the words of this letter?**

27) What is meant by **irrevocably** and by **according to their writing and their time?**

29) Why is Esther's name repeated and what is meant by **with all their power?**

of Purim. [30] Letters were sent to all the Jews, to the one hundred and twenty-seven provinces of Achashveirosh's kingdom, words of peace and truth; [31] to confirm these days of Purim in their times according to what Mordechai the Jew and Queen Esther had enjoined them and as they had ordained for themselves and their posterity, the matters of their fasts and their cry. [32] The commandment of Esther confirmed these matters of Purim and it was recorded in the book.

---

30) What are **words of peace and truth?**
31) What is referred to in **the matters of their fasts and their cry** and what sort of acceptance was asked for after they had already accepted the holiday?
32) What is meant by **the commandment of Esther?**
What did the second letters of Mordechai achieve more than the first ones he sent to the Jews?

Chapter 10

[1] King Achashveirosh levied a tax upon the land and upon the isles of the sea. [2] All the acts of his power and his might, and the account of Mordechai's greatness to which the king elevated him—are they not recorded in the book of the chronicles of the kings of Media and Persia? [3] For Mordechai the Jew was second to King Achashveirosh and great among the Jews, and accepted by most of his brethren; a seeker of good for his people and a spokesman of peace for all his posterity.

X 1-3 MORDECHAI'S GREATNESS

1) Why did Achashveirosh levy a tax and why is it mentioned here?
2) Why does the Megillah bother mentioning the accomplishments of Achashveirosh?

THE MALBIM

Rabbi Meir Yehudah Leibush Malbim

(5569-5640; 1809-1879)

The Early Years

Every student of *Tanach* is familiar with the commentary of the Malbim and sometimes finds it hard to believe that such a major work was created only a century ago. This universal admiration for his works, however, belies a personal history of conflict within and without Orthodox Judaism, against a background of tragedy and frustration.

Tragedy stalked him at an early age, when he lost his father, and continued to cast its shadow over him through an early marriage ending in divorce and throughout his years as a religious leader. Some Chassidim were initially suspicious of the modern style of his writings and his attitude to Chassidus despite the fact that he had, in his younger years, been a leading disciple of the greatest Kabbalist of the era, Reb Zvi Ziditchoiver. The anti-religious Maskilim who originally mistook him to be one of their own soon learned to fear the power of his tongue and pen, and used every method available to persecute him.

But just as tragedy appeared early in his life so did his brilliance as a Torah scholar. It was his reputation at age fourteen as a Torah genius which had made him so desirable a son-in-law and eventually resulted in his unsuccessful marriage to a wealthy man's daughter. The years after his divorce were spent in secluded study and at eighteen he was admitted to the court of the Ziditchoiver. There he mastered the classic works of Kabballah and even managed to complete an unpublished commentary of his own on Kabbalah.

Soon after he had completed his first published work, *Artzos Hachaim*, at the age of twenty—he began working on it when he was fifteen—the Malbim took the manuscript along with him in his travels across Europe and sought the endorsements of the leading Torah scholars. So impressed were they with the young man's brilliance that they heaped generous praise upon him in their letters of endorsement, of which one of the most enthusiastic is that of the Chasam Sofer, *zatzal.*

Positions of Leadership

His personal life, too, began to be blessed with success as he married a young widow, the daughter of the wealthy head of the Lintshitz Jewish community. Already famous throughout Europe as a great scholar and gifted *darshan*, the Malbim, in 1837, was offered the rabbinical leadership of Posna, left vacant by the passing of Rabbi Akiva Eiger, *zatzal*. But he had another offer from the community of Vereshneh and he decided to accept it.

For seven years he served with great distinction as the rabbi of the city and then went on to the Prussian city of Kempenah, where he served until 1858. In the summer of that fateful year he accepted the position of Chief Rabbi of Bucharest, then the second largest Jewish community in Romania. As Y. Yosef Cohen points out in his study on Romanian Jewry, some of the leaders of the Bucharest community championed his selection because they believed him to be an "enlightened" rabbi. A Yiddish newspaper published during that period by the Maskilim in Romania's largest community, Jassy, called for "the election of a modern rabbi in the city such as the one Bucharest had succeeded in gaining."

The Malbim had left Kempenah with great honors after the townspeople finally resigned themselves to his departure and ceased their intensive efforts to dissuade him from leaving a post they felt no one else could properly fill. Hundreds of its citizens had accompanied their rabbi for several miles beyond the city limits and eagerly listened as he spoke words of Torah and offered counsel on how they should run the community in the future.

But this was pale beside the fanfare with which he was greeted upon his arrival in Bucharest. Three hundred carriages rode out to welcome him, followed by all the rest of the community on foot. Even the Romanian government saw fit to send an honor guard of soldiers to receive him with the protocol reserved for the most important government ministers.

The Malbim, however, proved a very big disappointment to the champions of assimilation and compromise. Just as he had dedicated his creative talents to writing a commentary on *Tanach* to combat the Maskilim and reformers, he now devoted his talents as a speaker and leader to eliminating their influence on the Jewish life of his community. His enemies, including some disillusioned community leaders, persecuted him at every turn and climaxed their campaign against him with a report to the authorities slandering him as a foreign espionage agent. Romanian police arrested him in the middle of a lecture to his congregation on the Sabbath and he was soon court-martialed and sentenced to death. The intervention of Sir Moses Montefiore, who rushed from London to appeal to the Romanian ruler, saved him from death, but the opponents of the Malbim continued their pressure until they succeeded in having him banished from the land.

There is a fascinating footnote to the history of the Malbim's "most troubled and least productive years," which he spent in Bucharest. A certain Rabbi Margolis was exiled from Eretz Yisrael by the Turkish government in the First World War and made his way to Bucharest. While a guest of one of the local Jews he witnessed a strange scene. An elegantly dressed man, with the bearing of a noble gentleman and the face of a disturbed soul, entered the house and began drinking hot tea. He sat there for a long time and drank seemingly endless amounts of the steaming beverage. When Rabbi Margolis finally asked his host for an explanation of the odd fellow's peculiar conduct he was told, "This is the Malbim's grandson."

"This is a descendant of the Malbim!" exclaimed Rabbi Margolis.

"He's not really a grandson," explained the host, "but that is what everyone calls him. His grandfather was the main informer responsible for the Malbim's expulsion and near death, and the rabbi cursed him with insanity. The curse not only took its toll on the informer but continued in his family. This grandson is an intelligent man but during two months of every year he behaves irrationally and does things like drinking hot tea incessantly."

After the Bucharest affair the Malbim gained the opportunity of a respite from the arduous challenges of the rabbinate. His wealthy father-in-law had passed away, leaving him a substantial estate in Lintshitz. With his wife managing the inherited business and property, the Malbim could serve as rabbi of the community yet be independent enough to complete his classical commentary on *Tanach*. Not only his own writings occupied his attention during this period but also the writings of the Rishonim, the early commentaries whose manuscripts had never been printed. Together with the rabbi of Warsaw, Rabbi Dov Berish Meisles, *zatzal,* he founded the Shomrei Torah Society for the purpose of publishing these manuscripts. The first undertaking was the commentary of Rabbeinu Chananel on *Masechta Pesachim.*

These were the Malbim's happiest years, but they were soon to come to an end. When the business became too much for his wife to handle alone she hired a local Jew to help manage it. This fellow turned out to be an unscrupulous swindler and he succeeded in swallowing up the entire business, leaving the Malbim and his family penniless.

"I can forgive you everything," the Malbim told this swindler, "except that you have made it necessary for me to support myself once again under the heavy yoke of a rabbinical position."

As in Bucharest, justice was not long in coming. The swindler went mad, began barking like a dog, and was soon discovered dead at the city dump.

There was another factor that cast a cloud over his years in Lintshitz and eventually caused him to leave the city. The community was dominated by Chassidim who resented the Malbim's attitude to Chassidus and the inevitable clashes dulled his appetite for leadership in Lintshitz.

So it was that in 1869 the Malbim resumed his wandering by accepting the rabbinical post in Chersan. Three years later he was called to assume the leadership of a stronghold of the Maskilim, the White Russian city of Mohilov. Here there were echoes of the battles in Bucharest as the Malbim fearlessly spoke out against those who would dilute Torah Judaism. His 'enlightened' opponents in Mohilov followed in the footsteps of their colleagues in Bucharest by slandering the Malbim with the authorities. An expulsion order was issued and the Malbim was forced to leave all of Russia within forty-eight hours.

The German city of Koenigsberg was the Malbim's next position and here again he came into conflict with the enemies of traditional Judaism, this time in the form of Mendelssohn's reformist disciples. His three years there were relatively quiet ones but his disgust with the inroads of reform caused him to lend an interested ear to offers of positions in more satisfying surroundings. Just as he had in his younger years been offered such world famous positions as Posna and Uhel, which he could not accept because of previous commitments, the Malbim found himself, in his last years, called to fill the most outstanding positions and unable to do so. Vilna asked him to become the chief *darshan* of that great Jewish center but the government refused to approve his election. From across the seas came an offer from New York City to serve as its first Chief Rabbi at an annual salary of five thousand dollars, a sum far exceeding anything he had ever received in his previous positions. But his family argued that he was too old to undertake the long voyage and that he had already committed himself to the Krementshog community. Once again the opportunity of settling in a comfortable position had eluded him and the Malbim set out on the long journey to his new community.

After a glorious welcome in the Lithuanian city of Brisk the Malbim made his way to Kobrin, where he was taken seriously ill. Momentarily recovered, he pursued his journey and reached Kiev where he had a fatal relapse. On Rosh Hashanah, 5640, he returned his soul to its Maker.

His Works

When the Malbim departed this world at the end of a troubled life as a Jewish leader he had the satisfaction of knowing that his many *seforim* had received universal acclaim and had become part of the traditional literature of many thousands of Jewish homes. His first published work was the *Artzos Hachaim,* a scholarly commentary on the first twenty-four *simanim* of *Shulchan Aruch Orach Chaim* which he completed at the age of twenty. It was finally published in 1837, in Breslau, and included the enthusiastic endorsement of the Chasam Sofer, hailing its author's greatness. A year later he established his reputation as a homiletic genius with the publication in Kerestin of *Artzos Hashalom,* a series of *drashos* which was a forerunner of the style he was to use in his commentary on *Tanach*.

A charming story is told which reflects both the personality of the Malbim and the impact of his works. The late Rabbi Mordechai Chaim Slonim relates that the Malbim had traveled to the spas at Marienbad a short while after completing publication of his *Artzos Hashalom* and noticed that he was being followed. When the stranger approached and asked his name the Malbim became terrified that he might be a government agent who would arrest him for not carrying the documents required for travel. But the Malbim was never one to deviate from the truth and he frankly declared his identity. When the stranger countered with the announcement of his own name the Malbim's fear grew even greater. Standing before him was the author of one of the most dangerous attacks on traditional Judaism and a leading figure in the reformist camp so violently opposed to the Malbim's philosophy.

"I read your *Artzos Hashalom*," his challenger calmed him, "and a spirit of purity entered my heart. I want to repent my grave sins!"

"My *sefer* was written," the Malbim told him, "to counteract your book's ridicule of our holy Sages and your misinterpretation of their words. If you wish to truly repent you must do so with the poetic justice of distributing my newly published *sefer*, which puts the wisdom of the Sages into the proper light."

The penitent author thanked the Malbim for his advice and sent his *sefer* to his many acquaintances along with a personal letter of recommendation.

The Malbim's success in striking a responsive chord in Jewish hearts with his spoken and written *drashos* was attributed by one of the greatest Chassidic leaders to his heavenly motivation. The Munkatcher Rav, author of *Darkei Teshuvah*, heard his master, the Divrei Chaim of Sanz, testify that "all of the Malbim's *drashos* are *l'shem Shomayim*—intended only for the greater glory of G-d." Connoisseurs of Sanzian perfectionism may truly appreciate this as the ultimate compliment.

A turning point in the Malbim's life, which was to shape his destiny as an author, came in the year 1844. In the German city of Braunschweig the leaders of the reform movement assembled for a meeting which was to cast a long, dark shadow on Jewish history. In his introduction to his commentary on *Toras Ko-*

hanim the Malbim bitterly attacked these "shepherds who devour their sheep and call themselves the rabbis, preachers, cantors and *shochtim* of their communities." The Malbim realized that it was a time "to act for G-d, to erect for the Written and the Oral Torah a protective wall, with doors and bolts, to keep out the vile invaders who would defile them." He dipped his pen in tears as he wrote how "this wicked assembly treated scripture as mythology and compared its songs and phrases with the poetry of Homer and the Greeks." He echoed the "agonizing wail of the betrayed Torah" as he recounted how "the Talmud was for them a subject of sport; they denied it and defamed its Sages by declaring that they knew not the simple meaning of scriptural passages and were ignorant of Hebrew grammar."

These observations stirred the Malbim to action. "I girded my loins like a warrior," he concludes, "and began writing my commentary on *Tanach*."

Viewing this situation as his heaven-ordained personal challenge the Malbim dedicated all of his brilliance and energy to creating a commentary which would beat the Maskilim at their own game. He was determined to demonstrate how the Talmudical Sages based their explanations of scriptural passages according to a consistent and logical application of a language discipline handed down at Sinai.

His first work on *Tanach* was his commentary on Megillas Esther, published in 1845. In this he fulfilled the promise shown in *Artzos Hashalom* by brilliantly analyzing every word and phrase in his searching questions and then weaving his answers into a classical interpretation of the biblical story. The popularity of this work can be seen in the fact that by 1862 it had already been printed in three editions. Although he had produced another popular work, *Shirei Hanefesh*—a commentary on *Shir Hashirim*—whose third edition appeared in 1863, it remained for his commentary on *Yeshayahu* to truly mark the beginning of the magnum opus which would guarantee him immortal fame. Published in Warsaw in 1849, his *Chazon Yeshayahu* was prefaced with a detailed description of the Malbim's approach to explaining *Tanach*, and served as an introduction to his successive works.

The following decade saw the Malbim laboring over the keystone of his classic commentary on *Tanach*. Focusing on the Talmudical *midrashim* on *Sefer Vayikra* known as *Sifra Devei Rav* or *Toras Kohanim*, he set himself the goal of showing how all of the Sages' explanations are implicit in the words of the Torah if one is aware of the God-given rules of language so perfectly applied by them. He even compiled a staggering six hundred and thirteen rules of Hebrew grammar and usage under the title *Ayeles Hashachar* and listed examples of their application in *Toras Kohanim*. This 'encyclopedia' of the Talmudical use of the Holy Tongue eventually became the introduction to his complete commentary on *Toras Kohanim, HaTorah Vehamitzvah*, published in Bucharest in 1860, and offered a blueprint for his commentary on *Tanach*, which he completed years later.

Although the Malbim's imprint on history was that of the "master of *pshat*," who illuminated the meaning of even the vaguest passage of Scripture and the most difficult Talmudic *drashah*, he sometimes confuses the ordinary reader with his penchant for poetry. Not only did he compile an entire work of sacred poetry, *Shirei Kodesh—Mashal Umelitzah,* but he suffused the prefaces to his works with imagery and wordplay. He was careful, however, to assure the general reader that the commentaries themselves would be in language he could easily understand. Each of the nine *drashos* in *Artzos Hashalom* is prefaced by flowery phrases, which, the Malbim tells his readers, "were written for lovers of poetry... and anyone unfamiliar with such language and anxious to see the *drashah* itself should skip the preface and proceed to the *drashah*, which is written in simple language." The same self-conscious tone appears at the end of his preface to *Chazon Yeshayahu.* After a torrent of poetic prose he urges the reader "not to despair and not to retreat for now I shall speak to you as an ordinary man in a language you can understand and no longer shall you hear poetry from me."

Some smaller works also flowed from the prolific pen of the Malbim and one of them, a commentary on the Pesach Haggadah, printed in Warsaw, provides an outstanding example of his ability to interpret any Talmudic material related to Scripture.

His Reputation

Anyone undertaking such immense challenges as did the Malbim inevitably invites the suspicion of people unfamiliar with his character and motives. Despite the Chasam Sofer's endorsement of his scholarship and the Divrei Chaim's tribute to the Malbim's sacred motivations, his works were sometimes criticized by Chassidim who resented his modern innovations in explaining *Tanach*. In relation to these suspicions the renowned author Rabbi Yisrael Yaakov Klapholtz of Bnei Brak, a confidant of the later Belzer Rav, Reb Aharon, *zatzal*, relates a revealing story he once heard from the Rebbe about his grandfather, Reb Yehoshua, *zatzal*. The Belzer Chassidim of those days complained to their Rebbe about such Malbim devices as "question marks in his commentary on *Tanach*." Reb Yehoshua decided to investigate their complaints by sending a trusted agent to study the Malbim. This agent spent two months in the Malbim's home and made mental notes of his host's daily schedule, down to the minutest detail. As soon as he had completed his report to the Rebbe upon his return, the Chassidim entered to hear their master's verdict.

"Out!" the Rebbe angrily shouted. "I refuse to even hear one word about the Malbim because I am convinced that he is a *kadosh vetahor*—a pure and saintly Jew."

In the Torah circles of Lithuania the Malbim was highly respected for both his brilliance and piety. The famed Rav of Brisk, Reb Yehoshua Leib Diskin, *zatzal,* referred to him as the "Tzaddik of Kempin" and his successor, Reb Yosef Dov Soloveitchik, *zatzal,* was a great admirer of the Malbim. A charming tale of a visit by the Malbim to Brisk was told to a colleague of this writer, Rabbi Yitzchak Weinstein, by a very old Jew in Haifa. Approaching his one hundredth birthday, this Jew, Reb Ber, was asked to reveal the secret of his extraordinary longevity.

"I was the outstanding student in the Brisker Yeshiva for boys many, many years ago," Reb Ber began. "One day the great Malbim came to town and secluded himself with our Rav, Reb Yosef Dov, with whom he exchanged Torah thoughts. I boldly entered the room where they sat and the Rav introduced me to the Malbim as an outstanding yeshiva *bachur*. The Malbim spoke to me a while and then asked me if I desired his blessings. I replied that I truly wished he would bless me with three things—that I will have the will to study Torah, the ability to do so, and that I utilize these blessings to actually study. The Malbim granted my request but added that since I had only asked for spiritual blessings he would, on his own initiative, add a blessing for long life. Reb Yosef Dov added his own blessing to this effect and their blessings are responsible for my long life."

Reb Ber passed away in Haifa at the age of 103.

Brisk was one of the Malbim's last stations in his final journey and he was welcomed there by Reb Yosef Dov and all the prominent Jews of the city.

The Chafetz Chaim, *zatzal,* was another Torah giant unstinting in his praise of the Malbim. "How does one merit such a great mind as the Malbim's?" was his expression of admiration whenever he cited him as an example of multi-faceted genius. He first became acquainted with the Malbim when the latter served as rabbi of Koenigsberg and soon became friendly enough for the Malbim to pour out his heart to him about the bitter communal and family problems which had constantly plagued him. When the Chafetz Chaim visited him again during his brief stay in Kobrin he purchased from him a set of *Chumashim* with the Malbim's commentary. "I bought them from the author himself!" the Chafetz Chaim would exclaim with pride as he pointed to the *Chumashim* he so treasured ever after. In his *Mishnah Berurah* the Chafetz Chaim often quoted the halachic decisions expressed by the Malbim in his *Artzos Hachaim*.

His Impact

No statistics or records can adequately describe the Malbim's impact on Jewish history. The only justice which can be done is to declare that he succeeded in achieving the ambitious goals he had outlined in his self-declared war against the perverters of Scripture and slanderers of the Talmudic Sages. His triumph saved Torah Jewry from one of the greatest spiritual dangers it has ever faced. Let us listen once again as the Malbim, in his introduction to *HaTorah Vehamitzvah,* envisions his own role:

"For the Oral Torah I have prepared a shelter; I have built for it a high tower and a mighty fortress—my present work. Its arrows, like those of an expert archer, shall not return without success. It will battle at the gate with the foes of Tradition. Its quiver is filled with arguments and powerful proofs demonstrating that all its explanations are explicit in the simple meaning of Scripture and the profoundness of its language; that the *drashos* of our Sages constitute the only real meaning of scriptural passages according to the true and clear rules of language... In this work I have demonstrated that the Sages possessed tremendous stores of wisdom and intelligence and were masters of great rules and solid principles in grammar and expression... Here I have built a mighty tower for G-d upon which the warrior generals can stand and do battle against the 'Karaites' and those who deny the teachings of our Sages. Here they shall speak out boldly against the foes of the Oral Tradition, engage them in face to face confrontation, press their battle and marshal their forces until they will be convinced and finally understand the truth, that 'Moshe is true, his Torah is true and his Oral Tradition is true'—all given by the same Shepherd."

History has added its own poetic footnote to the chorus of truth foreseen by the Malbim. It has declared for generations of faithful students of *Tanach* that "the Malbim's Torah is true and his dreams have come true."

מגילת אסתר
עם
פירוש מלבי"ם

מגלת אסתר

עם

פירוש רש"י ז"ל, ושפתי חכמים

ונוסף עוד הפירוש הנפלא

מכבוד נזר ראשנו הרב הגאון האמיתי כליל החכמה והמדעים בקש"ת מו"ר
הרב ר' מאיר ליבוש מלבי"ם זצללה"ה :

מחבר פירוש היקר התורה והמצוה על ספר תורת כהנים, פירוש על
תורה נביאים וכתובים, ארצות החיים, על שו"ע או"ח, ארצות השלום,
שירי הנפש פירוש על שיר השירים, ועוד כמה ספרים.

מגלת אסתר א

א א וַֽיְהִ֖י בִּימֵ֣י אֲחַשְׁוֵר֑וֹשׁ ה֣וּא אֲחַשְׁוֵר֗וֹשׁ הַמֹּלֵךְ֙ מֵהֹ֣דּוּ
וְעַד־כּ֔וּשׁ שֶׁ֛בַע וְעֶשְׂרִ֥ים וּמֵאָ֖ה מְדִינָֽה׃

בימים

רש"י

(א) ויהי בימי אחשורוש. מלך פרס היה שמלך תחת א כורש לסוף שבעים שנה של גלות בבל: הוא אחשורוש. הוא ב ברשעו מתחלתו ועד סופו: המלך. שמלך ג מעצמו ולא היה מזרע המלוכה: מהדו ועד כוש וגו' המולך על מאה ועשרים ושבע מדינות כמו שמלך מהדו ועד כוש ד שעומדים זה אצל זה וכן (מ"א ה) כי הוא רודה בכל עבר הנהר מתפסח ועד עזה שהיה רודה בכל עבר הנהר כמו שהוא רודה

שפתי חכמים

א דק"ל איזה אחשורוש הוא אם אביו של דריוש הראשון זה לא היה מלך ואם בנו של דריוש א"כ יתר היה מלכותו הלא אחר דריוש מלך כורש ונמשך מלכותו עד סוף ע' שנה שעלה מבבל ומרדכי היה מעולי גולה ובזמן המלך הזה עדיין היה מרדכי בגולה לכ"פ מלך פרס וכו'. א"נ דק"ל למ"ל לכל הסימנים הל"ל ויהי בימי המלך אחשורוש בשנת המלך וכו' לכ"פ מלך פרס היה ומלך תחת כורש ע"כ היה צריך להבדילו מאחשורוש אחר שהיה במלכי פרס הקודמים ואמר שזה המלך האחרון מלך מהודו ועד כוש תוקף על פרס ומדי וכ"ה דעת הראב"ע ז"ל: ב דק"ל אם כוונתו רק להבדילו הל"ל רק ויהי בימי אחשורוש המלך מהודו ועד כוש הוא ל"ל לכ"פ הוא כו': ג דק"ל הל"ל המלך בקמ"ץ. לכ"פ המולך מעצמו כו' וכ"כ ברכות המ־לך ועדיין לא מלך ובאורו מעבר עד עכשיו לא ירש מלכותו: ד דק"ל הרי אמר שבע ועשרים ומאה מדינה למה פי' מהודו ועד כוש לכ"פ המולך על מאה וכו' ורש"י נמשך אחר גרסת דאלו בגמרא במגילה איכא פלוגתא בדבר וחד אמר כי רחוקים היו ומאמר דברכות הסכים כמ"ד קרובים היו כשב רש"י

השאלות

א כ"מ שאמר ויהי בימי בא לספר ענין זולתי בלתי נודע שהיה בימי איש הנודע ומפורסם, כמו ויהי בימי שפוט השופטים ויהי רעב וכדומה ולא שיספר מה שקרה לאותו האיש בעצמו. ואיך אמר פה בימי אחשורוש, היה הוא אחשורוש: מ"ש הוא אחשורוש מיותר כי לא נודע את מי רוצה לשלול: גם בכל המגלה קראו בתואר המלך אחשורוש זולת פה לבד קראו אחשורוש סתם שמבואר שמדבר מעת שלא מלך עדיין: מ"ש המולך משמע שמדבר על הוית ממשלתו והיל"ל אשר מלך:

פירוש

א (א) לבאר הפרשה הזאת צריך אני להקדים הקדמה אחת, הנה המלכים המלך בימים הקדמונים בממשלות המצריים הכשדיים והפרסיים והמדיים היתה על אחת משתי דרכים: א) המולך ע"י בחירת העם שהסכימו על איש אחד להמליכו עליהם: ב) המולך ביד חזקה שכבש מדינות ומלך עליהם בעל כרחם כמ"ש על נמרוד, ומזה עמדו אז שני מיני ממלכות: א) ממלכה מוגבלת, והוא שממשלת המלך על העם היתה לה גבול ידוע, וזה היה לרוב במלך שנתמנה ע"י בחירת העם, שאז בעת בחירתם אותו שמו חוק למשפט המלך אשר מלך עליהם עד כמה תתפשט כחו וממשלתו, וע"פ הרוב מלך כזה נשבע בעת מלכותו לשמור הנמוסים והדתות אשר במדינה: ב) ממלכה בלתי מוגבלת, והוא שהמלך היה לו רשות לעשות כחפצו ואף לפעמים שלא בעצת שרי העצה, וגם היה יכול לשנות דתות ולתקן המדינה ולחקוק חקים אחרים תחתיהם, באופן שהוא היה המלך והמחוקק בעצמו. והנה בין שני מיני המלכות האלה, חמשה הבדלים: א) המולך ממלכה מוגבלת, המלך היה שומר המדינה, והיה כאב המדינה לעשות משפטיהם ולהלחם מלחמותם וכל עניניהם, והם משועבדים לו לדברים הצריכים לצרך הכלל כמו המס וכדומה, אבל המולך ממלכה בלתי מוגבלת בחזקה כמו סנחריב ונבוכדנצר, המדינה היתה משועבדת אליו, וכולם היו נחשבים עבדיו והיה לו רשות לעשות בהם כחפצו כאשר יעשה האדון בעבדו מקנת כספו: ב) המולך ממלכה מוגבלת, האוצרות וגנזי המלכות היו שייכים אל המדינה, ומי שמלך ממלכה בלתי מוגבלת, האוצרות היו שייכים לו לבדו, כמו פרעה ונבוכדנאצר: ג) המולך ממלכה מוגבלת לא היה אפשר לו לעשות דבר כללי אם לא בהסכמת שרי העצה, ובממלכה בלתי מגבלת היה יכול לתקן ולהרוס הכל לבדו בלי נטילת עצה ורשות כלל: ד) שהראשון היה נתון תחת דתי המדינה ולא היה אפשר לו לעבור על דתות הקבועים, והשני הוא היה המחוקק והיה יכול לתקן חוקים אחרים כנ"ל: ה) המולך ממלכה מוגבלת לא היה אפשר לו לשנות עיר המלוכה לקבוע המלכות במקום אחר, רק היה צריך לישב על כסא מלכות המלכים אשר לפניו בעיר אשר זכתה בה מקדם, אבל המולך בלי הגבלה היה יכול לבנות כחפצו: ע"פ הקדמה הזאת נבא אל הבאור, הנה אחשורוש כפי קבלת חכמינו היה תחלה הדיוט, ואח"כ ע"י עשרו מלך על מדי ופרס ונתחזק במלכותו, עד שכבש כל המדינות קכ"ז במספר ביד חזקה. והנה כל האפרכיות האלה היו שייכים תחלה למלכות בבל, ועד עתה עמד כסא המלכות בבבל, כמו שנאמר בדניאל, בהיכל מלכותא די בבבל, אבל בשושן לא היה כסא המלוכה, כמש"ש הייתי בשושן אשר בעילם המדינה

אסתר א

ב בימים ההם כשבת | המלך אחשורוש על כסא
מלכותו אשר בשושן הבירה: ג בשנת שלוש למלכו
עשה משתה לכל־שריו ועבדיו חיל | פרס ומדי
הפרתמים

שפתי חכמים

רש"י רק חד מ"ד ותפס לשון סרכות: ה דק"ל וכי דוקא בשבתו על כסא עשה. ועוד מנ"מ אם ישב או עמד. לכ"פ כשנתקיים וכו'. א"נ דק"ל כשבת המלך משמע בתחלת מלכותו

רש"י

רודה מתפשט עד עזה: (ב) כשבת המלך אחשורוש וגו'. כשנתקיים המלכות בידו. ורבותינו פרשוהו בענין אחר במס' מגילה: (ג) הפרתמים. שלטונים בל' פרס

פירוש

המדינה, ולא הזכיר שהיתה עיר מלוכה, ובעת שכבש כל הממלכות האלה, למען תתקיים המלכות בידו, לקח את ושתי שהיתה מזרע נבוכדנצר לו לאשה, והיא היתה יורשת עצר, ומצדה היה המלכות מגיע לו גם בירושה, עפ"ז היה המלכות נכון בידו, או מצד הכבוש שכבשם ביד חזקה ומצד זה היה יכול למלוך עליהם ממלכה בלתי מוגבלת או מצד הנחלה ע"י ושתי אבל מצד זה היתה מלכותו מוגבלת, ויען שבתחלת מלכותו נפתו המדינות לקבל עול מלכותו ולהכנע תחתיו בחשבם שהמלכות מגיע לו בירושה ע"י ושת, ומצד זה היה רחוק ממלכתו מלכות מוגבלת, והוא רצה להשתרר עליהם בחזקה בממלכה בלתי מוגבלת, היה זה עקר התחבולה במה שהושיב הכסא בשושן, ובמה שעשה המשתה הגדול הזה, ובמה שצוה להביא את ושתי לפניו, כל אלה היו עצות עמוקות להוציא מגמתו אל הפועל להשתרר עליהם גם השתרר, ולכן הקדים ויהי בימי אחשורוש הוא אחשורוש המולך וכו', מספר כי אחשורוש לא היה מזרע המלוכה, וגם לא עלה על מלכותו בהדרגה עד שתחלה יהיה מלך על מדינה אחת עד שיכבוש שהיה הדיוט תחלה ואח"כ התגבר לאט לאט, רק ויהי בימי **אחשורוש**, בימים ההם שעוד היה אחשורוש הדיוט, בימים ההם בעצמם הוא **אחשורוש** המולך מהודו **ועד כוש**, באופן שלא זכרו שמלך במדינה פלונית מלך מהודו ועד כוש, ורק זכרו שאחשורוש הדיוט מולך מהודו ועד כוש, וגם בימים ההם **מלך על שבע ועשרים ומאה מדינה**, ולא היה בין הדיוטתו למלכותו העצום משך זמן, רק בימי הדיוטתו פתאום נתהוה מלך עצום ומושל עמים רבים:

(ב) **בימים**, עתה מספר איך תיכף בראשית מלכותו התחזק כ"כ עד שערב לבו לשנות כסא המלכות שהיה עד עתה בבבל, והושיבו בשושן, ושם את שושן לבירה ועיר מלוכה, ובזה הראה: א) את תקפו שהשב תיכף למלוך ממלכה בלתי מוגבלת עד שלא פחד מבני מלכותו שימרדו עליו במה ששנה כסא המלכות, ב) את גדלו וגאותו, כי הנה הדיוט העולה למלוכה, הלא זה כבודו לישב על כסא מלכים הקדומים, לא שישב על כסא שיעשה לעצמו כי בזה יגרע כבודו, אבל הוא התנשא כ"כ, עד שיסד לעצמו כסא מלכות מחדש, ושנה גם כן את עיר הממלכה שהיה בשושן, כאלו לא בהסכמתם ורצונם נתמנה על בבל וכל המלכות, רק בחרבו ובקשתו ירשם, ובזה כולם נכנעים ויורדים תחת שושן אשר בפרס מלכותו, ומוסף שהתוקף הזה לא הראה אחר שהחזיק במלכות ימים רבים, רק תיכף בימים ההם, כבר היה דומה **כשבת המלך אחשורוש**, כאלו הוא מלך מתולדתו ויושב **על כסא מלכותו** המיוחס לו, מבלי שצריך אל כבוד כסא המלכים שקדמוהו:

(ג) **בשנת**, למען הוציא תקנו זה מכח אל הפועל להיות מלכותו בלתי מוגבלת, התחכם **בשנת שלוש למלכו**, זה המלכות אשר חשב למלוך ביד חזקה לז"א למלכו, **עשה משתה** למען שבמשתה הזאת יקים מזמות לבבו, והנה בסדר הקרואים הראה את תכלית כונתו, שהקדים תחלה **שריו ועבדיו חיל צבא פרס** ומדי ולאחריהם הושיב את **הפרתמים ושרי המדינות** אשר היו שם שרים לפניו, ר"ל לפני כבשו הממלכות האלה, ובזה הראה שאינו חושב כי ברצונם ובבחירתם נתמנה שאז הלא שרי המדינות הגדולות קודמים לשרי המדינה הקטנה שמלך בתחלה וכ"ש לעבדיו וחיל הצבא, אבל הראה כי בחרבו ובקשתו כבשם, עבור שריו ואף חיל הצבא שהם היו הכובשים קודמים במעלה וחשיבות אף לפני שרי

השאלות

ב בימים ההם מיותר שהלא כבר אמר ויהי בימי. גם המלך אחשורוש מיותר שכבר נזכר בפסוק הקודם והול"ל והיה כשבתו. גם גוף הספור שישב על כסא מלכותו ושהית בשושן לאין צורך:

ג לא נודע טעם נכון לאיזה צורך עשה המשתה הזה. וביחוד למה האריכו בו כותבי המגלה בכל פרטיו. גם סדר הקרואים פלא שהזכיר תחלה השרים והעבדים וחיל הצבא, ושוב חוזר אל הפרתמים ושרי המדינות, והם ודאי קודמים להעבדים ובכלל שרים יחשבו גם הם. גם מלת לפניו מיותר, גם מ"ש פה למלכו וגבי לקיחת אסתר אמר למלכותו:

הַֽפַּרְתְּמִים וְשָׂרֵי הַמְּדִינוֹת לְפָנָֽיו׃ ד בְּהַרְאֹתוֹ אֶת־עֹשֶׁר
כְּבוֹד מַלְכוּתוֹ וְאֶת־יְקָר תִּפְאֶרֶת גְּדוּלָּתוֹ יָמִים רַבִּים
שְׁמוֹנִים וּמְאַת יֽוֹם׃ ה וּבִמְלוֹאת ׀ הַיָּמִים הָאֵלֶּה עָשָׂה
הַמֶּלֶךְ לְכָל־הָעָם הַנִּמְצְאִים° בְּשׁוּשַׁן הַבִּירָה לְמִגָּדוֹל
וְעַד־קָטָן מִשְׁתֶּה שִׁבְעַת יָמִים בַּחֲצַר גִּנַּת בִּיתַן הַמֶּֽלֶךְ׃
ו ח֣וּר° ׀ כַּרְפַּס וּתְכֵלֶת אָחוּז בְּחַבְלֵי־בוּץ וְאַרְגָּמָן עַל־
גְּלִילֵי כֶסֶף וְעַמּוּדֵי שֵׁשׁ מִטּוֹת ׀ זָהָב וָכֶסֶף עַל רִֽצְפַת
בַּהַט־וָשֵׁשׁ וְדַר וְסֹחָֽרֶת׃ ז וְהַשְׁקוֹת בִּכְלֵי זָהָב וְכֵלִים

°נח עם הדגש °ובמלאות קרי °ח' רבתי

מכלים

רש"י

פרס: (ד) ימים רבים. עשה להם ו משתה: (ה) גנת. מקום זרעוני ירקות: ביתן. נטוע אילנות: (ו) חור כרפס ותכלת. מיני בגדים צבועים פרש להם למצעות: אחוז בחבלי בוץ וארגמן. מרוקמים בפתילי בוץ וארגמן אותן פרש להם על גלילי כסף ועל עמודי שש: מטות זהב וכסף. ערך ז ליסב עליהם לסעודה: על רצפת. קרקעות של בהט ושש וגו' מיני אבנים טובות פירשו רבותינו. ולפי משמעות המקרא כך שמם: (ז) והשקות בכלי זהב

שפתי חכמים

מלכותו והדר כתיב בשנת שלוש למלכו. לכ"פ כשנתקיים המלכות בידו דהיינו בשנת שלוש למלכו: ו פי' אבל אינו דבוק למה דסמך לו דהיאך הראה להם יקר תפארת גדולתו ימים רבים: ז דק"ל מטות לסעודה למאי מבעי' לכ"פ עך ליסב

השאלות

ד לאיזה צורך הראה את עשרו לפני רבים עמים, ולמה כפל ואת יקר תפארת גדולתו. גם ימים רבים מיותר:

ה מה היה כונתו במשתה השני שעשה · ומלת הנמצאים מיותר. ולמה בכ"מ אמר מקטן עד גדול שבא להשוות הקטן אל הגדול, ופה אמר מגדול ועד קטן שבא להשוות הגדול אל הקטן. ולאיזה ענין מספר שהיה בחצר גנת הביתן. גם כל מה שהאריך בפסוק ו' ז' ח' לא נודע ענינו:

פירוש

שרי המדינות, שלא היו נחשבים לשרים רק לפניו, לפני כבשו אותם, אבל עתה נתונים נתונים שמה תחתיו לעבדים ירודים ושפלים:

(ד) בהראותו, כבר הקדמנו כי המולך ממלכה מונחלת, כל האוצר וההון הנמצא בגנזי המלכות לא לו היה, אך שייכים להמדינה והממלכה, ולא לו להתפאר בהו, ולכן ברצותו להשתרר בממלכה בלתי מונחלת הוכרח להחזיק באוצר המלוכה להחזיקו כשלו, והראהו לפני רבים עמים להתפאר בהו כאיש המתפאר בקנין כספו, וז"ש בהראותו את עושר כבוד מלכותו, כאלו העושר הזה לא של המדינה הוא רק עומד לכבוד לו שע"י הגיע למלוכה, ויען שלכל מלך צריך שיהיה לו עושר, אבל למלך עצום המושל ממשל רב בהכרח שירבו אוצרותיו לפי גדולתו, לזה הראה ביחוד יקר תפארת גדולתו, וזה לא עשה יום אחד ולא יומים רק ימים רבים, עד שעלו לק"פ יום, שבזה גלה דעתו שמחזיק באוצר המלוכה ורוצה לפרוץ בו פרץ כברכונו וקנינו:

(ה) ובמלואת, עוד התחכם כי באחרית ימי המשתה שעשה אל השרים עשה משתה כללית לכל עם שושן, להורות כי קטן וגדול שוים אצלו כי כולם עבדיו ואין לאחד התנשאות על חבירו, ועז"א מגדול ועד קטן להשוות הגדול אל הקטן, ואמר לכל העם הנמצאים, כי אחר שהוא בא מחוץ לשושן והושיב כסאו בשושן קרא לבני שושן הנמצאים, ועשה משתה זה בחצר המלך, מקום אשר לפי נמוסי פרס לא יבואו שמה רק השרים והפרתמים, והוא הראה כי העם וההמון לא נופלים אלו מן השרים, אחר שכולם עבדיו, ואדרבה בני שושן ששם כסא המלכות להם יאות כבוד ותפארת כלכל השרים:

(ו) חור, עתה תושב בעושר והיקר אשר נראה לו במשתה הזה, שיען היה בחצר הפתוח בלי תקרה ונגד סביב, עשה שמה אהלים פרושים סביב מחור כרפס ותכלת, וגם החבלים שקשר האהלים בהם היו של בוץ וארגמן, והעמודים שאליהם נקשרו חבלי היריעות היו של שיש ועמדו ונשענו על גלילי כסף, ב) המטות שישבו עליהם המסובים היו של זהב וכסף, ג) גם הרצפה היתה של בהט ושש ואבנים יקרות:

(ז) והשקות, הכלים ששתו בהן היו של זהב, ולא זאת אלא וכלים מכלים שונים. פי' מהרא"ח שבכל

כלי

מִכֵּלִים שׁוֹנִים וְיֵין מַלְכוּת רָב כְּיַד הַמֶּלֶךְ׃ ח וְהַשְּׁתִיָּה כַדָּת אֵין אֹנֵס כִּי־כֵן ׀ יִסַּד הַמֶּלֶךְ עַל כָּל־רַב בֵּיתוֹ לַעֲשׂוֹת כִּרְצוֹן אִישׁ־וָאִישׁ׃ ס ט גַּם וַשְׁתִּי הַמַּלְכָּה עָשְׂתָה מִשְׁתֵּה נָשִׁים בֵּית הַמַּלְכוּת אֲשֶׁר לַמֶּלֶךְ אחשורוש

שפתי חכמים

ליהנ עליהם: ח הוסיף למ"ד במלת והשקות כדי שיהיה מקור כי במלת זה הוא צווי וידוע הוא שמשפט המקור לעולם שיבא עליו אחד מאותיות בכל"ם וכן הוסיף למ"ד בפ' ויקהל לעשות אותה והותר כתב רש"י ולהותר כוונתו ג"כ שלא יהא צווי והביא שם לראיה כמו והכבד שפירושו ולהכבד והכות את מואב ולהכות. ובפ' וארא הביאם שהם הסרי הלמ"ד לפי שכן הוא משפט המקור הנזכר: ט פי' מלת רב הוא שם כמו הרבה כמו רב לכם בני לוי שפירש"י הרבה אבל

רש"י

זהב. ח כמו ולהשקות: שונים. משונים זה מזה וכן ודתיהם שונות. ורבותינו דרשו מה שדרשו: ויין מלכות רב. ט הרבה. ורבותינו אמרו שהשקה אותם כל אחד ואחד יין שהוא זקן ממנו: (ה) כדת. לפי שיש סעודות שכופין את המסובין לשתות כלי גדול ויש שאינו יכול לשתותו כי אם בקושי אבל כאן אין אונס: יסד. ל' יסוד כלומר כן התקין וצוה: על

פירוש

כלי היו קבועים כלים שונים כמו קנקן זהב שבו היין והגביעים לשתות בהם וכדומה באופן שלפני כל אחד היו כל כלי השתיה וכולם של זהב, עד שלא הוצרך אחד ליקח כלי מחברו, וזה מורה על רוב הכלים, ולא תאמר שהיו הכלים מספיקים בעבור שלא היה יין הרבה, לז"א ויין מלכות רב, היין היה רב בכמות כיד המלך, וגם טוב באיכות, שעז"א יין מלכות עד שרבו השותים בעבור טובו ומתקו:

השאלות

ט למה עשתה ושתי משתה ביחוד, וקראה בשם משתה נשים. ולאיזה צורך מספר זאת ומודיע המקום שהיה בבית המלכות. וגם אשר למלך אחשורוש מיותר. גם צריך להבין השנוים, למה פה ובפסוק י"א ט"ז י"ז קראה ושתי המלכה, שמורת שמלכותה לא היה מצד עצמה, ובפסוק י"ב וט"ו קראה המלכה ושתי:

(ח) והשתיה, ובכל זאת היתה השתיה בלי אונס, כי בסעודה שאין הכלים מספיקים אונסים את המסובים למהר לשתות חלקו, כדי שיקחו את כוסו למזוג להאחרים אבל פה היה לכ"א כלי שתיתו בפ"ע ולא אנסוהו אל השתי כי לא הוצרך אחד מהם לכלי חברו, וזה מורה על רוב כלי זהב שהיו שם, ואף שככר היה מנהג בני פרס לכבד הגדול בשתיה [כמ"ש בברכות הני פרסאי בסדר הסבה בקיאי טפי מינן] אבל פה לא אנסו לזה רק כ"א שתה בפני עצמו כפי רצונו, ולבל יהיה זה לבוז אל הגדולים והעדר כבוד, יסד כן המלך על כל רב וגדולי ביתו, שהם מחוייבים לעשות כן, ובאופן שהם עצמם מחלו על כבודם, כדי לעשות כרצון איש ואיש:

(ס) גם, כבר באַרנו בפסוק א' שאחשורוש בעת שתפש כל המלכות שהיתה תחלה תחת שבט בבל ופקודת כשדים, לקח את ושתי לו לאשה, ועי"כ הודו כולם במלכותם, יען שהמלוכה מגיע לו בנחלה ע"י ושתי שהיא יורשת בבל, ועתה שחשב מחשבות למלוך ממלכה בלתי מוגבלת, שע"ז חרד כל ההדרס באשר בשמתו את כסאו לשושן ובעשית המשתה כנ"ל, ברצה להשיב את עצמו כאלו כבש הממלכות האלה בחרבו וביד חזקה ימלוך עליהם, ורצה בשרי המדינות יסכימו עמו בזה שינהיג המלוכה בלי הגבלה רק ימשול ברצונו, הנה עתה היו כבושי ושתי כסילון ממהיר בעיניו כי ע"י כבושי ושתי נחשב כאלו מעצמם קבלוהו למלך ע"י יורשת ושתי, וממילא דינו כמלך הנעשה בבחירת העם, שמלכותו מוגבלת ע"פ דתות ונימוסי עממים. לכן חשב מחשבות והשכל להראות כי לא לקח את ושתי מצד יחוסה ולא על ידה הגיע למלוכה, כי בעת כבש המלכות מיד בבל פסקה מלכות בבל וושתי באשה לידו כשבוית חרב ולא ע"י יחוסה לקחה רק על ידי יפיה, ולא על ידה בא למלוכה, כי נהפוך הוא שהיא מלכה על ידו, באופן שלא יצדק לקראה בשם המלכה ושתי, רק ושתי המלכה, כי אין מלכותה מצד עצמה רק ע"י אחשורוש, ושמה קדם למלכותה, והאות הראשון לזה היה במשתה אשר עשתה, שאם היתה יורשת בבל והוא מלך על ידה, הלא היה ראוי שהמשתה גם היא משתה אל השרים, אחר שהיא העיקר במלוכה, וגם שיהיה המשתה בבית מלכותה המיוחד לה מצד עצמה שהיא המולכת מצד עצמה, אבל לא היה כן, רק גם ושתי המלכה מצד שהאלים שעיקר ענינה הוא ושתי המלכה בשמה קודם למלכותה ואין מלכותה רק על ידו, לזה לא עשתה רק משתה נשים לא אל השרים והעמים, וזאת שמה במשתה היה רק בבית המלכות אשר למלך אחשורוש, באופן שמורה שהיא אין לה בית מלכות בפ"ע, רק לו לבדו יאתה המלוכה:

ביום

אֲחַשְׁוֵרוֹשׁ: י בַּיּוֹם הַשְּׁבִיעִי כְּטוֹב לֵב־הַמֶּלֶךְ בַּיָּיִן אָמַר
לִמְהוּמָן בִּזְּתָא חַרְבוֹנָא בִּגְתָא וַאֲבַגְתָא זֵתַר וְכַרְכַּס
שִׁבְעַת הַסָּרִיסִים הַמְשָׁרְתִים אֶת־פְּנֵי הַמֶּלֶךְ אֲחַשְׁוֵרוֹשׁ:
יא לְהָבִיא אֶת־וַשְׁתִּי הַמַּלְכָּה לִפְנֵי הַמֶּלֶךְ בְּכֶתֶר מַלְכוּת
לְהַרְאוֹת הָעַמִּים וְהַשָּׂרִים אֶת־יָפְיָהּ כִּי־טוֹבַת מַרְאֶה
הִיא: יב וַתְּמָאֵן הַמַּלְכָּה וַשְׁתִּי לָבוֹא בִּדְבַר הַמֶּלֶךְ אֲשֶׁר
ביד

°בריהוז קרי

רש"י

על כל רב ביתו. על כל שרי הסעודה שר האופים ושר הטבחים ושר המשקים: לעשות כרצון איש ואיש. י לכל אחד ואחד רצונו: (י) ביום השביעי. רבותינו אמרו שבת כ היה: (יב) ותמאן המלכה ושתי. רבותינו אמרו לפי שפרחה בה צרעת ל כדי שתמאן ותהרג לפי שהיתה מפשטת בנות ישראל ערומות ועושה בהן מלאכה בשבת נגזר עליה שתפשט ערומה

שפתי חכמים

אבל רבותינו דרשו רב רב בשנים: י דק"ל דהי יעשה כרצון איש זה לא יוכל לעשות כרצון איש אחר כי אין רצון כולם שוים. לכ"פ לכל אחד רצונו לא שיעשה רצון כולם בעת אחד ובנושא אחד: כ בפ"ק דמגילה ביום השביעי כטוב לב המלך ביין אטו עד יום השביעי לא טב לביה ביין אמר רב יום השביעי שבת היה כו' נמצא שעיקר כוונת הכתוב להורות שכאשר טב לביה ביין בשבת אירע מעשה דושתי כדי לשלם לה מדה כנגד מדה כמו שמפרש והז"ל ודיוקא דל' הכי הוא אטו עד יום השביעי לא טב לביה ביין אלא ע"כ דפירוש דקרא כאשר טב לביה ביין ביום השביעי הוא הגורם לטב לביה כי כל יום טב לביה רק זה אירע כאשר טב לביה ביום השביעי א"כ קשה מה בא הכתוב להשמיענו מ"מ אי ביום השביעי הוה או ביום הראשון אע"כ כאי יום השביעי שבת היה וקרא אתא לאשמועינן שבמדה שאדם מודד מודדים לו: ל דיוקא דרבותינו מהדי פרוצה

השאלות

י איך סכלות גדול מזה, שמושל אדיר כזה יצוה להביא אשת חיקו, להראותה לפני המון גוים והמון לאומים כי יפת מראה היא. ובשגם לקבלת חז"ל שצוה להביאה ערומה. וביותר יפלא איכות הבאתה אשר נראה שצוה תיכף להביאה בע"כ ביד הסריסים, כמביאים אחת הנבלות, עד שנבחר לה מות מחיי הבוז והקלון. גם למה האריך בספור זה בשמות הסריסים, ובאר המשרתים את פני המלך, מה צורך לנו בהודעה זאת:

יא לפני המלך מיותר. ולמה לא אמר להביא את ושתי בכתר מלכות לפני המלך, שהלא הכתר תלבש קודם שתבא לפני המלך:

יב מ"ש לבא בדבר המלך אשר ביד הסריסים משמע שהוא נתינת טעם שמצד זה לא רצתה לבא. גם להבין הכפל ויקצוף וחמתו בערה בו:

פירוש

(י) ביום השביעי, ולמען יהיה זאת ליסוד מוסד ולאבן הראשה שושתי אין לה חלק במלכות, ומלכותה היא מצד הכתר לבד שעי"ז ישיג מגמתו להיות מולך ממלכה בלתי מוגבלת, התחכם במה שצוה להביא ושתי לפניו, להראות שלא מצד יחוסה לקחה, רק מצד שיפת מראה היא, לא זולת זה, כי יחוס מלכותה נפסק בעת הכתוב והצריך להוציא זה לאור בחמשה ענינים: א) שצוה למהומן וכו' שבעת הסריסים שאם היתה נחשבת כמולכת בפני עצמה, איך יובילוה ע"י הסריסים הלא ראוי שילכו לקראתה כל שרי המלוכה: ב) שגם לא בחר שתבא ע"י הסריסים המשרתים אותה, רק ע"י הסריסים המשרתים את פני המלך אחשורוש, שזה שפלות גדול לפניה, שמהשיבה אחת מפילגשיו, אשר סריסיו יביאוה לפניו:

(יא) להביא, ג) שצוה להם להביא שהל' מראה שיביאוה בעל כרחה כאחת שפחותיו, ד) שצוה שיביאוה באופן שידעו הכל כי מביאים את ושתי המלכה לא המלכה ושתי, שמן נואה לפני המלך ידעו כל העמים שאין מלכותה עצמי לה, והוא ע"י שיביאוה לפני המלך בכתר מלכות, ר"ל שלא תלבש הכתר עד אשר תבוא לפני המלך, ור"ל לפני המלך עת שתהיה לפניו אז תהיה בכתר מלכות לא קודם לכן, ובזה יכירו הכל שאין ראוי לה ללבוש הכתר בהיותה לבדה כי הדיוטית היא, ה) תכלית מטרת חפצו להראות העמים והשרים שלא לקחה בעבור יחוסה רק בעבור יפיה כי טובת מראה היא שאם היה לוקחה בעבור יחוסה ובעבור שע"י זכה למלכות לא יתכן שיראה את יפיה, כי הלא בין יפה בין כעורה היה לוקחה אחר שעמה לקח הכל המלוכה, והלא זה בזיון אל המדינות אם מראה יפיה, כאלו היופי הטוב יותר מן המלכות שהשיג על ידה, אבל בזה גלה כי אין מחשיב אותה למלכה מצד עצמה, וחכם במלכות מצד עצמו בכחו וגבורתו, ובזה רצה להגיע לחפצו למלוך מלוכה בלתי מוגבלת:

(יב) ותמאן, מבאר כי מה שושתי לא רצתה לבא היה על כי הבינה כוונו שרוצה להורידה ממעלתה שתחשב
עד

בְּיַד הַסָּרִיסִים וַיִּקְצֹף הַמֶּלֶךְ מְאֹד וַחֲמָתוֹ בָּעֲרָה בוֹ׃ ס
יג וַיֹּאמֶר הַמֶּלֶךְ לַחֲכָמִים יֹדְעֵי הָעִתִּים כִּי־כֵן דְּבַר הַמֶּלֶךְ
לפני

שפתי חכמים

פירוש שהיה מדכתיב עשתה משתה בית המלכות ביד הסריסים מבע"ל. אלא גם היא לדבר עבירה נתכוונה כדי להסתכל ביופיה א"כ למה לא באה אלא לפי שפרחה כו' והא דאמרו פרחה צרעת ולא ע"א בירושלמי מפיק לה בג"ש כתיב הכא אשר נגזר עליה וכתיב גבי עוזיה כשנתנגע נגזר מבית ה' מה להלן צרעת אף כאן צרעת: ם דייקו מדאמר להביא את ושתי המלכה לפני המלך בכתר מלכות ולא אמר בלבוש מלכות וכתר מלכות על ראשה מלמד שכן היה אומר להביא את ושתי המלכה ולא יהיה עליה כלום אלא כתר מלכות וכ"ה בהדיא בילקוט: ג דק"ל מאי כולי האי דלקא ליה שמשיה לכ"פ ששלחה לו כו': ם דק"ל וכי דבר המלך תמיד לפני כל יודעי דת וזולת זה לא היה מדבר לכ"פ כי

רש"י

ם ערומה בשבת: ויקצף. ששלחה לו דברי נגאי: (יג) כי כן דבר המלך. כי כן מנהג ם המלך בכל משפט

ק

פירוש

עד שהם שים לה חלק בהמלכות מצד נחלת אבותיה, וז"ש ותמאן יען שהיא לפי דעתה המלכה ושתי שמלכותה מצד עצמה, ע"כ לא רצתה לבא מפני טעמים: א) בדבר המלך יען שפקד עליה שתבא באופן שיתראה שאין לה חלק במלוכה ולא תלבש הכתר רק כשהוא לפניו, ב) אשר ביד הסריסים אשר צוה להביא ע"י הסריסים שהוא בזיון וקלון. והנה בזה הפרה כל עצתו שרצה להחזיק במלכות מצד עצמו והיא עמדה נגדו לאמר שמלכותו לא נצמח רק על ידה, ועז"א ויקצף המלך מאד, ר"ל כי הבדל יש בין קצף ובין חמה, שהקצף הוא בגלוי והחמה מורה על שמירת הקנאה בלבו בלי יגלה מן השפה ולחוץ, ופה היו שני ענינים: א) הקצף הגלוי, על שסרבה לעשות מצותו שזה היה בפרהסיא, ב) החמה הפנימיית אשר בערה בלבו על שעל ידה נתבטלו כל מחשבותיו וכל מה שטרח עד הנה בהסעודה למען ימלוך ממלכה בלתי מוגבלת היה עתה לאפס, ויען שזה לא יכול להגיד, כי עלות האלו היו נסתרים בלבו, לא הראה הקצף הזה, רק חמתו בערה בו:

(יג) ויאמר המלך, מתוך דברי המלך ומתשובת ממוכן נראה בעליל, שהמלך עם כל חמתו עליה רצה לזכותה ועל כל פשעים תכסה אהבה. והנה יש הבדל בין משפט אשר ישפטו בין המלך ובין אחד מעבדיו, למשפט אשר ישפטו בין כל האדם בין איש לרעהו, כי אל משפטי המלך היו קבועים שופטים מיוחדים הנקראים יודעי העתים, שהשופטים האלה מלבד שהיו צריכים לדעת הדתות וחוקי המשפט, היו צריכים לדעת את העתים, לדון לפי השעה והזמן, שאם חטא מי נגד המלך בעת שישב על כסא מלכותו פשעו יותר גדול מאם חטא נגדו בעת שעובר ממקום למקום, וכ"ש אם חטא נגדו בעת כזאת שכל גדולי המדינה היו לפניו שעונו גדול וכבד יותר, אבל משפטים שבין איש לרעהו ידונו לפני כל יודעי דת ודין לבד לפי חוקת המשפט והמלך ראה שאם יצוה לדון משפט זה במשפט יודעי העתים, שבזה מחשיב כאלו הדיוט חטא נגד המלך דינה משפט מות, ע"כ אמר המלך אל החכמים יודעי העתים שמשפט זה אין ענינו לבא לפניהם רק יכול לשפוט לפני כל יודעי דת ודין, כי אין זה משפט של הדיוט שחטא נגד המלך כי היא מלכה כמוהו, ואין לו יתרון עליה, ואחר שהוא מלך והיא מלכה מצד תולדתה, הוא רק משפט שבין איש לאשתו, כי שניהם שוים במעלה, וכל יודעי דת ודין יכולים לשפוט דבר זה כשאר משפט שבין איש לאשתו, ח"ש ליודעי העתים שדבר המלך הלז יכול להשפט לפני כל יודעי דת ודין דעלמא, ואמנם במה שכפל דת ודין בזה רצה לזכותה לגמרי, כי עם שדת יבא גם על משפט הנמוסי אשר בדברים שבין איש לרעהו, ר"ל שאחר שבא נרדף עם דין שכולל דברי ריבות שבין איש לחבירו, יהיה דת שם נבדל על נמוס המוסרי, כי דת יבא לרוב על הדתות האלהיים או המוסריים. והנה במשפט הלזה שצוה להביא את ושתי לפניו להראות את יפיה לפני רבים עמים, מצד הדין יש לחייבה כי גם אם ידונו אותם כאיש ואשתו בלי השקף על המלוכה, היה הדין אז כמו שהוא עד היום בארצות המזרח שהאשה משועבדת תחת בעלה וצריכה להכנע לעשות רצונו ואם תעבור עמה תענש, אבל מצד הדת המוסרי הזכה בדינה, כי הדת המוסרי היה שהפרסיות והמדיות היו לנשים סגורות בהיכליהם, לא יראו לפני האנשים, כמ"ש במשנה (שבת פ"ו מ"ו) הערביות יוצאות רעולות והמדיות פרופות, והוא צוה לה לבא להראות את יפיה לפני המונים שזה נגד הדת המוסרי, ובזה אם ידונו זה המשפט כמשפט שבין איש לאשתו אין האשה חייבה לעבור על הדת המוסרי, ועז"א לפני כל יודעי דת ודין, שצריכים במשפט זה לדעת גם הדת, ואמר אח"כ כדת מה לעשות שיבקשו במשפט על הדת המוסרי:

השאלות

יג מי הם יודעי העתים ומי הם היודעי דת ודין ובאור הכתוב הזה מוקשה ומהו ההבדל בין דת ודין. ולמה אמר אח"כ כדת מה לעשות ולא אמר כדין:

והקרוב

לִפְנֵי כָּל־יֹדְעֵי דָּת וָדִין׃ יד וְהַקָּרֹב אֵלָיו כַּרְשְׁנָא שֵׁתָר
אַדְמָתָא תַרְשִׁישׁ מֶרֶס מַרְסְנָא מְמוּכָן שִׁבְעַת שָׂרֵי ׀
פָּרַס וּמָדַי רֹאֵי פְּנֵי הַמֶּלֶךְ הַיֹּשְׁבִים רִאשֹׁנָה בַּמַּלְכוּת׃
טו כְּדָת מַה־לַּעֲשׂוֹת בַּמַּלְכָּה וַשְׁתִּי עַל ׀ אֲשֶׁר לֹא־
עָשְׂתָה אֶת־מַאֲמַר הַמֶּלֶךְ אֲחַשְׁוֵרוֹשׁ בְּיַד הַסָּרִיסִים׃ ס
טז וַיֹּאמֶר מוּמְכָן° לִפְנֵי הַמֶּלֶךְ וְהַשָּׂרִים לֹא עַל־הַמֶּלֶךְ
לְבַדּוֹ עָוְתָה וַשְׁתִּי הַמַּלְכָּה כִּי עַל־כָּל־הַשָּׂרִים וְעַל־כָּל־
הָעַמִּים אֲשֶׁר בְּכָל־מְדִינוֹת הַמֶּלֶךְ אֲחַשְׁוֵרוֹשׁ׃ יז כִּי־

°ממוכן קרי

יצא

רש"י

משפט לשום את הדבר לפני כל יודעי דת ודין: (יד) והקרב אליו. לערוך ע דבריו לפניהם אלו הם כרשנא שתר וגו': (טו) כדת מה לעשות. מוסב על ויאמר המלך לחכמים: (טז) עותה. ל' עון: (יח) כי יצא דבר המלכה על כל הנשים. זה שבזתה את המלך על כל פ הנשים להבזות אף הן את בעליהן

שפתי חכמים

ס מנהג המלך כו': ע דק"ל מה ענין זה לכאן לכ"פ לערוך דבריו כו': פ דק"ל דהלא לא עשתה שום דבר רק שאמרה לבא לא באותה שיעשו הנשים דבר. לכ"פ זה שבזתה

השאלות

יד מז"ש והקרוב אליו, ולמה כפל תארם בשלשה ענינים:

טו למה אמר ביד הסריסים:

טז מה רצה ממוכן בכפלו על כל השרים ועל כל העמים, שאם החטא הוא רק מה שהנשים יבזו בעליהן. מה הבדל אם נשי השרים או העמים יבזו בעליהן

יז איך יתכן שעל חטא זה שהנשים יבזו בעליהן תומת המלכה, הלא יכול לתת דת מעתה להיות כל איש שורר בביתו, ומהו כי יצא דבר המלכה:

פירוש

(יד) והקרוב, אחר שהקדים שמשפט זה אינו משפט מלך, רק משפט שבין איש לאשתו בחר להציע המשפט הלז לפני שבעת השרים האלה מצד ד' טעמים: א) והקרוב אליו שהם יושבים קרובים אליו ולא רצה שיתפרסם המשפט הזה רק אחר שהם בל"ז כבר שמעו את כל אשר רצה שהם ישפטו בדבר וישאר סוד ביניהם, ב) בחר בהם מצד שהם שבעת שרי פרס ומדי וראוי שישפטו משפט זה מפני מעלתם, ג) שהם רואי פני המלך תמיד ומכירים קריצותיו ורמיזותיו וידעו מה בלבו שרוצה לזכותה, ד) היושבים ראשונה במלכות שיושבים במלכות מזמן רב, וכבר בחנו תולדות הימים ומבחן הזמנים כדרך השופטים הישישים הבקיאים ומומחים בדבר:

(טו) כדת, כבר בארנו שהיה מגמתו שישפטו ע"פ הדת המוסרי שע"פ הלא זכאי בדינה, ולמען לא ידונו אותה כהדיוט המורד במלך שבזה אין מועיל טענה זאת, אמר: א) במלכה ושתי, שהיא מלכה מצד עצמה ויחוסה ואין משפטה עם המלך רק כמשפט אשה נגד בעלה, ב) אשר לא עשתה את מאמר המלך אחשורוש, יש לה תירוץ יען שהיה ביד הסריסים וכדי בזיון וקצף שמלכה מהולדתה יביאוה הסריסים:

(טז) ויאמר ממוכן, כאשר ראה ממוכן שהמלך רצה לזכותה לאמר שאינו משפט הנוגע למלך שהוא משפט כללי, כי כבוד המלך הוא כבוד כל המדינה, ורק משפט פרטי בין איש לאשתו, וגם רצה להסתיר הדבר במ"ש והקרוב אליו, השיב לפני המלך והשרים בפרהסיא, לאמר לא על המלך לבדו שהוא משפט פרטי רק משפט כללי הנוגע לכל המדינה, וגם לאמת שהמלך רצה לזכותה במ"ש שהיא המלכה ושתי שמלכותה מצד עצמה, השיב שהיא ושתי המלכה שמלכותה אינה עצמי לה, רק על ידי המלך היא מלכה. ובזה הוא משפט שבין הדיוט למלך, וגם אינו משפט הנוגע למלך לבדו. רק הטעם, א) לכל השרים, שהוא מה שבזה רצתה להשפיל כל כבוד מלכות אחשורוש ושמן הדין ראוי שמלכותו תהיה מלכות בלתי נגבלת אחר שזכה בהמלכות ע"י כבוש, והיא רצתה להגביל מלכותו לאמר שהגיע למלכות על ידה, זה דבר הנוגע לכלל המלוכה, ואת שרים השאה על כל העמים במה שנשיהם יבזו בעליהן, ולא בחלק אחד ממלכותך רק אשר בכל מדינות המלך, שהדבר כולל בין כלל המלוכה בין כלל המדינות:

(יח) כי יצא, עתה באר דבריו ומפרש שהלא איך הוא נוגע לכלל העמים, כי בזאת אשר ושתי לא היו רק

ברום

יֵצֵא דְבַר־הַמַּלְכָּה עַל־כָּל־הַנָּשִׁים לְהַבְזוֹת בַּעְלֵיהֶן
בְּעֵינֵיהֶן בְּאָמְרָם הַמֶּלֶךְ אֲחַשְׁוֵרוֹשׁ אָמַר לְהָבִיא אֶת־
וַשְׁתִּי הַמַּלְכָּה לְפָנָיו וְלֹא־בָאָה׃ יח וְהַיּוֹם הַזֶּה תֹּאמַרְנָה ׀
שָׂרוֹת פָּרַס־וּמָדַי אֲשֶׁר שָׁמְעוּ אֶת־דְּבַר הַמַּלְכָּה לְכֹל
שָׂרֵי הַמֶּלֶךְ וּכְדַי בִּזָּיוֹן וָקָצֶף׃ יט אִם־עַל־הַמֶּלֶךְ טוֹב יֵצֵא
דְבַר־מַלְכוּת מִלְּפָנָיו וְיִכָּתֵב בְּדָתֵי פָרַס־וּמָדַי וְלֹא יַעֲבוֹר
אֲשֶׁר לֹא־תָבוֹא וַשְׁתִּי לִפְנֵי הַמֶּלֶךְ אֲחַשְׁוֵרוֹשׁ וּמַלְכוּתָהּ

יתן

שפתי חכמים

פ מחס כו' כלומר מתוך מעשיה תלמדנה הנשים לעשות גם הם: צ דק"ל דבר המלך מבעי"ל לכ"פ גזרת מלכות כו': ק דק"ל שלא הדת לא דבר גופני הוא שבו יכתוב וכל"ל ויכא

רש"י

בעליהן: (יח) תאמרנה שרות פרס ומדי. לכל שרי המלך את הדבר הזה והרי זה מקרא קצר: וכדי בזיון. ויש בדבר הזה הרבה בזיון וקצף: (יט) דבר מלכות. גזרת צ מלכות של נקמה שלוח להרגה: ויכתב בדתי פרס ומדי. בספרי ק חוק ומנהג המלכות: ולא יעבור. חוק זה מביניהם שיהא זה

תום

פירוש

שרות פרס ומדי, והם שמעו וידעו גוף הענין והויכוח שהיה ביניהם והם ידעו שמה שלא רצתה לבא היה מצד שרצה להורידה ממעלתה להכחיש מלכותה והם לא יבזו בעליהן, כי לפי דעת ושתי, דבר גדול בקש ממנה, רק הם יספרו גוף הענין להשרים שמזה יתגלגל כבוד המלך לאמר שמלכותו מוגבלת, אבל נשי העמים שהם לא היו שם, ולא ידעו גוף הענין, לא ישמעו רק פשטות הספור שאחשורוש קרא לושתי ולא רצתה לבא, ובזה ילמדו ק"ו להבזות בעליהן, וז"ש כי יצא דבר המלכה על כל הנשים, בזה שיתפשט דבר המלכה בפי המספרים אשר ישמעו הדבר אחר ימים אחדים איש מפי איש ולא ידעו גוף המעשה, יפעל זה לרוע שיבזו בעליהן בעיניהן, שאם יצוה הבעל לאשתו לעשות לו עבודה, תעיז פניה ותשיב לו: א) הלא המלך אחשורוש שהוא מלך. ב) שאמר להביא את ושתי המלכה שהיא אינה מלכה מצד עצמה רק מצדו, ג) שאמר רק להביא לפניו שהוא דבר קטן ומ"מ ולא באה, וכ"ש אתה שאינך מלך ואני איני מלכה על ידך רק דומה לך במעלה ואתה מבקש ממני לא לבא לפניך, רק שאעבוד עבודה קשה, כ"ש שאיני צריך לשמוע לך. ובזה יתדלדלו הנשים משמוע לבעליהן, והמעשה הלז תהיה למשל ולשנינה בפי כולם, וזה הוא הנגע לכל העמים:

(יח) והיום הזה, עתה באר מה שנוגע להשרים, כי שרות פרס ומדי שהן היו במשתה הלז והן שמעו את דבר המלכה וכל הויכוח שהיה ביניהם בפרטות, והם עוד היום הזה תאמרנה כל דבר המלכה לכל שרי המלך, באופן שהיום הזה אשר הגבלת לקיים בו מנמתך שיסכימו השרים עמך שתמלוך ממלכה בלתי מוגבלת, ותוכל לנתך במה שנשי השרים יספרו לבעליהן, כי ושתי מחזקת שיש לה חלק במלכותך, והמלוכה לך ירושה על ידה, ואם לא תהרגנה הרי תסכים עמה, ויושבת כל ענתך. וממילא וכדי בזיון בין העמים שהנשים יבזו בעליהן, וקצף בין השרים שיקציפו את מלכותך שתשאר ממלכה מוגבלת:

(יט) אם על המלך טוב, אחר שהגיע כל מה שעשתה ושתי וההפסד שנמשך על ידה, וגלה דעת המלך כל מה שהיה עם לבבו במשתה הזאת וכי ושתי הפרה עצתו, בא ביועץ הכס והודיעו איך יתוקנו שני הקלקולים האלה ע"י מיתת ושתי, וראשון יעצו איך יחזיק במעוז שמעתה תהיה מלכותו מלכות בלתי מוגבלת, ועז"א יצא דבר מלכות מלפניו, יעצו שמעתה יעמיד חק חדש אשר כל דבר מלכות לא יצאו עוד מן השרים המחוקקים כמו שהיה עד הנה שלא היה רשות להמלך לשפוט או לתקן דבר בעצמו אם לא ע"פ השרים ויועצי המדינה מעתה לא יהיה כן רק כל דבר מלכות אשר יצא, מלפניו לבדו יצא,

ולא

השאלות

יח מלות והיום הזה אין להן הבנה. וגם לא נזכר מה שיאמרו שרות פרס ומדי. ומהו הכפל של בזיון וקצף:

יט מ"ש יצא דבר מלכות מלפניו אין לו מובן מהו הדבר מלכות. וביחוד מ"ש ויכתב בדתי פרס ומדי, שהלא בדתות העמים לא יכתב רק דת הקיים לעולם שע"פ יפסקו הדין להבא אבל הריגת ושתי אינו דת קיים רק משפט לפי שעה, ומהו ולא יעבור:

יִתֵּן הַמֶּלֶךְ לִרְעוּתָהּ הַטּוֹבָה מִמֶּנָּה׃ כ וְנִשְׁמַע פִּתְגָם
הַמֶּלֶךְ אֲשֶׁר־יַעֲשֶׂה בְּכָל־מַלְכוּתוֹ כִּי רַבָּה הִיא וְכָל־
הַנָּשִׁים יִתְּנוּ יְקָר לְבַעְלֵיהֶן לְמִגָּדוֹל וְעַד־קָטָן׃ כא וַיִּיטַב
הַדָּבָר בְּעֵינֵי הַמֶּלֶךְ וְהַשָּׂרִים וַיַּעַשׂ הַמֶּלֶךְ כִּדְבַר מְמוּכָן׃
כב וַיִּשְׁלַח סְפָרִים אֶל־כָּל־מְדִינוֹת הַמֶּלֶךְ אֶל־מְדִינָה
וּמְדִינָה כִּכְתָבָהּ וְאֶל־עַם וָעָם כִּלְשׁוֹנוֹ לִהְיוֹת כָּל־אִישׁ
שֹׂרֵר בְּבֵיתוֹ וּמְדַבֵּר כִּלְשׁוֹן עַמּוֹ׃ ס

אחר

רש"י

חוק ודת לכל הבוזה את בעלה: אשר לא תבוא ושתי. ולכך ר נהרגה: (כב) ומדבר כלשון עמו. כופה את אשתו ללמוד את לשונו אם היא בת לשון אחר

שפתי חכמים

ויבא בדתי פרס ומדי. לכ"פ בספרי חוק כו': ר דק"ל מה יתקנו בזה שיכתב אשר לא תבא ושתי שלא גרועי גרעי שממנה שלמדנה הנשים לעשות גם הנה כן. לכ"פ ולכן נכרגב

השאלות

כ הלא יפלא מ"ש ונשמע פתגם וכו' כי רבה היא, מה הוא הדבר הגדול הזה שהרג אשת חיקו, ומי יעצור בעדו. וביחוד מ"ש וכל הנשים יתנו יקר שמורה שלכן יתרגה כדי שישמע בכל המלכות וילמדו הנשים לתת יקר לבעליהן, וזה עצה סכלה ומגונה מאד שהמלך יהרוג אשת חיקו בשביל דבר כזה. גם מ"ש מגדול ועד קטן ולא אמר מקטן ועד גדול, ועיין למעלה (פסוק ה'):

כב למה מספר ששלח לכל מדינה ומדינה ככתבה. גוף הספרים הם דברי סכלות שיהיה כל איש שורר בביתו. גם מה שפקד שידבר כלשון עמו לא מצאו כל אנשי חיל ידיהם, מה רצה בפקודתו זאת:

פירוש

ולא זאת אלא ויכתב בדתי פרס ומדי, שכל פסק שילא מן המלך יכתב בדתי פרס ומדי להשאר דת קבוע שע"פ ישפטו כל דין כיולא בו, ולא יעבור רק ישאר דת קבוע לנלח, כמו שהוא גם היום אלל המלכים שפסקיהם ישארו דת קיים במדינה (גאבינעטס ארדערע) והדבר מלכות הראשון יהי אשר לא תבא ושתי לפני המלך, [ויכתב בדתי פרס ומדי הוא מאמר מוסגר ומוסב על כל הפסקים שילאו מן המלך להבא], וגם בזה יען נכונה כי אם ימית את ושתי עדיין יאמרו הלא מ"מ לא באתה לפני המלך, והמלך לא יכול להכריחה שתבא לפניו, לכן יען שהמלך יתן דת שלא תבא ושתי לפניו, שעי"ז יאמרו שלא היא היתה המעכבת, רק שאח"כ היה ברלונה לתקן עותתה ולבא ולא יכלה לבא לפניו מפני דת המלך שלא תבא. ועוסף לזה ומלכותה יתן המלך לרעותה הטובה ממנה. כלל בזה שתי כוונות, אחת כמ"ש המפרש שלא יבים עוד על יחוס אבותיה, רק שתהיה טובה ממנה בעלמה לא מלד אבותיה, וזאת שנית, אמר אליו בל תירא פן גם השרית תמרוד בך, כי השנית תלמד מוסר מן ושתי ותירא לעשות כמוה פן כמקרה ושתי גם היא יקרנה, וז"ש הטובה ממנה, המ"ס הוא מ' הסבה שעל ידה תוסר ותהיה טובה:

(כ) ונשמע, עתה באר איך עי"ז ירויח לתקן כל מה שנעוות עתה, כי על ידי שישים חוק שמעתה ילא דבר מלכות מלפניו בלי עלת הסגנים, עי"ז מעתה ונשמע פתגם המלך אשר יעשה, מה שיעשה המלך בעלמו גם בלי עלת השרים ישמע בכל מלכותו ואין מי שימרה את פיו יען כי רבה היא, כי פתגם המלך היא עלמו יהיה דת קבוע ולא יעבור, ובזה תרויח למשול ממלכה הבלתי מוגבלת. ב) וע"י שישים משפט בושתי ירויח שכל הנשים יתנו יקר לבעליהן, הגם שהאחד גדול והאחד קטן, ר"ל שגם כשהיא גדולה ממנו ביחוס תתן לו יקר:

(כא) וייטב, אחר שלדבר הזה שימלוך ממלכה בלתי מוגבלת היה לריך הסכמת השרים, אחר שהשרים הסכימו עם המלך בזה, ומעתה נסתלק כח השרים, ונשאר הנהגת הדת להמלך לבדו, ויעש המלך כדבר ממוכן בלי עורך אל הסכמת השרים:

(כב) ע"פ זה נתן הדת הראשון שכל איש ידבר כלשון עמו, וזה עשה בחכמה ודעת, כי עד עתה היה בחוקי פרס שכל העמים הנכנעים תחתם כשהיו כותבים אל המלך וכן המכתבים שהגיעו מן המלך אליהם היה לריך להיות בלשון פרס שהוא שפת האום המולך, ומלד זה היו כולם לריכים ללמוד לשון פרס, ואחר שההשורוש החזיק עתה, שלא המדינה היא השולטת רק הוא עלמו הוא המולך על כולם.

מפילה

ב א אַחַר הַדְּבָרִים הָאֵלֶּה כְּשֹׁךְ חֲמַת הַמֶּלֶךְ אֲחַשְׁוֵרוֹשׁ
זָכַר אֶת־וַשְׁתִּי וְאֵת אֲשֶׁר־עָשָׂתָה וְאֵת אֲשֶׁר־
נִגְזַר עָלֶיהָ׃ ב וַיֹּאמְרוּ נַעֲרֵי־הַמֶּלֶךְ מְשָׁרְתָיו יְבַקְשׁוּ
לַמֶּלֶךְ נְעָרוֹת בְּתוּלוֹת טוֹבוֹת מַרְאֶה׃ ג וְיַפְקֵד הַמֶּלֶךְ
פְּקִידִים

רש"י

אחר: (א) זכר את ושתי. את יפיה ונעצב: (ג) ויפקד המלך פקידים. לפי שכל פקיד ופקיד ידועים

פירוש

ממילא אין הבדל בין מדינת פרס ליתר מקומות ממשלתו, שכולם נכנעים תחתיו ועבדים לו כאלה, ממילא אין לכתב ולשון פרס יתרון על יתר לשונות הגוים, כי אין המלכות נקראת מעתה על שם פרס רק ע"ש אחשורוש, וע"ז כתב אל כל עם ועם כלשונו, ונתן הדת שכ"א ידבר כלשון עמו, והדת השני נתן שכל איש יהיה שורר בביתו, כי עד עתה היה בחוקי פרס שהאשה תכנע אל האיש לכבדו לבד, והוא נתן הדת שישתרר עליה וימשול בה כאדון בשפחתו, ויכול לעשות בה דין ומשפט כעם קנין כספו, וכמו שהוא עוד היום בחלק ממדינות אפריקא. ושני דתות האדפים האלה היו מגבילים לעומת שני הדברים שהזכיר ממוכן, שלעומת ימלוך לבדו בבלי הגבלה, נתן הדת שכל הלשונות יהיו שוים, ולעומת שכל הנשים יתנו יקר לבעליהן נתן הדת להיות כל איש שורר בביתו:

השאלות

א מה רצה במה ששלש פה, את ושתי, את אשר עשתה, ואת אשר נגזר עליה:

ב עצת הנערים נבערה, שאל מלך כמוהו יבקשו אשה מן הרחובות וקיקלון על כבודו. תחלה אמר יבקשו שמורה הבאות בטוב לבן, ושוב אומר ויפקד ויקבצו שמורה בעל כרחן:

ג ולמה הגבילו שינתנו ליד הגא. ולמה הזכיר שנתנו תמרוקיהן שזה אינו מענין העצה:

אולם מה שהקדים הפרשה הזאת לספור המגלה, ונתחייבנו לקראה בפורים כאילו גם היא שייכה אל ספור הנס, אחשוב בו שני טעמים, א) והוא הטעם העקרי אצלי, כי כלל הספור הזה הוא יסוד מוסד לספורים הבאים אחריו, כי לולא התאמץ המלך למלוך מלכות בלתי מוגבלת, לא היה באפשרי להיות לו לקיחת אסתר, כי לא היו שרי העצה מסכימים שיקבצו למלך נערות בתולות לברור מהם אשה, ואף כי לקחת אשה אשר לא ידע עמה ומולדתה, ולא הגדלת המן שלא היה יכול לעשות זה בלי רשות השרים, וכ"ש הגזרה הכוללת להשמיד אומה שלמה, ועז"א אלמלא אגרות ראשונות לא נתקיימו אגרות אחרונות, ר"ל אלמלא לא יצא הדת הראשון שהמלך שליט על הדתות והנמוסים לבדו ואין זולתו, לא היה באפשר שילכו האגרות האחרונות, אחר שהיה צריך נטילת רשות משרי העצה. זאת שנית, אחר שהנס הזה לא היה בו דבר היוצא מהיקש הטבעי, כי שהאשה היפה בנשים תפנה רצון המלך בעצה יקרה על הרוב, ולא יהיה זה נס ופלא, רק אם נשקיף היטב על המלך אשר בו היה המאורע, כי אם יקרה זה לרוב במלכים הקטנים, לא יהיה זה בקל אצל מלך הנורא למלכי ארץ. ומגד זה הקדים להודיע. א) גודל מלכותו שמלך על קכ"ז מדינות, ב) גבורתו שכבשם כולם בזמן קצר, ג) עשרו הנראה מהמשתה הגדול, ד) חכמתו איך התנהג בתחבולות להסיר לב ראשי עם הארץ למלוך עליהם בלי הגבלה, ה) טבעו ותכונתו שהגם שאהב את ושתי עד מות, מ"מ מפני אהבת הטוב הכללי יבזו נשי המדינה בעליהן בעיניהן, או אהבת המועיל שישתרר במלכות בלתי מוגבלת, ביטל אהבת הערב שאהב את ושתי, ובכל זה גלוי לכל רואה שמה שאסתר שנתה לבו להשיב את הספרים מהשבת המן, לא אהבת הערב השתו, רק מאת ה' היתה זאת:

ב (א) זכר את ושתי, מספר שאחר ששך חמת המלך ועלה בדעתו לקחת אשה אחרת למלכה, פחד בלבבו מפני שלשה דברים, א) שזכר את ושתי, את יפיה ויחוסה ומעלותיה וחשב כי קשה שימצא אשה כמוה, ב) זכר את אשר עשתה, וירא לקחת אשה פן גם ימצא מיוחסת ויפ"ת כושתי תעשה גם היא כמעשה ושתי, ולא יכון במשפט כסאו שיהרוג גם זאת שיאמרו שהוא הורג את נשיו, ג) זכר את אשר נגזר עליה, וירא שגם תמצא אשה ראויה אליו לא תרצה להנשא לו כי תתירא שלא יהרוג גם אותה.

(ב) ויאמרו וכאשר הודיע פחדו למשרתיו, יעצוהו עצה נכונה להסיר שלשה הספקות אלה; שלעומת מה שזכר את ושתי ואת יפיה, אמרו יבקשו לאדני המלך שיבקשו אשה הראויה למלך. גם אל יביטו על היחוס רק שיהיו נערות טובות מראה, כי מלך גדול כזה למה ישגיח על היחוס:

(ג) ונגד מה שזכר את אשר נגזר עליה ופחד לבבו שלא תרצה האשה להנשא לו, אמרו שאחר שבקשו מאלה אם הבאים ברצונם ולא ימצאו אשה נאותה אליו, אז יפקיד פקידים ויקבצו את כל נערה ביד חזקה

פְּקִידִים֮ בְּכָל־מְדִינ֣וֹת מַלְכוּתוֹ֒ וְיִקְבְּצ֣וּ אֶת־כָּל־נַֽעֲרָֽה־
בְ֠תוּלָה טוֹבַ֨ת מַרְאֶ֜ה אֶל־שׁוּשַׁ֤ן הַבִּירָה֙ אֶל־בֵּ֣ית הַנָּשִׁ֔ים
אֶל־יַ֥ד הֵגֶ֛א סְרִ֥יס הַמֶּ֖לֶךְ שֹׁמֵ֣ר הַנָּשִׁ֑ים וְנָת֖וֹן תַּמְרֻקֵיהֶֽן׃
ד וְהַֽנַּעֲרָ֗ה אֲשֶׁ֤ר תִּיטַב֙ בְּעֵינֵ֣י הַמֶּ֔לֶךְ תִּמְלֹ֖ךְ תַּ֣חַת וַשְׁתִּ֑י
וַיִּיטַ֧ב הַדָּבָ֛ר בְּעֵינֵ֥י הַמֶּ֖לֶךְ וַיַּ֥עַשׂ כֵּֽן׃ ס ה אִ֣ישׁ יְהוּדִ֔י הָיָ֖ה
בְּשׁוּשַׁ֣ן הַבִּירָ֑ה וּשְׁמ֣וֹ מָרְדֳּכַ֗י בֶּ֣ן יָאִ֧יר בֶּן־שִׁמְעִ֛י בֶּן־קִ֖ישׁ
אִ֥ישׁ יְמִינִֽי׃ ו אֲשֶׁ֤ר הָגְלָה֙ מִיר֣וּשָׁלַ֔יִם עִם־הַגֹּלָה֙ אֲשֶׁ֣ר
הָגְלְתָ֔ה עִ֖ם יְכָנְיָ֣ה מֶֽלֶךְ־יְהוּדָ֑ה אֲשֶׁ֣ר הֶגְלָ֔ה נְבוּכַדְנֶאצַּ֖ר

°סגו״ל בלא מקף

מלך:

רש״י

ידועות לו נשים יפות שבמדינתו: תמרוקיהן. הן דברים המחליקין, כמו (ויקרא ו׳) ומורק ושוטף. שמן ערב ומיני סמנים ובשמים המטהרין ומעדנין את הבשר: (ה) איש יהודי. על שגלה עם גלות יהודה, כל אותן שגלו עם מלכי יהודה היו קרויים ש יהודים בין הגוים ואפי׳ משבט אחר הם: איש ימיני מבנימין

שפתי חכמים

נתרגם פי׳ שהיו כותבים שלכך נתרגם: ש דק״ל קרי ליה יהודי

השאלה

ה איש יהודי, יל״ד שהי״ל ויהי איש יהודי בשושן, ולמה מספר יחוסו:
ו למה מאריך הספור שהגלה מירושלים:

פירוש

חזקה, (וגם התחכמו שיפקיד ע״ז פקידים חדשים, שהפקיד החדש לא יערבו לבם לתת לו שוחד להסתיר ולהעלים עין מבנות העשירים), ונגד החשש הנ״ל מה שזכר את אשר עשתה וירא פן תעשה כמעשה ושתי, יעצוהו שיקבצו הנערות אל יד הגא, ושלא יביאו התמרוקים מביתם רק ונתון תמרוקיהן, ע״י הסריסים. ומלבד זה יכנעו תמיד אל הסריסים ולא תגבהנה בלבבן כושתי שהיה לה להרפה מה ששלח לה המלך ביד הסריסים:

(ד) והנערה גם אם אינה מיוחסת רק אם תיטב בעיני המלך:

וייטב הדבר בעיני המלך, פה לא הוצרך לעצת השרים כמו למעלה, כי כבר נתן בידו הכח לעשות הכל לבדו כנ״ל:

(ה) איש יהודי הכתוב בא לספר צדקת מרדכי ואסתר, איך בשלשה זמנים היתה אסתר נזהרה ונלקחת בעל כרחה, א) בזמן הראשון שנלקחה מביתה, ב) בזמן השני במשך י״ב חדש שישבה תחת יד הגי, ג) זמן השלישי בעת נלקחה אל היכל המלך. עתה התחיל לספר מתחלת לקיחתה מביתה, שמרדכי הסתירה משך זמן רב, הגם שהיה לו סכנה בדבר כי פקודת המלך בודאי היתה שכל מי שי״ל בת יפה יביאנה, וכשעבר על פקודת המלך אחת דתו להמית ובכל זאת לא מסרה ברצונו, והוצב בזה שמונה ענינים, א) איש יהודי היה בשושן הבירה, שאם היה מרדכי דר במדינה אחרת לא היתה הסכנה גדולה כ״כ, כי היה יכול לומר שלא שמע מפקודת המלך, אבל הוא היה בשושן ושם היה מקום הקיבוץ ומודע לכל בני העיר, וגם אם היה דר בשושן זה תקרוב היה לו תירוץ שעדן לא שמע, עז״א איש יהודי היה מכבר בשושן שדר שמה מימי קדם, וכזה מתחייב ראשו למלך, ב) ושמו מרדכי כי אם היה איש שפל ונבזה היה לו אמתלא שנכלם למסור בתו למלך בידעו פחיתות מדרגתו, לכן אמר שהיה איש הנודע בשמו ויחוסו ושם שבשו לכבוד ולתפארת, ובשגם שהיה מזרע המלוכה מבני שאול:

(ו) אשר הגלה, ג) חטאו היה יותר גדול מצד שהיה מן הגולים, כי ידוע שאם איש גר אשר יסתופף בצל המלך מצד החסד יעבור ואשם נגד דת המלך, יענש יותר מאם יחטא אחד מאזרחי הארץ, וגם לא יכול לתת אמתלא שמצד זה בעצמו שהוא מן הגולים לא ערב לבו לתת בתו למלך, כי הגולים נבזים ע״פ רוב, לז״א שהיתה מן הגולה שהגלתה עם יכניה, שאז גלו שרי יהודה ותפארת ציון, ואלה היו החשובים תמיד:

ויהי

מֶלֶךְ בָּבֶל׃ ז וַיְהִי אֹמֵן אֶת־הֲדַסָּה הִיא אֶסְתֵּר בַּת־
דֹּדוֹ כִּי אֵין לָהּ אָב וָאֵם וְהַנַּעֲרָה יְפַת־תֹּאַר וְטוֹבַת
מַרְאֶה וּבְמוֹת אָבִיהָ וְאִמָּהּ לְקָחָהּ מָרְדֳּכַי לוֹ לְבַת׃
ח וַיְהִי בְּהִשָּׁמַע דְּבַר־הַמֶּלֶךְ וְדָתוֹ וּבְהִקָּבֵץ נְעָרוֹת רַבּוֹת
אֶל־שׁוּשַׁן הַבִּירָה אֶל־יַד הֵגָי וַתִּלָּקַח אֶסְתֵּר אֶל־בֵּית
הַמֶּלֶךְ אֶל־יַד הֵגַי שֹׁמֵר הַנָּשִׁים׃ ט וַתִּיטַב הַנַּעֲרָה בְעֵינָיו
וַתִּשָּׂא חֶסֶד לְפָנָיו וַיְבַהֵל אֶת־תַּמְרוּקֶיהָ וְאֶת־מָנוֹתֶהָ
לָתֵת לָהּ וְאֵת שֶׁבַע הַנְּעָרוֹת הָרְאֻיוֹת לָתֶת־לָהּ מִבֵּית
הַמֶּלֶךְ

שפתי חכמים

יסודי וקרי ליה ימיני. לכ"פ על שגלה כו': ת דק"ל כי איך תוכל להיות לו לבת מאשר שאינה מזרעו וצ"ל לקחה מרדכי והיתה לו כבת כמו ותהי לו כבת גבי בת שבע (שמואל ב' י"ב). לכ"פ אל תקרי לבת אלא לבית, כ"ה בפ"ק דמגילה

רש"י

מבנימין היה כך פשוטו. ורבותינו דרשו מה שדרשו: (ז) לו לבת. רבותינו פירשו ת לבית לאשה: (ט) ויבהל את תמרוקיה. זריז ומהר בשלה משל כולן: שראויים לתת לה. לשרתה וכן עושין לכולן, ורבותינו

השאלות

ז כפל הלשון. וגם אינו מסודר במה שהפסיק באמצע במ"ש והנערה יפ"ת.

ח מ"ש ויהי בהשמע ובהקבץ הכל דברי מותר, הלא עיקר בא להודיע שנלקחה אסתר. ומה נ"מ אם נלקחו נערות רבות קודם או לא:

ט ותיטב ותשא חסד הוא כפל ענין. מה ענין ויבהל מה הבהלה הזאת. למה נזכרו פה מנות. ולא נזכר שנתנו מנות לנערות אחרות. גם לא נזכר שנתנו להאחרות ז' נערות. ומלת הראויות מורה שראוים לה לבדה:

פירוש

(ז) ויהי אומן, ד) שהיה נודע לכל שהוא האומן אותה, וגם אסתר היתה נודעת בשם עד שנקראת הדסה ע"י מדותיה הטובים, וגם היתה בת דודו וממילא הוא פקיד עליה והיא תחת רשותו, ומכל אלה הצדדים היה בסכנה גדולה אם יודע שמחביאה מפני המלך. ה) כי אין לה אב ואם, וממילא רק ממנו יבקשו דין וחשבון לא מזולתו, ו) והנערה יפת תאר, ולא יהיה לו שום כפרה אם ימצאו שהחביא נערה יפה כזאת, ולא היה יכול לאמר שהנערה גדולה היא ותשב שמעצמה הלך אל בית המלך, כי במות אביה ואמה לקחה מרדכי לו לבת וא"א שתלך בלעדי רשותו:

(ח) ויהי, (ח) נוסף על כל אלה כבר היה שנשמע דבר המלך ודתו, כי שתי פקודות יצאו מן המלך, האחת יצאה הפקודה שיבקשו למלך נערות ממי שימסרם ברצון, וזה קרא דבר המלך, ואחר כך יצאה הפקודה השנית, שיקבצו נערות בע"כ [כנ"ל פסוק ב' וג'] וזה קרא דתו, כי עם הפקודה השנית ודאי חייבו להשבר ומסתיר את בתו משפט מות, מבואר שלא חשש תחלה אל התועלת עת יצא דבר המלך שהנערה שתמצא חן תלקח לאשה, ואף לא אח"כ אל הסכנה בצאת הדת שיקחו בע"כ, וזאת שנית ובהקבץ נערות רבות שכבר נקבצו נערות רבות מחוץ לשושן אל שושן, ואז ודאי גדול שוגם איש שושן כרואה כל זאת ומעלים בת יפת תואר אשר אצלו, ומ"מ מכל זה לא נתפעלו הצדיקים האלה, רק ותלקח אסתר בחזקה ולא נהגה מרדכי מדעתו:

(ט) ותיטב, והנה אחר כל ההצעה הזאת, שראו בעליל שאסתר נלקחה ביד חזקה, הלא היה ראוי שידוש אונה ואת אומנה משפט מות, כי עברו מצות המלך, מ"מ ע"י כי ותיטב הנערה בעיניו וראה שהיא ראויה למלוכה, ע"ז ותשא חסד לפניו, והוא עשה אתה חסד למחול על עונה ושלא להעניש, ויבהל עתה מספר איך תיכף כשראה אותה הבין שהיא תהיה המולכת, ומגיד זה שינה בה בארבעה דברים, א) כי כל בתולה אשר נקבצה לידו לא התחיל תיכף לתת תמרוקיה רק המתין עד תחלת התקופה כמו שיתבאר (בפסוק י"ב), אבל באסתר בהל ומהר לתת תמרוקיה למען ישלמו הי"ב חדש תיכף ותבא קודם אל המלך, ב) ואת מנותיה שנתן לה מנות ביחוד מה שלא נתן לשום נערה כי ידע שהיא תמלוך, ג) ואת שבע הנערות, כי המלכה היו לה שבע נערות לשמשה, וגם שלא מלכה עדיין נתן לה שבע הנערות הראויות לתת אח"כ בעת שתמלוך, כי לא נסתפק כלל במלכותה, ד) וישנה ששנה לא לבד

אותה

המלך וישנה ואת־נערותיה לטוב בית הנשים: י לא־
הגידה אסתר את־עמה ואת־מולדתה כי מרדכי צוה
עליה אשר לא־תגיד: יא ובכל־יום ויום מרדכי מתהלך
לפני חצר בית־הנשים לדעת את־שלום אסתר ומה־
יעשה בה: יב ובהגיע תר נערה ונערה לבוא ׀ אל־
המלך אחשורוש מקץ היות לה כדת הנשים שנים
עשר חדש כי כן ימלאו ימי מרוקיהן ששה חדשים
בשמן המר וששה חדשים בבשמים ובתמרוקי הנשים:
יג ובזה הנערה באה אל־המלך את כל־אשר תאמר
ינתן לה לבוא עמה מבית הנשים עד־בית המלך:

בערב

רש"י

ולטותים דרשו א מה שדרשו: **וישנה.** שינה אותה: (י) **אשר לא תגיד.** כדי שיאמרו שהיא ממשפחה בזויה וישלחוה שאם ידעו שהיא ממשפחת שאול המלך היו מחזיקים בה: (יא) **ומה יעשה בה.** זה אחד משני צדיקים שניתן להם רמז ישועה דוד ומרדכי דוד שנאמר (שמואל א יז לו) גם את הארי גם הדוב הכה עבדך אמר לא בא לידי דבר זה אלא לסמוך עליו להלחם עם זה, וכן מרדכי אמר לא אירע לצדקת זו שתלקח למשכב ערל אלא שעתידה לקום להושיע לישראל לפיכך היה מחזר לדעת מה יהא בסופה: (יב) **תר.** זמן: (יג) **כל אשר תאמר**

שפתי חכמים

דמגילה ומפרש מה לבית פי' לאשה: א דיוקו מדכתיב הראויות לתת לה משמע שהיו נותנים לכל אחת הראויות לא דאל"כ הל"ל ואת שבע הנערות מבית המלך. וכן איתא במדרש היה מוסר לכל אחת שב"ע נערות אם היתה שתורם אומרת

השאלות

י למה **לא** תגידה את מולדתה:

יא למה התהלך מרדכי כל יום ויום לדעת את שלום אסתר, הלא ידע שלא תכנס לבית המלך עד מלאת יב"ח:

יב למה **היו** ימי המירוק י"ב חדש:

יג ובזה הנערה **לא** נודע אם **היא** השלמת הפסוק הקודם שחסר ממנו נשוא המאמר. **ולמה נתנו לה את כל אשר תאמר:**

פירוש

אותה אלא גם **את** נערותיה שינה לטוב **בית הנשים**, וזה כולל שני דברים, א) שנתן להם החדרים היותר טובים ומרווחים, ב) שנתן להם מטוב המאכלים וכדומה:

(י) **לא הגידה**, עתה באר הזמן השני שהראית אסתר שהיא לקוחה שלא ברצונה, שאחר שהקדים איך שהנהגה בכבוד בכל הזמן הזה כבוטחים שהיא תמלוך, בכל זאת לא פתחה לבה ע"ז ולא רצתה להגיד עמה **ומולדתה**, וזה היה בעצת מרדכי, כי חשב שעי"כ יגרשנה המלך מביתו כי לא יקח אסופי מן השוק לו לאשה: (יא) **ובכל יום**, וגם בזה היתה בסכנה גדולה כי היתה ראויה לעונש במה שהראית שהיא אנוסה **עד** שבעבור זה היה מרדכי מבקר בכל יום **לדעת את שלומה ומה יעשה בה**, ר"ל אם יענישוה או יגרשוה, כי האמין בודאי שלא תפטר בלי עונש על מרדה במלך ומ"מ שמה לפיה מחסום ולא הגידה: (יב) **ובהגיע**, עתה מספר זמן השלישי שהראית שהיא אנוסה, שגם ביאתה לבית המלך היה באונס גלוי לכל, וע"ז מקדים לספר כי כל נערה אחר שמלאו ימי מרוקיהן שהיו יב"ח [וזה היה לבחון את בריאת גופה, כי הגם שהיא יפת תואר יוכל להיות שיש בה חולי פנימית, ולכן בחנו אותה בארבע תקופות השנה **כי** יש חולאים שלא יחולו רק באחת מן התקופות ואחר יסורו, ואלה נקראים ימי המירוק והנקיה, וששה חדשי החורף היו מושחות בשמן המור המחמם האיברים, ובימי הקיץ מרגילות בבשמים מריחים המסירים העפושים המצוים בעת"ה הללו]:

(יג) **ובזה**, אמר שזה כל ההתקשרות שהיה בין המלך והנערה, היה תמיד הנערה לא בקש המלך רק

היופי

יד בָּעֶרֶב ׀ הִיא בָאָה וּבַבֹּקֶר הִיא שָׁבָה אֶל־בֵּית הַנָּשִׁים
שֵׁנִי אֶל־יַד שַׁעֲשְׁגַז סְרִיס הַמֶּלֶךְ שֹׁמֵר הַפִּילַגְשִׁים לֹא־
תָבוֹא עוֹד אֶל־הַמֶּלֶךְ כִּי אִם־חָפֵץ בָּהּ הַמֶּלֶךְ וְנִקְרְאָה
בְשֵׁם׃ טו וּבְהַגִּיעַ תֹּר־אֶסְתֵּר בַּת־אֲבִיחַיִל ׀ דֹּד מָרְדֳּכַי
אֲשֶׁר לָקַח־לוֹ לְבַת לָבוֹא אֶל־הַמֶּלֶךְ לֹא בִקְשָׁה דָּבָר
כִּי אִם אֶת־אֲשֶׁר יֹאמַר הֵגַי סְרִיס־הַמֶּלֶךְ שֹׁמֵר הַנָּשִׁים
וַתְּהִי אֶסְתֵּר נֹשֵׂאת חֵן בְּעֵינֵי כָּל־רֹאֶיהָ׃ טז וַתִּלָּקַח
אֶסְתֵּר אֶל־הַמֶּלֶךְ אֲחַשְׁוֵרוֹשׁ אֶל־בֵּית מַלְכוּתוֹ בַּחֹדֶשׁ
הָעֲשִׂירִי הוּא־חֹדֶשׁ טֵבֵת בִּשְׁנַת־שֶׁבַע לְמַלְכוּתוֹ׃
יז וַיֶּאֱהַב הַמֶּלֶךְ אֶת־אֶסְתֵּר מִכָּל־הַנָּשִׁים וַתִּשָּׂא־חֵן
וָחֶסֶד לְפָנָיו מִכָּל־הַבְּתוּלֹת וַיָּשֶׂם כֶּתֶר־מַלְכוּת בְּרֹאשָׁהּ

וימליכה

רש"י

שאמר. כל שחוק ומיני זמר: (יד) אל בית הנשים שני. השני: (טז) בחדש העשירי. עת צנה שהגוף נהנה מן הגוף זימן הקב"ה אותו עת חיבה כדי לחבבה עליו: (יז) מכל הנשים. הבעולות שאף נשים

פירוש

ביופי ובבריאות הגוף, ועת עלתה ימי מרוקיה שנודע שאינה הולכת בזה הנערה באה אל המלך, כי לא בקשה ממנה מעלה אחרת, ומצד המלך היה מה שכל אשר תאמר בלכתה מבית הנשים עד בית המלך ינתן לה לבא עמה, שהיה לה רשות לבקש בכל הדרך מתנות וכדומה והיו נותנים לה כל משאלות לבבה, ובזה הראתה שהיא מתרצית ללכת ברצונה ואינה אנוסה, כי בצד המתנות מסרה עצמה למשכב, שעז"א ובזה הנערה באה ברצונה:

השאלות

טו למה הזכיר פה שנית יחוס **אסתר**, **ושאביחיל** היה דוד מרדכי. למה לא בקשה דבר ואם היה במקרה למה מספר זאת כותב הספר. לאיזה צורך **אומר** פה ביחוד שנשאה חן וכבר אמר זה למעלה:
יז מי הן הנשים ומי הן הבתולות. **ושינוי הלשון** אהבה וחן וחסד:

(יד) **בערב** ר"ל שבערב היא באה ובבוקר היא שבה להיות גרורה בבית הפילגשים ולא תבא עוד אל המלך, מ"מ התרצו והלכו ברצון טוב בהפך לנפש:

(טו) **ובהגיע**, אומר ראה כי באסתר היה הפך מכל הנשים, הנה מה שהביאה היא אל המלך מצדה, לא היה היופי והבריאות לבד רק היה בידה חוסן ויקר מה שהיתה **בת אביחיל**, שהיו תכונותיה ומדותיה טובות ושכלה שלם מצד תולדותה מאביה הצדיק, והוא היה **דוד מרדכי** שגדלה והוציא כוונתיה אלה הטובים אל פועל השלימות, זאת הביאה היא אל המלך, אבל מה שלקחה מן המלך מצדו, שמצד זה הבא ברצונה בלי אונס **לא בקשה דבר**, כי הראית בפועל שהיא אנוסה ואינה מתרצית אליו, וע"כ אמר **ובהגיע תור אסתר לבא**, שרק התור הגיע ואנסה לזה, ולא לבה הרצה לבא, ולכן לא רצתה מאומה **רק** מה שנתן לה הגי בעצמו, שזה הכריחה לקחת, ואף שבזה חייבה ראשה למלך זה הטעם השלישית, מ"מ **ותהי אסתר נושאת חן** וזה כסה על כל פשעיה:

(טז) **ותלקח**, עתה סיים שגם בסוף בואה לחדר המלך היה באונס, שעז"א ותלקח בעל כרחה, וספר שהיא לא נלקחה אל בית המלך הכולל רק **אל בית מלכותו** החדר המיוחד למלך:

(יז) **ויאהב**, באין ספק היו לאחשורוש נשים ופילגשים גם מכבר, ואצלם שייך אהבה, ואצל הבתולות שבאו להמליך אחת מהם שייך נשיאת חן כדי להמליכה, ובפניהם הכתיר עליה על כולנה עד שגם בעצמו הכתר על ראשה ברוב אהבתו אותה וימליכה תיכף:

ויעש

וַיַּמְלִיכֶהָ תַּחַת וַשְׁתִּי׃ יח וַיַּעַשׂ הַמֶּלֶךְ מִשְׁתֶּה גָדוֹל לְכָל־
שָׂרָיו וַעֲבָדָיו אֵת מִשְׁתֵּה אֶסְתֵּר וַהֲנָחָה לַמְּדִינוֹת עָשָׂה
וַיִּתֵּן מַשְׂאֵת כְּיַד הַמֶּלֶךְ׃ יט וּבְהִקָּבֵץ בְּתוּלוֹת שֵׁנִית
וּמָרְדֳּכַי יֹשֵׁב בְּשַׁעַר־הַמֶּלֶךְ׃ כ אֵין אֶסְתֵּר מַגֶּדֶת
מוֹלַדְתָּהּ וְאֶת־עַמָּהּ כַּאֲשֶׁר צִוָּה עָלֶיהָ מָרְדֳּכָי וְאֶת־
מַאֲמַר מָרְדֳּכַי אֶסְתֵּר עֹשָׂה כַּאֲשֶׁר הָיְתָה בְאָמְנָה
אִתּוֹ׃ ס כא בַּיָּמִים הָהֵם וּמָרְדֳּכַי יֹשֵׁב בְּשַׁעַר־הַמֶּלֶךְ
קָצַף בִּגְתָן וָתֶרֶשׁ שְׁנֵי־סָרִיסֵי הַמֶּלֶךְ מִשֹּׁמְרֵי הַסַּף

ויבקשו

רש"י

שיש בעולם קבץ : (יח) והנחה למדינות עשה . לכבודה הניח להם מן המס שעליהם : ויתן משאת . שלח דורונות להם והכל כדי לפתותה ב אולי תגיד מולדתה . ואע"פ כן , (כ) אין אסתר מגדת מולדתה . לפי שמרדכי יושב בשער המלך המזרזה והמרמזה

שפתי חכמים

אומרת שחורה תנא עמה אם היתה קוראה אמרה קוראה תנא עמה : ב כך דרשו בפ"ק דמגילה ודייקי מדסמיך ליה להאי קרא ובהקבץ בתולות שנית אין אסתר מגדת כו' , וא"ת היאך אתה יכול לומר שלא היה יודע אחשורוש מאיזו עם היתה ושלא כמה דלעוזין היו בישראל שהיו אומרים שהיא ישראלית אלא

השאלות

יח למה קראו משתה אסתר , הלא ידוע שהיה בשביל לקיחת אסתר · ולמה נתן הנחה ומשאת :

יט מה היה הקבוץ הזה שנית אחר שכבר המליך את אסתר ומה ענין פה מה שמרדכי יושב בשער המלך :

כ ולמה הוזר שאסתר אין מגדת עמה ומולדתה וכבר אמר זה, ושטחות הלשון מורה שתלוי בפסוק הקודם ולא נודע יחוכם זה אל זה , ולמה בפסוק יו"ד אמר עמה ומולדתת ופה אמר מולדתה ואת עמה :

כא למה הזכיר פה שנית שמרדכי יושב בשער המלך וכבר הזכירו למעלה :

פירוש

(יח) ויעש עתה מספר שנס אחר שכבר המליכה המלך והיא לא הגידה עדיין עמה ומולדתה , עשה המלך תחבולות רבות כדי שתגיד מאיזה עם היא , ובכן עשה בג' דברים , א) מלד הכבוד שעשה משתה גדול לכל שריו ועבדיו , וקרא למשתה זאת בשם משתה אסתר שהיא היא העושה משתה זאת , וחשב אולי בזה יתעורר בה אהבת הכבוד , שתבוש לפני השרים שהיא אסופי ואין יודעים מולדתה ותגיד , ב) מלד הטוב לעמה , שהנחה למדינות עשה , מספק שמא היא מדינה שאסתר נולדה שם , ובזה תתעורר להגיד מדינתה בידעה כי אז ייטיב ביתר שאת לבני מדינתה ועמה , ג) ויתן משאת יקרות כיד המלך , ובזה תתעורר להעשיר בני מולדתה ותגיד מולדתה כדי שגם הם יקבלו משאת :

(יט) ובהקבץ, גם אם היתה יראה להגיד מולדתה , כי אולי היא מעם שפל ונבזה ויגרש אותה המלך , הנה כבר קבץ את הבתולות הנשארות שעדיין לא נבעלו ושלחם לביתן , באופן שהיה לבה בטוח שלא יבחר עוד המלך באחרת , ועוד זאת כי מרדכי נתעלה להיות יושב בשער המלך על כסאות למשפט כאחד השרים , שזה עשו לו בעבור שמאתו אותה בביתו , ובזה הלא בטחה בכ"ש שיעשו לו גדולה וכבוד אם ידעו כי היא בת דודו :

(כ) אין, וכ"ז לא הועיל רק אין אסתר מגדת מולדתה ואת עמה, והנה התלה הקדים עמה למולדתה, כי שם היה המבוקש לדעת מי היא, והדך נשאול תחלה על עמה ואח"כ על מולדתה . ופה היו מתבוקש כדי להטיב עם בני עמה , ובזה שאלו תחלה על מולדתה שהם קודמים לקבל הטוב שהיא ואח"כ על עמה שגם עמהם ייטיבו בעבורה , וספר לדקתה שאף בעלתה לגדולה שמעה לדברי מרדכי כבעת שהיתה תחת רבותו בבית האומן :

(כא) בימים ההם, טרם יבא אל ספור הגזרה אשר היה לישראל, הקדים רפואה למכה , להורות כי המכה היתה למען הכות רק למען ירפא , כמו שמקיז דם שמכין תחלה הדברים הצריכים להשקיט מרוצת הדם ולעצרו ולהשיב נפשו אחר ההקזה , ועז"א כל המחלה אשר שמתי במצרים לא אשים עליך כי אני ה' רופאך , ר"ל שלא אשים ענין המחלה ע"ד שמותים במצרים שהיה עיקר הכונה למען הכות בשבע , רק אשים המחלה מצד שאני ה' רופאך , ומצ' זה יקדים הרפואה למכה . כי זאת עיקר הכונה , ע"כ

וַיְבַקְשׁוּ לִשְׁלֹחַ יָד בַּמֶּלֶךְ אֲחַשְׁוֵרֹשׁ׃ כב וַיִּוָּדַע הַדָּבָר
לְמָרְדֳּכַי וַיַּגֵּד לְאֶסְתֵּר הַמַּלְכָּה וַתֹּאמֶר אֶסְתֵּר לַמֶּלֶךְ
בְּשֵׁם מָרְדֳּכָי׃ כג וַיְבֻקַּשׁ הַדָּבָר וַיִּמָּצֵא וַיִּתָּלוּ שְׁנֵיהֶם עַל־
עֵץ וַיִּכָּתֵב בְּסֵפֶר דִּבְרֵי הַיָּמִים לִפְנֵי הַמֶּלֶךְ׃ ס
ג א אַחַר ׀ הַדְּבָרִים הָאֵלֶּה גִּדַּל הַמֶּלֶךְ אֲחַשְׁוֵרוֹשׁ אֶת־
הָמָן בֶּן־הַמְּדָתָא הָאֲגָגִי וַיְנַשְּׂאֵהוּ וַיָּשֶׂם אֶת־

כסאו

שפתי חכמים

אלא בשביל שנושאת חן בעיני כל רואיה והיו האומות מתגרות ואומרות זו ממשפחתי וזאת אומרת כמו כן לפיכך לא היה לו לעמוד על הבירור, כך כתוב ברש"י בספר עין יעקב: ג דק"ל מה הגיד לנו הכתוב שלא גדלו עד שבא המעשה הזאת

רש"י

והמרמזה על כך: (כא) לשלח יד. להשקותו סם המות: (כב) ויודע הדבר למרדכי. שהיו מספרים דבריהם לפניו בלשון טורסי ואין יודעים שהיה מרדכי מכיר בשבעים לשונות שהיה מיושבי לשכת הגזית: (כג) ויכתב בספר דברי הימים. הטובה שעשה מרדכי למלך: (א) אחר הדברים האלה. שנבראת ג רפואה זו להיות להשועה לישראל: גדל המלך

פירוש

ב"כ אחר שהקדים ההכנה הראשונה שזמן ה' לרפואת הכר עמו במה שהזמין להם אחות בבית המלך ויפה את אסתר לובשת כתר מלכות, ספר ההכנה השניה מה שהזמין למרדכי זכות וחסד בבית המלך שהציל נפשו ממות, והקדים לספור זה מה שמרדכי יושב בשער המלך לשתי כונות, אחת שזה עורר הקנאה משומרי הסף שחרה אפם על שמרדכי יושב בגדולה וכבוד והם עומדים על רגליהם לשמור הסף כדרך השומרים, ב) שמעשה זה בעצמו סבב ה' שישב מרדכי בשער המלך כדי שיודע לו קצף הסריסים, ובאופן שישיבת מרדכי שם היתה סבה לצרת ישראל שעי"ז נתגרה בו המן, והיא עצמה היתה סבה לגאולתן, וזה גם האחד שעשה ה' שמרדכי ימצא שם והיה סבה לרפואת המכה העתידה. (הגם הב') שקצף בגתן ותרש שהיו שומרי הסף, ולמשמרת זה בוחרים אנשים נבחנים לאוהבי המלך, וה' סבב שיקצפו על לא דבר, כי אחר שהיו סריסים מה להם לקנאות בגדולת מרדכי. ג) גוף המעשה מה שבקשו לשלוח יד במלך גדול כזה, כי אם יקרה שסרים יעיזו למרוד במלכם הוא כשופט להמליך איש מביניהם, ולא שיעשו זאת שני סריסים אשר יודעים כי בנפשם הוא:

(כב) גם הב' שנודע הדבר למרדכי, ע"י השגחת ה' המשגחת נעלמים. הד' שהגם שמרדכי לא אמר לאסתר שתגיד זאת בשמו, והיא שמעה לקולו בכל דבר כמו שהקדים ואת מאמר מרדכי אסתר עשה, ופה שנתה דבריו ותאמר למלך בשם מרדכי:

(כג) ה) ויבקש הדבר וימצא, ר"ל וימצא הדבר, שנמצא גוף הסם שרצו להמיתו, שזה דבר רחוק המציאות כי ודאי הסתירו אותו הסם במטמונים: ו) ויכתב, היה בהשגחת ה' שלא שלם לו המלך שכרו תיכף, רק כתבו בספר לזכרון כדי שיעמוד זאת למרדכי לישועה ליום פקודה, והיה בזה השגחה פרטית שלא נכתב בספר ד"ה הכולל, שהוא נמצא תמיד ביד המשנה, שאז ודאי היה המן מוחקו משם, רק נכתב בספר דברי הימים המיוחד למלך, שלא השיג אותו המן, וגם שנכתב לפני המלך שיש בפניו שאל"כ היה נקל שהסופר יזייף ויגרע בו דבר:

ג (א) אחר הדברים האלה. באור המפרשים כי אחר שנשכח מאחשורוש שאסתר הגידה זאת בשם מרדכי, וזה המלך היה הפך מאד ביחוד לשלם גמול למטיביו, ולא מצא דבר במה שישלם לאסתר עבור שהצילה נפשו ממות, חשב כי אך בזאת יאות לה במה שייטיב להשרים אשר יעצוהו לקחת את אסתר שהראשון מסריסיו היה ממוכן, והוא יעצהו לבקש לו נערות בתולות וע"י בא את אסתר, ולכן העלהו על במתי עב, וגם כי אחר שנשכח ממנו מי היה המגלה מדבר בגתן ותרש, היה נקל להמן אשר שעתו הצליחה לו לפתות לב המלך שהוא היה המגיד דבר, ולכן העלהו לגדולה, ובאופן שהמן התלבש בטלית שאינו שלו, והכבוד הלז היה באמת מגיע למרדכי אך מאת ה' היתה נסבה שחמול על ראש הרשע לפי שעה עד בא עת להחזיר העטרה לבעליה: גדל וינשאהו מנמוסי המלכים שלא לגדל איש הדיוט פתאום משפל המדרגה

עד

השאלות

כג לפני המלך מיותר:
א למה גדל את המן כ"כ. ולמה דוקא אחר הדברים האלה. ומהו הכפל גדל וינשאהו:

כִּסְא֔וֹ מֵעַ֕ל כָּל־הַשָּׂרִ֖ים אֲשֶׁ֥ר אִתּֽוֹ׃ ב וְכָל־עַבְדֵ֨י הַמֶּ֜לֶךְ
אֲשֶׁר־בְּשַׁ֣עַר הַמֶּ֗לֶךְ כֹּרְעִ֤ים וּמִֽשְׁתַּחֲוִים֙ לְהָמָ֔ן כִּי־כֵ֖ן צִוָּה־
ל֣וֹ הַמֶּ֑לֶךְ וּמָ֣רְדֳּכַ֔י לֹ֥א יִכְרַ֖ע וְלֹ֥א יִשְׁתַּחֲוֶֽה׃ ג וַ֠יֹּאמְרוּ
עַבְדֵ֥י הַמֶּ֛לֶךְ אֲשֶׁר־בְּשַׁ֥עַר הַמֶּ֖לֶךְ לְמָרְדֳּכָ֑י מַדּ֙וּעַ֙ אַתָּ֣ה
עוֹבֵ֔ר אֵ֖ת מִצְוַ֥ת הַמֶּֽלֶךְ׃ ד וַיְהִ֗י °בְּאָמְרָם֙ אֵלָיו֙ י֣וֹם וָי֔וֹם
וְלֹ֥א שָׁמַ֖ע אֲלֵיהֶ֑ם וַיַּגִּ֣ידוּ לְהָמָ֗ן לִרְאוֹת֙ הֲיַֽעַמְדוּ֙ דִּבְרֵ֣י

°כאמרם קרי

מרדכי

רש"י

המלך וגו' את המן. שהקב"ה בורא רפואה למכתן של ישראל קודם שיביא המכה עליהם: (ב) כרעים ומשתחוים. שעשה עצמו אלוה לפיכך ומרדכי לא יכרע ולא ישתחוה: (ד) היעמדו דברי מרדכי. האומר

השאלות

ב מה רצה למעט במ"ש אשר בשער המלך הל"ל וכל עבדי המלך כורעים. מדוע אמר כי כן צוה לו, הלא להם צוה לא לו. מדוע לא השתחוה מרדכי:

ד מ"ש היעמדו דברי מרדכי כי הגיד להם אשר הוא יהודי, אין לו מובן, הלא בזה לא היו מסופקים שהוא יהודי, והיה צ"ל היעמדו דברי מרדכי שהגיד להם שלא ישתחוה:

פירוש

עד רום המעלות, רק יעלהו מדרגה אחר מדרגה, כמו שבארתי זאת ביחוד בפ' מקץ אצל הגדלת יוסף ע"י פרעה, וכן ספר יוסף לאחיו (בראשית מה) וישימני לאב לפרעה, ואח"כ ולאדון לכל ביתו ואח"כ ומושל בכל ארץ מצרים, וכן עשה אחשורוש תחלה גדלו שהעלהו להיות שר ואחר כך וינשאהו מדרגה אחר מדרגה עד שהעלהו **ששם את כסאו למעלה מכל השרים שהיו אתו** במדרגה העליונה, שמהו לראש כלם:

(ג) **וכל**, אח"כ נתן לו רבו יתירא שכל עבדי המלך אף שיושבים **בשער המלך יכרעו וישתחו לו**, כי מנמוסי המלכים אשר במקום אשר המלך שם לא ינהגו כבוד לשום אדם, כי בזה מיקל כבוד המלך אם יכבד אחד מעבדיו לפניו [וכמ"ש שאוריה החתי מרד במלכות בית דוד מפני שקרא ליואב בפני דוד אדוני] ואחשורוש מחל על כבודו וצוה שגם בשער המלך יכרעו להמן, **יען כי כן צוה לו המלך** ומחל על כבודו, וגם שלא היה זה רק לכבוד המן שבזה היה בידו למחול רק היה מצות המלך, וגם לא להמן צוה זאת שיפקיד ע"ז ויעניש את העובר מצד עברו מצות המלך. **ומ"מ מרדכי לא יכרע** גמר בלבו שלא לכרוע בשום אופן, והטעם שנמנע מרדכי מכרוע לו, בארו המפרשים מפני שהיתה השתחויה הזאת כענין קבלת אלהות, שכן היה דרך העמים הקדמונים מאמיני ההזיות ליחס אל כל איש שמצאו בו איזו מעלה יתירה בחכמה או גבורה ועושר לאמר שהוא מבני אלים ושכוכב או כח עליון שופע עליו כמ"ש בנבוכדנצר (דניאל ב) ולדניאל סגיד ומנחה וניחוחין אמר לנסכה ליה, ולכן נמנע מרדכי מזה באשר הוא יהודי. זאת שנית, שגזרת המלך לא היה רק על מי שיש בו ב' תנאים, עבד המלך, ויושב בשער המלך. ומרדכי הגם שנמצא בו תנאי אחד שיושב בשער המלך לא היה מעבדי המלך, באשר הוא יהודי, והיהודי אינו נעשה עבד בנמוסי פרס, ושני הטעמים נכללים במ"ש כי הגיד להם אשר הוא יהודי:

(ד) **ויהי**, העבדים לא משנאה הלשינוהו להמן, רק מאשר הטיל עליהם לשמור מצות המלך ולמחות בעוברי רצונו, וע"כ לא הלשינוהו עד שהתרו בו תחלה, שעז"א **ויהי כאמרם אליו**. זאת שנית שהתמידו בהתראה **יום יום** ולא שמע אליהם, אז הגידו להמן, **לראות היעמדו**, ר"ל שמרדכי הגיד להם שלכן אינו משתחוה להמן בעבור שהוא יהודי ואינו יכול להשתחוות לו מצד דתו. אולם תרוצו זה צודק שלא ישתחוה לו בעת שהמן הולך מרחוק ואינו רואה, שאז אינו משתחוה רק מצד שעשה עצמו אלוה, אבל אם משתחוה לו בעת שהמן רואה אותו, שאז אין זה לשם אלהות רק מצד שררותו, כי לכל שר וגדול הדרך להשתחוות בפניו, ואם גם בעת שהמן יראה לא ישתחוה לו יודע כי לא מחמת יהדותו ודתו עשה זאת, רק מצד שמורד במלכות, וז"ש **שהגידו להמן לראות** היינו שהמן יראה על מרדכי, ובזה ידעו **אם יעמדו דברי מרדכי** ותרוצו **אשר הגיד להם** שלכן אינו משתחוה **בעבור שהוא יהודי**, שאם בעת יראה המן וילך בקרוב אליו, ישתחוה לו, אז יעמדו דבריו על כור המבחן, וידעו כי מחמת דתו נמנע להשתחוות שלא בפניו, ואין עליו עון אשר חטא, אבל אם גם בעת יראה המן לא ישתחוה, שאז דבריו ותרוצו מה שהוא יהודי לא **יעמדו** כי הגם שהוא יהודי לא תמנעהו דתו מהשתחוות לשר וגדול בפניו, אז ידעו כי מורד במלכות הוא:

וירא

מָרְדֳּכַי כִּי־הִגִּיד לָהֶם אֲשֶׁר־הוּא יְהוּדִי׃ ה וַיַּרְא הָמָן כִּי
אֵין מָרְדֳּכַי כֹּרֵעַ וּמִשְׁתַּחֲוֶה לוֹ וַיִּמָּלֵא הָמָן חֵמָה׃ ו וַיִּבֶז
בְּעֵינָיו לִשְׁלֹחַ יָד בְּמָרְדֳּכַי לְבַדּוֹ כִּי־הִגִּידוּ לוֹ אֶת־עַם
מָרְדֳּכָי וַיְבַקֵּשׁ הָמָן לְהַשְׁמִיד אֶת־כָּל־הַיְּהוּדִים אֲשֶׁר
בְּכָל־מַלְכוּת אֲחַשְׁוֵרוֹשׁ עַם מָרְדֳּכָי׃ ז בַּחֹדֶשׁ הָרִאשׁוֹן
הוּא־חֹדֶשׁ נִיסָן בִּשְׁנַת שְׁתֵּים עֶשְׂרֵה לַמֶּלֶךְ אֲחַשְׁוֵרוֹשׁ
הִפִּיל פּוּר הוּא הַגּוֹרָל לִפְנֵי הָמָן מִיּוֹם ׀ לְיוֹם וּמֵחֹדֶשׁ

לחדש

רש"י

לאומר שלא ישתחוה עולמית כי הוא יהודי והוזהר על עבודת אלילים: (ז) הפיל פור. הפיל מי שהפיל ולא פירש מי ומקרא קצר הוא: הוא הגורל. הכתוב מפרש ומהו הפור הוא גורל הפיל הגורל באיזה חדש

פירוש

(ה) וירא המן, עתה שראה המן, ובכל זאת אין מרדכי כרע ומשתחוה לו, בזה ראה והבין כי אין מרדכי כורע ומשתחוה לו מצד עצמו שיש לו שנאה עליו, ואינו נרה בכבודו, כי עתה שהמן רואה אותו לא תוהם ההשתחויה להשר או הכוכב שנופש עליו כמו אם משתחוה אליו בהיותו ברחוק מקום, רק לו בעצמו מצד שהוא שר וגדול, עז"א ומשתחוה לו דוקא, ואז נתמלא המן חמה:

השאלות

ה למה לא חרה אף המן עד שראה בעיניו וכי לא האמין להם:

ו מה חטאו עם מרדכי. האיש אחד יחטא וכל עדתו ישמיד:

ז מלות לפני המן מיותר, וגם מ"ש מיום ליום ומחדש לחדש אין לו באור, גם הלא בדבר כזה ההשגחיי בהכרח ימצא טעם, למה נפל דוקא הגורל על י"ג אדר:

(ו) ויבז, מספר רשעות המן וגאותו, שהגם שעיקר הקצף היה על מרדכי, אחר שנראה בעיניו שלא מצד דתו נמנע להשתחוות לו רק משנאתו אותו, מ"מ אחר שעבדי המלך הגידו לו את עם מרדכי. שהם ספרו שמניעת ההשתחויה הוא כולל את עם מרדכי מצד דתם הישראלית ומצד זה היה לו שנאה על כלל ישראל ודתם, ויבקש להשמיד את כל היהודים מצד שהם עם מרדכי ומתתפשים בדתו, ורצה להכחיד כלל הדת ההיא באבדן השומרים אותו:

(ז) בחדש, הוא הגורל לפני המן. הגורל הזה היה מין ממיני הגורלות שנקרא שמו פור, והגורל הזה היה רגיל לפני המן להגריל בו בכל עת, וע"י הגורל הזה הגריל מיום ליום, הנה הגורל היה בשלשה עשר בניסן (כמ"ש בפסוק י"ב) ובודאי מהשבת המן היה לנקום בעם ה' תיכף והתחיל בגורלו מן ארבעה עשר בניסן שהוא יום המחרת ולא עלה בידו ושוב הגריל על ט"ו ט"ז ניסן תמיד דהוו הגורל עד סוף ימי החדש, וכיון שהגיע להדש הבא התחיל מיום א' של אייר ודהו הגורל מיום ליום עד יום האחרון שהוא י"ג אייר, כי הגורל מוכרח ליפול על יום אחד מימים הנגרלים, והיה בהשגחת ה' שיפול על יום המאוחר, כדי שיכינו ישראל זמן, ואח"כ השב המן בלבו אולי החודש אינו מצליח והתחיל להגריל על החדשים והתחיל מניסן שעומד בו ולא עלה הגורל, וכן דהו הגורל מחדש לחדש עד החדש האחרון שהוא אדר, ושוב לא הגריל על ימי החדש כי כבר בגורל הראשון יצא יום י"ג, וכא גורלו על י"ג אדר, ואם היה מגריל על החדשים תחלה, וממילא היה נופל ג"כ על אדר שהוא חדש המאוחר ואח"כ היה מגריל על הימים היה בא הגורל על יום האחרון של חדש אדר. אבל יען הגריל על הימים תחלה, ולא היה במחשבתו להגריל על החדשים נפל על היום האחרון מיום י"ד שהתחיל בו שהוא יום י"ג הבא. ועז"א מיום ליום ומחדש לחדש. תחלה דהוא הגורל מיום אל יום ואח"כ מחדש אל חדש, עכ"פ מן הגורל הזה כבר היה לו לראות שעלת ה' הופיע בגורל הזה להרויח זמן להשועת ישראל, ועז"א הוא הגורל לפני המן, שהגורל הזה היה מוכן לפני המן לתפלתו:

ויאמר

לחדש שנים־עשר הוא־חדש אדר: ס ח ויאמר המן
למלך אחשורוש ישנו עם־אחד מפזר ומפרד בין
העמים בכל מדינות מלכותך ודתיהם שנות מכל־עם
ואת־דתי המלך אינם עשים ולמלך אין־שוה להניחם:
ט אם־על־המלך טוב יכתב לאבדם ועשרת אלפים
ככר־כסף אשקול על־ידי עשי המלאכה להביא אל־

גנזי

רש"י

חדש יצליח: מיום ליום. באיזה יום בחדש יצליח: (ח) ואת דתי המלך. לתת מס לעבודת המלך: אין שוה. אין חפץ כלומר אין בצע: (ט) יכתב לאבדם. יכתב ספרים לשלוח לשרי המדינות לאבדם:

ויסר

השאלות

ח הלא יפלא איך יסכים מושל עמים להשמיד אומה שלמה על לא חמס בכפם, וביותר יפלא אם באמת ברשעתו הסכים על זאת, איך תמה אח"כ לאמר מי הוא זה אחר אשר מלאו לבו לעשות כן, וכי דבר גדול כזה לא שוה בעיניו אף לזכור את אשר פעל ועשה, וגם אם הרשיע לעשות זאת מדוע שפך חמתו על המן, ומדוע הניחו לכתוב כלל המגלה בימים ההם, שבה נזכר המלך לדראון עולם, גם במלשינות המן לא נזכרו היהודים בשמם רק ישנו עם אחד, ולא נזכר ההשמדה רק לאבדם, ומהו הכפל מפוזר ומפורד, ולמה אמר ודתיהם ל' רבים ומדוע לא אמר שונות מכל דת עם כי הדת ישונה מדת אחר לא מעם אחר:

ט יפלא מאד וכי עושי המלאכה הם הממונים על אוצרות המלך וגנזיו, הלא ליד הסוכנים ראוי שישקלם, גם היתכן שימכר המלך עם ונפשות אישיו במחיר, לא נשמע כזאת בכל דברי הימים הקודמים, ואם נתחייבו להשמידם למה יקח כסף מחירם:

פירוש

(ח) ויאמר המן, המבואר שהמן גנב את לב אחשורוש בשני דברים, אחד שלא הודיע לו מי הוא העם הזה שמלשין עליהם, שאם היה אחשורוש יודע שהם היהודים שהיו מפורסמים לעם חכם ונבון לא היה שומע לעצתו, וכן אף על עם אחר היותר שפל ונבזה אם היה אומר לו שכונתו להשמידם, ג"כ לא היה שומע לו, אבל המן בערמתו אמר ישנו עם אחד, עם בלתי מפורסם, עד שאיני יכול לכנותו בשם, ויען שרצה להלשינם שמזיקים לכלל העמים, אם באמונתם ואם בהנהגה המדינית, וידוע שאם עם לבדד ישכון במדינה מיוחדת אף שיהיו היותר גרועים לא יזיקו לעמים אחרים השוכנים במדינות אחרות, וכן אם אף ישכנו בין עמים אחרים במדינותיהם, אם על"פ בכל מדינה שוכנים בה יש להם ערים נבדלים, ג"כ אין שכונתם מזיק ולא יקפיד המלך לאבדם, ע"כ הקדים שהוא עם מפוזר להוציא שאין להם מדינה מיוחדת, וגם מפורד להוציא שגם במדינות ששוכנים שם לא ישכנו בערים פרטיים רק מפורדים ומעורבים בכל שכונה ושכונה, ולא בקצת מדינות רק בכל העמים אשר בכל מדינות מלכותך ובאופן שהיזק הנמשך מהם כולל כל העמים, ועתה התחיל לספר שני ההיזקות הכלליות הנמשכות מהם: א) באמונות, כי דתיהם שונות מכל עם, וכלל בזה שלשה דברים, א) שנוי הדת הישראלי מיתר הדתות, ב) שהגם שכל דת ודת בהכרח יהיה משונה מדת זולתו, מ"מ לא ישתנה רק בעקריו ושרשיו, אבל בפרטיהם יתחברו וישתתפו, אבל בדת הישראלי נמצאו בו דתות שונות ומצות רבות חלוקות עד שנחשב להרבה דתות וכל הדתות האלה הנבדלות משונות מכל דתי העמים, ולא יתדמו אליהם בשום דבר. ג) שלא לבד שדת הישראלי משונה מדתות העמים, אבל הם משונים גם מכל העמים בעצמם, כי הדת תבדיל אותם מן העמים במאכליהם ומלבושיהם והנהגתם, עד שע"י הדת משונים גם בחיי האנושית מכל עם, ונגד הקבוץ המדיני אומר ואת דתי המלך אינם עושים, שגם בדבר שאינו נגד דתם רק בעניני ממון אינם עושים דת המלך, ומהם לומדים כל העמים למרוד במלך ופקודיו, ואחר שחשב ההפסד הגדול המגיע על ידם, אומר כל תחשוב שיש לך מהם איזו תועלת שבעבורו תניחם, אמר בכלל ולמלך אין שוה להניחם, שאין לך שום תועלת שישוה נגד ההיזק שתמצא בהנהגתם:

(ט) אם, זאת הדבר השני שגנב לבו שלא אמר לו שרוצה להשמידם רק לאבדם, שפשוט באמרו הוא לאבד צורת האומה שהיא דתם לבטל דתם ולהכריחם לשמור דתות של יתר העמים, או יותר עניים כלה שיעשו שהטלות שיבטל ענין כשם הוא וחוקיהם ונמוסיהם, ולא כוון אחשורוש כלל אל הריגה

ואבוד

גִּנְזֵ֥י הַמֶּֽלֶךְ׃ י וַיָּ֧סַר הַמֶּ֛לֶךְ אֶת־טַבַּעְתּ֖וֹ מֵעַ֣ל יָד֑וֹ וַֽיִּתְּנָ֗הּ
לְהָמָ֧ן בֶּֽן־הַמְּדָ֛תָא הָאֲגָגִ֖י צֹרֵ֥ר הַיְּהוּדִֽים׃ יא וַיֹּ֤אמֶר הַמֶּ֙לֶךְ֙
לְהָמָ֔ן הַכֶּ֖סֶף נָת֣וּן לָ֑ךְ וְהָעָ֕ם לַעֲשׂ֥וֹת בּ֖וֹ כַּטּ֥וֹב בְּעֵינֶֽיךָ׃
יב וַיִּקָּרְאוּ֩ סֹפְרֵ֨י הַמֶּ֜לֶךְ בַּחֹ֣דֶשׁ הָרִאשׁ֗וֹן בִּשְׁלוֹשָׁ֨ה עָשָׂ֥ר
יוֹם֮ בּוֹ֒ וַיִּכָּתֵ֣ב כְּֽכָל־אֲשֶׁר־צִוָּ֣ה הָ֠מָן אֶ֣ל אֲחַשְׁדַּרְפְּנֵֽי־
הַמֶּ֨לֶךְ וְאֶל־הַפַּח֜וֹת אֲשֶׁ֣ר ׀ עַל־מְדִינָ֣ה וּמְדִינָ֗ה וְאֶל־שָׂרֵי֙
עַ֣ם וָעָ֔ם מְדִינָ֤ה וּמְדִינָה֙ כִּכְתָבָ֔הּ וְעַ֥ם וָעָ֖ם כִּלְשׁוֹנ֑וֹ בְּשֵׁ֨ם
הַמֶּ֤לֶךְ אֲחַשְׁוֵרֹשׁ֙ נִכְתָּ֔ב וְנֶחְתָּ֖ם בְּטַבַּ֥עַת הַמֶּֽלֶךְ׃
יג וְנִשְׁל֨וֹחַ סְפָרִ֜ים בְּיַ֣ד הָרָצִים֮ אֶל־כָּל־מְדִינ֣וֹת הַמֶּלֶךְ֒
לְהַשְׁמִ֡יד

רש"י

(י) ויסר המלך את טבעתו. הוא מתן כל ד דבר גדול שישאלו מאת המלך להיות מי שהטבעת בידו שליט בכל דבר המלך: (יג) ונשלוח ספרים. ויהיו נשלחים

שפתי חכמים

הואיל וכ"פ אחר שנכרזת רשאה כו׳: ד דק"ל הוא בקש לאבד את היהודים והמלך נתן לו הטבעת מה שלא שאל ולא בקש

השאלות

י למה מספר שנתן הטבעת ביד המן, ולמה קורא פה ביחוד בשם יחוסו ובכנוי צורר היהודים:

יא מ"ש הכסף נתון לך הל"ל יהיה לך כי לא נתן לו רק מחל לו:

יב אחר שהעת לקיים דבר הדת להרוג היהודים היה בי"ג אדר הבא, מדוע זה מהר לקרא תיכף לסופרי המלך בו ביום, והלא עוד חזון למועד:

פירוש

ולאבד נפשות, ועשרת אלפים אמר בל תחשוב כי אתכוון להוציא ע"ז הוצאה רבה ולהחזיק פקידים הממונים על כך, ונכוני לב אשר יהרגו במלאכה הזאת להעבירם מדתם, כי עושי המלאכה הזאת שהם המדינות אותם יעשוהו כ"כ בשמחה עד שהם עוד ישקלו כסף עבור זה שעבר בהכות על ידי עושי המלאכה הזאת. (אהיה אנכי ביכולת) לשקול עשרת אלפים ככר כסף אל גנזי המלך, כי הם ישקלו כסף כדי שיעשו מלאכה זאת, שיחשב בעיניהם לשכר ואוצר, ובזה רמה את המלך שכל העמים ישמחו בזה להשיב תועים אל דרך:

(י) ויסר, עתה מספר כי המלך לא חשב בדבר זה מאומה, כי אחר שגנב לבו ולא הגיד לו מי העם, ולא שדעתו להשמידם, אם היה המלך עצמו חותם האגרות היה רואה כי מרמה בדבר ולא היה מסכים עמו, אבל המלך מבטיחו בו מסר הטבעת לידו לחתום בשמו, והוא שנה וכתב להרג ולאבד, וע"כ אמר שלא המלך היה החייב בדבר רק שהמן היה הצורר היהודים, והוא כתב הכל מדעתו, ע"פ משטמת אבותיו השמורה אתו עד עלה יען שהוא אגגי:

(יא) ויאמר, מגלה שגם תימת המלך בל יחשוב אדם שעשה זה בעבור הכסף, כי אדרבה לפי מחשבתו ברוצה ליפר העם ולאבד רוע דתם ומדותיהם אמר לו שהוא יתן לו הכסף הצריך להוצאה על זו פלוגרותיו, ויתן בידו הכסף עם העם לעשות בו הטוב בעיניו כפי שימצא דרך שישר להסיר המכשלה היוצאה מרוע דתם והנהגתם לכוב להם:

(יב) ויקראו, עתה מספר ערמת המן, איך חשב תחבולות להוציא דבשו אל הפועל. שאחר ברמה את המלך והשיג הטבעת, ירא פן אחר ימים יודע למלך מי הם העם, ומה הוא רוצה לעשות בהם ויפר עצתו, ע"כ מהר לכתוב הספרים בו ביום, ומספר כי סופרי המלך כתבו בכל אשר צוה המן לא כאשר צוה המלך, כי המלך לא ידע מזאת כלל. והנה בכל מדינה נמצאו כמה עמים, ולכן כתב לכל מדינה שתי אגרות, א) לאחשדרפן, ב) להפחה, ולכל עם אשר במדינה כתב לשר אשר הוא גדול אל העם, ומן הרגיל שכל מדינה יש לה כתב מיוחד ולכל עם ועם יש להם לשון מיוחד, אבל לרוב כל בני המדינה מהיהודים בכתבם, לכן אמר שכתב לכל מדינה ככתבה ולכל עם כלשונו:

(יג) ונשלוח, זאת שנית שלח הספרים תיכף ביום ההוא ביד הרצים, כדי שלא ירגיש המלך לחזור בדבר

זה

לְהַשְׁמִיד לַהֲרֹג וּלְאַבֵּד אֶת־כָּל־הַיְּהוּדִים מִנַּעַר וְעַד־זָקֵן
טַף וְנָשִׁים בְּיוֹם אֶחָד בִּשְׁלוֹשָׁה עָשָׂר לְחֹדֶשׁ שְׁנֵים־
עָשָׂר הוּא־חֹדֶשׁ אֲדָר וּשְׁלָלָם לָבוֹז׃ יד פַּתְשֶׁגֶן הַכְּתָב
לְהִנָּתֵן דָּת בְּכָל־מְדִינָה וּמְדִינָה גָּלוּי לְכָל־הָעַמִּים לִהְיוֹת
עֲתִדִים לַיּוֹם הַזֶּה׃ טו הָרָצִים יָצְאוּ דְחוּפִים בִּדְבַר הַמֶּלֶךְ
וְהַדָּת נִתְּנָה בְּשׁוּשַׁן הַבִּירָה וְהַמֶּלֶךְ וְהָמָן יָשְׁבוּ לִשְׁתּוֹת
וְהָעִיר שׁוּשַׁן נָבוֹכָה׃ ס

ומרדכי

רש"י

ונשלוח ה ספרים איפטר"א פרמי"ש בלעז והוא מגזרת (שופטים יא כה) אם נלחום נלחם (שמואל א ב טו) הנגלה נגליתי (הושע י כז) נדמה נדמיתי: בשלשה עשר לחדש שנים עשר. ביום י"ג לאותו חדש שהוא י"ב לחדשי השנה: (יד) פתשגן. לשון ארמי ספור הכתב דריטמאנ"ט בלעז: להנתן דת. טופס הכתב שהיה אומר להנתן חוק גזרת המלך: גלוי לכל העמים. דבר זה: (טו) והדת נתנה בשושן. מקום שהיה המלך שם ניתן ו החוק בו ביום להיות עתידים ליום י"ג לחדש אדר לכך: והעיר שושן נבוכה

שפתי חכמים

בקש ממנו. לכ"פ הוא מתן כו': ה לאפוקי שאינו ט"ז האיתן ומביא ראיה מגזרת אם נלחום כו': ו דק"ל הרי בכל מדינה ניתן הדת ולמה אמר בשושן לכ"פ מקום שהמלך כו': דק"ל

השאלות

יד מה היה הפתשגן הכתב, וכי הכתב הראשון לא נודע באורו רק ע"י השני, והלא הפתשגן היה פתוח וממ"ש גלוי לכל העמים משמע שהראשון היה חתום וסתום ומדוע היה זה, ומה היה הכונה שיהיו עתידים, ולא אמר למה ועל מה:

טו למה לא נתנה הדת בשושן עד שיצאו הרצים והלא שושן קודם לכ"מ, איך ישב המלך לשתות אחר שמכר עם גדול להשמיד ולאבד, אין זה כי אם לב אכזר, ומה זה מ"ש והעיר שושן נבוכה שלא נודע באורו:

פירוש

לא יוכל להשיב את הספרים כי כתב אשר נכתב בשם המלך אין להשיב, וגם בחר שהשמד הכללי יהיה בכל המדינות ביום אחד כדי שלא יהיה להם פליט ופלטה, וגם לא באר בכתבו שהגזרה כוללת כל המדינות, כמו שבאר מרדכי בכתביו, כדי שכל שר ופחה יחשוב שרק במדינתו נגזר זאת, ויירא יותר לשנות דבר [ועיין לקמן ח' בארתי יתר השנוים שבין מכתבי המן למכתבי מרדכי]:

(יד) פתשגן, לדעתי עשה בזה ערמה כפולה, כי הספרים שלח לשרי המדינות היו חתומים בחותם המלך, וכתוב עליהם מלמעלה שלא יפתחו רק עד שיבא יום י"ג אדר, כמו שהמנהג עוד היום אצל המלכיות, ועז"א ונחתום בטבעת המלך שהיו החתומים למעלה באופן שלא ידע איש מה היה כתוב בהם, רק עם הספרים האלה החתומים שלח עוד אגרות פתוחות פתשגן הכתבים החתומים, וזה היה בגלוי לכל העמים, שיהיו עתידים ליום י"ג אדר למלחמה, שבאותו יום יפתחו האגרות החתומות וידעו על מי זמי ילחמו, ובזה השכל עצה עמוקה, א) כי רצה שעד אותו זמן לא תודע הגזרה הזאת לשום אדם כי האגרות יהיו חתומים, ועי"כ לא יוכלו היהודים לבקש עזר והצלה, ולא להעמיד מליצים בבית המלך, וגם המלך לא ידע הדבר עד אחר מעשה, ב) שע"י עצה זו היה בטוח שלא יברחו היהודים למדינות אחרות ולא יסתירו את עצמם כי אחר שלא יודע עד אותו זמן למה יהיו עתידים, ממילא גם היהודים יהיו עתידים ליום ההוא בכל עיר ועיר עם יתר העמים, ובפתוח האגרת ויודע כי עליהם נגזר השמד יקומו עליהם ויהרגום:

(טו) הרצים, גם הטריח למהר על הרצים שילכו תיכף כדי שלא יוכל המלך לחזור, ולא עוד אלא הדת לא נתנה בשושן עד צאת הרצים כדי שלא יודע להמלך תחלה, כי חשש פן ישלח המלך אחר כתב הדת ורצה להחזירו, וספר עוד נראיה, שהמלך לא ידע מכל זאת מאומה כי ישב עם המן לשתות, ואם היה זה בידיעתו ליתן דת לאבד אומה שלמה ואיך ישב אז לשתות הלא גם בין הדמים דיני נפשות הנמוס שלא לשתות יין ביום שגזרו על איש עונש מיתה אף כי בעת נמכרה אומה שלמה להשמיד, וספר שהעיר שושן היו נבוכים בדבר כי לא ידע שום איש מה נכתב בהספרים החתומים, והפתשגן אין מבואר על מה יהיו

עתידים

ד א וּמָרְדֳּכַי יָדַע אֶת־כָּל־אֲשֶׁר נַעֲשָׂה וַיִּקְרַע מָרְדֳּכַי
אֶת־בְּגָדָיו וַיִּלְבַּשׁ שַׂק וָאֵפֶר וַיֵּצֵא בְּתוֹךְ
הָעִיר וַיִּזְעַק זְעָקָה גְדוֹלָה וּמָרָה׃ ב וַיָּבוֹא עַד לִפְנֵי
שַֽׁעַר־הַמֶּלֶךְ כִּי אֵין לָבוֹא אֶל־שַׁעַר הַמֶּלֶךְ בִּלְבוּשׁ שָׂק׃
ג וּבְכָל־מְדִינָה וּמְדִינָה מְקוֹם אֲשֶׁר דְּבַר־הַמֶּלֶךְ וְדָתוֹ
מַגִּיעַ אֵבֶל גָּדוֹל לַיְּהוּדִים וְצוֹם וּבְכִי וּמִסְפֵּד שַׂק וָאֵפֶר
יֻצַּע לָרַבִּים׃ ד וַתָּבוֹאינָה נַעֲרוֹת אֶסְתֵּר וְסָרִיסֶיהָ וַיַּגִּידוּ
לָהּ וַתִּתְחַלְחַל הַמַּלְכָּה מְאֹד וַתִּשְׁלַח בְּגָדִים לְהַלְבִּישׁ

°יתיר יו״ד

את

שפתי חכמים

ז דק״ל סיאך העיר שהיא עליס ואכניס נבוכה. לכ״פ היהודים שבה: ח אע״ג דתרי דעות ניינהו בס״ק דמגילה ובמדרש ילקוט. כתב רש״י שניהם יחד דס״ל דהא והא גרס כי אלת מצא הצלס לא נגזרה עליהם כליה כ״כ ווולת מצא בסעודה היה עדיין הש״י מאריך אפו ובזה נחתם גזר דינם נמלא אופן הגזרה היה בעבור הצלם וחתימת הגז״ד היה בעבור הסעודה וכן הוכיח מהר״ר שלמה אלקבץ בהקדמת

סברו

רש״י

נבוכה. ז היהודים שבה: (א) ומרדכי ידע. בעל החלום אמר לו שהסכימו העליונים לכך לפי שהשתחוו ללצם בימי נבוכדנצר ושנהנו ח מסעודת אחשורוש: (ב) כי אין לבוא. אין דרך ארץ לבוא אל שער המלך בלבוש שק: (ג) דבר המלך ודתו. כשהשלוחים נושאי הספרים עוברים שם נתנה הדת בעיר:

פרשת

פירוש

מתידים, באופן שעלתה עלתו, אם במה שנעלם דבר מן המלך, אם במה שנאמר דבר סתר בכל עיר, רק ה׳ הפיר עלתו ע״י מרדכי כמו שיבואר:

ד (א) ומרדכי, יושב בשמים ישחק, ועם כל המחשבות מחשב שיסאר הדבר בסוד, נודע הדבר למרדכי ע״י השגחת ה׳ וידע כל הדברים שעברו בינו ובין המלך, וכן איך רמה את המלך וכל עלילותיו ותחבולותיו, ובזה הכין א״ע לשני דברים, א) שקרע את בגדיו וילבש שק ואפר לתשובה ותפלה, להפיק רצון מאשר בידו לב מלכים, ואח״כ לאמצעיים טבעיים, והיתה עלתו הראשונה שלא יהיה הדבר בסוד, רק שיודע בין לגויי הארצות ובין להמלך, כי עי״כ יעמדו מליצים להשבית הדבר ולכן יצא ברחובות קריה חעק לאסוף אליו המונים שיתפרסם הדבר:

(ב) ויבא, אח״כ בא לפני שער המלך כדי שיודע הדבר בחצר המלך אם לאסתר אם לסמלך עצמו, כי אין לבא, יש בזה ב׳ כוונות, א) שמלד זה לא נכנס פנימה, ב) שמלד זה היה דבר מתודש במה שעמד בשק לפני השער שאין רגילים ללכת בשק גם באותו המקום ויתפרסם בחצר המלך:

(ג) ובכל, הנה קודם שפרסם מרדכי הדבר לא ידע מזה איש, אבל אחר שהרעיש מרדכי עיר ומלואה, נתפשט הדבר איש מפי איש למקומות פנימיים בכל מדינה, כי לא נודע הדבר לשום אדם זולת ע״י צעקת מרדכי (כי האגרות הנשלחים היו חתומים) ועז״א דבר המלך ודתו מגיע, ר״ל במקום אשר נודע גם הדת שהוא מה שהיה כתוב באגרות החתומים. וע״כ לא נאמר פה בכל עיר ועיר כי לא הגיע הדבר לכל המקומות רק לעיר אחת במדינה אבל גדול ליהודים תשובה ותפלה ואבלות:

(ד) ותבואנה, ע״י שבא מרדכי בשער המלך, ותשלח רצתה לשמוע הדבר מפי מרדכי מה זאת ושלחה בגדים שילבש על השק באופן שיסיר שקו מעליו שלא יהיה על בגדיו רק תחת בגדיו ויוכל לבוא בשער המלך, ולא קבל כי לא רצה להפסיק רגע מתחנונים, שזה כעוזב בטחונו מה׳ ובוטח על עזרת בשר

ושקרא

השאלות

א מהו הרבותא שמרדכי ידע, הלא היה הדת גלוי לכל העמים, ואם שידע מן פרשת הכסף זה אין נ״מ לגוף הענין אחר שראה שנחרצה הגזרה. למה יצא לצעוק ברחובות קריה, וזה מדרך הסכלים הלא היה לו לבקש עצות בחכמה, לא להרעיש עיר ומלואה:

ב למה בא עד שער המלך:

ג פסוק זה הלא מקומו למעלה אחר הרצים יצאו דחופים, כי ע״י הרצים נודע לכל, למה לא אמר פה ובכל עיר ועיר כמ״ש להלן (ח׳ י״ז) ולמה כפל דבר המלך ודתו:

ד אחר ששלחה שילבש בגדים פשיטא שיסיר שקו:

אֶת־מָרְדֳּכַי וּלְהָסִיר שַׂקּוֹ מֵעָלָיו וְלֹא קִבֵּל׃ ה וַתִּקְרָא
אֶסְתֵּר לַהֲתָךְ מִסָּרִיסֵי הַמֶּלֶךְ אֲשֶׁר הֶעֱמִיד לְפָנֶיהָ
וַתְּצַוֵּהוּ עַל־מָרְדֳּכָי לָדַעַת מַה־זֶּה וְעַל־מַה־זֶּה׃ ו וַיֵּצֵא
הֲתָךְ אֶל־מָרְדֳּכָי אֶל־רְחוֹב הָעִיר אֲשֶׁר לִפְנֵי שַׁעַר־
הַמֶּלֶךְ׃ ז וַיַּגֶּד־לוֹ מָרְדֳּכַי אֵת כָּל־אֲשֶׁר קָרָהוּ וְאֵת ׀
פָּרָשַׁת הַכֶּסֶף אֲשֶׁר אָמַר הָמָן לִשְׁקוֹל עַל־גִּנְזֵי הַמֶּלֶךְ
בַּיְּהוּדִיִּים° לְאַבְּדָם׃ ח וְאֶת־פַּתְשֶׁגֶן כְּתָב־הַדָּת אֲשֶׁר־
נִתַּן בְּשׁוּשָׁן לְהַשְׁמִידָם נָתַן לוֹ לְהַרְאוֹת אֶת־אֶסְתֵּר
וּלְהַגִּיד לָהּ וּלְצַוּוֹת עָלֶיהָ לָבוֹא אֶל־הַמֶּלֶךְ לְהִתְחַנֶּן־לוֹ
וּלְבַקֵּשׁ מִלְּפָנָיו עַל־עַמָּהּ׃ ט וַיָּבוֹא הֲתָךְ וַיַּגֵּד לְאֶסְתֵּר
אֵת דִּבְרֵי מָרְדֳּכָי׃ י וַתֹּאמֶר אֶסְתֵּר לַהֲתָךְ וַתְּצַוֵּהוּ אֶל־

°יתיר י׳ד

מרדכי

רש"י

(ז) פרשת הכסף. פרוש הכסף:

אל

השאלות

ה למה בחרה בהתך ואשר העמיד לפניה מיותר לשון ותצוהו על מרדכי אינו מדוקדק, כי צווי נקשר עם על מורה שאיש אחד ישגיח או יהיה ממונה על דבר אחר והיל"ל ותשלחהו אל מרדכי, ומהו הכפל מה זה ועל מה זה:

ז מהו את כל אשר קרהו, הלא הוא מקרה הכלל כולו ומה ענין פרשת הכסף היל"ל הכסף:

ח אם היה זה פתשגן הכתב שהיה גלוי לכל העמים, הלא שם לא נזכר להשמידם, ואם היה מן הספרים שהגיעו ליד שרי המדינות איך הגיע כתב זה למרדכי. אחר שאומר להראות את אסתר למה אומר להגיד הלא אחר שתראה אין צריך להגיד עוד:

י ותאמר ותצוהו, כפל ללא צורך:

פירוש

(ה) ותקרא, אחר שהבינה שיש בזה סוד כמוס, שלחה להתך שהיה אצלה נאמן רוח מכסה דבר, כי הוא מסריסי המלך אשר העמיד לפניה ביחוד והיא סודה, ויען שלא ידעה אם יאמין לו מרדכי לחשוף מסתוריו לפניו, לכן ותצוהו על מרדכי, היינו שיחקור מן הלך סבת הדבר, ונוסף ג"כ שיחקור מה זה ועל מה זה, כדרך הרופא האומן הבא לרפאות החולי שחוקר מהות החולי, וגם הסבה שבעבורה בא החולי, ר"ל הרעה בעצמה וגם סבתה, כי א"א להסיר המסובב אם לא בהסתלק הסבה תחלה. וכ"פ מהר"א אשכנזי:

(ו) רחוב העיר, לחקור הדבר:

(ז) את כל אשר קרהו, תחלה הגיד גם הסבה, שהוא היה המסבב לזה ע"י שלא השתחוה להמן, וגם הגיד פרשת הכסף, ר"ל שבהכסף הזה שאמר לשקול, היו בו שני פרופים, כי לפני אחשורוש אמר שעושי המלאכה יתנו העשרת אלפים ככר כסף, והיה אחשורוש מדמה שהוא בעבור השמחה שיהיה להם בדבר הזה יתנדבו רכוש לאוצר המלך. והמן כוון באמת שמן השלל והמלקוח שמגיע ממנו מכס למלך, יהיה עשרת אלפים סך המכס, באופן שרמה את אחשורוש:

(ח) ואת פתשגן, הדת היא הספרים החתומים שבם היה כתוב להשמידם, וספרי הדת האלה לא היו ביד מרדכי כי היו מונחים חתומים תחת יד פחת שושן, רק הפתשגן היה בידו שניתן בגלוי להיות עתידים, ומלת להשמידם מוסב אל הדת, ר"ל מן הדת אשר נתן בשושן להשמידם, שהוא הספרים החתומים, נתן לו פתשגן הכתב להראות את אסתר שכבר נעשה בהכרח הזה דבר אחר שכתוב בפתשגן שיהיו עתידים למלחמה ליום נכון, ולהגיד לה ר"ל ע"פ הסימן הזה יוכל להגיד לה בעל פה, כי כוונת הפתשגן הוא שיהיו עתידים להשמיד את היהודים, וע"כ לצוות עליה לבא אל המלך להציל שארית ישראל:

(י) ותאמר, אסתר יראה לשלוח התך שנית אל מרדכי פן יכירו גם אנשי המן שהולך ושב בשליחות מן

מרדכי

מָרְדֳּכָי׃ יא כָּל־עַבְדֵי הַמֶּלֶךְ וְעַם מְדִינוֹת הַמֶּלֶךְ יֹדְעִים
אֲשֶׁר כָּל־אִישׁ וְאִשָּׁה אֲשֶׁר־יָבוֹא אֶל־הַמֶּלֶךְ אֶל־הֶחָצֵר
הַפְּנִימִית אֲשֶׁר לֹא־יִקָּרֵא אַחַת דָּתוֹ לְהָמִית לְבַד
מֵאֲשֶׁר יוֹשִׁיט־לוֹ הַמֶּלֶךְ אֶת־שַׁרְבִיט הַזָּהָב וְחָיָה וַאֲנִי
לֹא נִקְרֵאתִי לָבוֹא אֶל־הַמֶּלֶךְ זֶה שְׁלוֹשִׁים יוֹם׃ יב וַיַּגִּידוּ
לְמָרְדֳּכָי אֵת דִּבְרֵי אֶסְתֵּר׃ יג וַיֹּאמֶר מָרְדֳּכַי לְהָשִׁיב אֶל־
אֶסְתֵּר אַל־תְּדַמִּי בְנַפְשֵׁךְ לְהִמָּלֵט בֵּית־הַמֶּלֶךְ מִכָּל־

היהודים

רש"י

(יג) אל תדמי בנפשך. אל תחשבי כמו (במדבר לג כו) יהיה כאשר דמיתי. אל תדמי בנפשך אל תהי סבורה להמלט ביום ההרגה בבית המלך שאין את רוצה לסכן עצמך עכשיו על הספק לבא אל המלך שלא ברשות ׃

ומי

פירוש

מרדכי לאסתר, וע"כ אמרה להתך ותצוהו שילך להגיע הדברים אל מרדכי ע"י שליח אחר ׃

(יא) כל עבדי, השיבה לו שתי טענות, טענה האחת כי אם תכנס עתה תהיה בספק סכנה, וגם לא תגיע למחוז חפצה לבקש בעד עמה, א) כי כל עבדי המלך יודעים, ולא יהיה תירוץ שלא ידעה דת המלך שהנכנס שלא ברשות חייב מיתה, ב) כי כל עם מדינות המלך יודעים, ובזה אף שירצה למחול על חטאה לא יוכל, אחר שהוא הבא פרהסיא כמו שהיה בושתי, ולא תאמר שהגזרה אינה כוללת את כל הנכנסים לז"א אשר כל איש ואשה מבלי הבדל יהיה מה שיהיה, וכן בל תאמר שהגזרה אינה רק על הנכנס שלא לצורך, אבל הנכנס לצורך דבר גדול כדבר הזה להציל עם לקוחים למות, לא יומת: לז"א אשר יבא אל המלך אשר רק לא יקרא כל שלא יקרא אין הבדל בדינו, רק אחת דתו להמית, ר"ל בין שיהיה הנכנס ראוי לנשיאת פניו או לא, ובין שיהיה עסקו נחוץ או לא, אין הבדל בדתם וכולם חייבים מיתה, ממילא הנכנס שלא ברשות הנהו בן מות חיכף, לבד מאשר יושיט לו המלך את שרביט הזהב מכפר שוא והיה, ובכל זאת הלא כבר נתחייב מיתה רק המלך עשה עמו חסד, ומעתה אם אכנס שלא ברשות אף שימחול לי המלך, די שאציל את נפשי ולא אוכל לבקש עוד בעד אחרים, זאת הטענה האחת. טענה הב', כי להציל לקוחים למות צריך לנסות כל האמצעים אף היותר רחוקים אולי ישלח ה' ע"י עזרו מקדש, אבל כל זה אם אין דרך היותר קרוב להצלה, אבל כשיש דרך היותר בטוח שלא צריך לאחוז הדרך היותר נכון, ועז"א אמר שאני לא נקראתי לבא אל המלך זה שלשים יום, הלא זדאי בימים אחדים יקרא אותי, ואז יהיה יותר בקל לבקש בעד העם, וטוב יותר להמתין עד שאקרא:

(יב) ויגידו, השלוחים שלא התך :

(יג) אל תדמי, הודיע לה בשליחות הזה כמה פנות יקרות: א) כל שאנו רואים דבר היוצא מן הרגילות והטבעי צריכים אנו לשית על לב כי ה' עשהו להיות זה אמצעי הצלה לאיזה תכלית השגחיי, וסבה לאיזה מסובב, ועפ"ז אמר שהצלחת אסתר שהעלה מבפל מצבה אל בית המלכות הוא רחוק מן הענין הרגיל, בהכרח היה בדבר ה' לאיזו תכלית, והאר שראינו שאז קרה לישראל הצרה הכוללת, מבואר כי הזמינה ה' לרפאות על ידה שבר עמו, ב) לכל צרה הבאה על ישראל יש עת מוגבל וזמן ויום הכסה מוכן לתשועה ע"י ההכנות והסבות שהכין ליפועה, ואם לא יושעו ע"י סבה אחת בהכרח יעמיד להם ה' סבה אחרת להצלתם כי לא יטוש ה' את עמו, ג) כל דבר שאין מציאותו בעבור עצמו רק בעבור דבר אחר, מציאותו וקיומו תלוי בדבר ההוא אשר בעבורו הוא נמצא, כמשל הבונה גנת החורף לגדל נטעים ולמחים שיתנו פרים בחורף בבקין, הנה לא יהיה מציאת הבנין שהוא רק בעבור הגידול של החורף, ואם יספיס בדעתו שיניח לגדל צמחים ההלם נקין, אז ממילא יהרוס את הבנין, כי בקין יש סבות אחרות המועילות אל הגידול ע"י תום

השאלות

יא למה פרטה ביחוד עבדי המלך ועם המלך מהו אחת דתו, היל"ל יומת, השאלה היותר נפלאה איך לא חרפה נפשה למות בשמעה אבד כלל ישראל, מ"ש ואני לא נקראתי הוא תפל מבלי מלח ודברי מותר :

יב ויגידו מי הם המגידים ודברי חז"ל ידועים :

יג בנפשך מיותר :

השמש

הַיְּהוּדִֽים׃ יד כִּ֣י אִם־הַחֲרֵ֣שׁ תַּחֲרִ֘ישִׁי֮ בָּעֵ֣ת הַזֹּאת֒ רֶ֣וַח
וְהַצָּלָ֞ה יַעֲמ֤וֹד לַיְּהוּדִים֙ מִמָּק֣וֹם אַחֵ֔ר וְאַ֥תְּ וּבֵית־אָבִ֖יךְ
תֹּאבֵ֑דוּ וּמִ֣י יוֹדֵ֔עַ אִם־לְעֵ֣ת כָּזֹ֔את הִגַּ֖עַתְּ לַמַּלְכֽוּת׃
טו וַתֹּ֥אמֶר אֶסְתֵּ֖ר לְהָשִׁ֥יב אֶֽל־מָרְדֳּכָֽי׃ טז לֵךְ֩ כְּנ֨וֹס אֶת־
כָּל־הַיְּהוּדִ֜ים הַנִּמְצְאִ֣ים בְּשׁוּשָׁ֗ן וְצ֣וּמוּ עָ֠לַי וְאַל־תֹּאכְל֨וּ
וְאַל־תִּשְׁתּ֜וּ שְׁלֹ֤שֶׁת יָמִים֙ לַ֣יְלָה וָי֔וֹם גַּם־אֲנִ֥י וְנַעֲרֹתַ֖י
אָצ֣וּם כֵּ֑ן וּבְכֵ֞ן אָב֤וֹא אֶל־הַמֶּ֙לֶךְ֙ אֲשֶׁ֣ר לֹֽא־כַדָּ֔ת וְכַאֲשֶׁ֥ר

אבדתי

רש"י

(יד) ומי יודע אם לעת כזאת הגעת. ומי יודע אם יחפוץ בך המלך לשנה הבאה שהוא זמן ההריגה: לעת כזאת. שהוא היה עומד בניסן וזמן ההריגה באדר לשנה הבאה: הגעת למלכות. אם הגיעי לגדולה שאת בה עכשיו: (טז) אשר לא כדת. שאין דת ליכנס אשר לא יקרא. ומדרש אגדה אשר לא כדת שעד עתה באונס ועכשיו ברצון: וכאשר אבדתי אבדתי. וכאשר התחלתי לילך, לאבוד אלך ואמות. ומ"א כאשר אבדתי מבית אבא אובד ממך שמעכשיו שאני ברצון נבעלת אני אסורה לך:

שפתי חכמים

ספרו מעט סלוי שכן דעת רש"י בפ"ק דמגילה: ט פי'

עד

ויעבר

השאלות

יד מהו בעת הזאת וביחוד מה מהר עליה הלא עוד חזון למועד ובתוך כך תקרא אל המלך, ומ"ש אם לעת כזאת אין לו באור:

טז מהו וצומו עלי וכי עליה יצומו, ומה זה כאשר אבדתי אבדתי, איך נאבדה עד הנה:

פירוש

השמש והאויר וא"ל לתגור וחמוס השיי, ע"ש זאת הוה להסתר דעת, כי אחר שכל מציאותה במעלה הזו להיות בבית מלכות, אינה בעבור עצמה רק בעבור הצלת היהודים, ובע"כ הזמין ה' גם סבות אחרות להוקות שבאם תפשע אסתר ותחשוך מלהציל עם ה' יצילם ע"י הסבות האחרות, ממילא צריך לה לחשוב כי מציאותה בגדולה וכבוד הוא רק בעבור שיהיה על ידה ההצלה בעת ההיא המוגבל שהיא עתה, ואם תעבור העת ההיא ולא תתאזר חיל להציל בין כך יגיעו הסבות האחרות, כי לא יעזוב ה' נחלתו ביד אשה אחת שי"ל בחירה לטוב ורע, ובהכרח יש עוד סבות ואז לא יתמך לך אחר שכבר הגיעה הישועה ממקום אחר, וז"ש אל תדמי בנפשך להמלט בית המלך, ור"ל אל תחשבי כי מה שאת בית המלך הוא דבר תלוי בנפשך ושמציאות גדולתך היא בשביל עצמך, לא בשביל היהודים והצלתם, עד שתחשבי שאת היא עקר והצלת היהודים ימשך ממך במקרה, כי נהפך הוא, שעיקר היא הצלת היהודים ומן הצלתם נמשך גדולתך כמ"ש בהקדמה ה', ועז"א בנפשך:

(יד) כי אם, ומזה המשיך אחר שמציאותה בבית המלך הוא רק שתהיה סבה לתשועת ישראל, ובהכרח לא עליה לבד תמך כל הצלתם, רק אם תתרשל בהכרח יקומו ויגיעו הסבות האחרות להשועה, ועז"א כי אם החרש התרישי בעת הזאת רוח והצלה יעמוד ליהודים ממקום אחר, כמ"ש בהקדמה ב', וממילא את ובית אביך תאבדו, אחר שמציאותך במעלה הזאת יהיה אז לבטלה כמ"ש בהקדמה ג', ובאר הדבר ומי יודע אם לעת כזאת הגעת למלכות, ר"ל בל תחשבי כי תהיי להם עזר לתשועתם אחר ימים אחדים, שתהיי קרובה מן המלך, כי יוכל להיות שאותך לא הזמין ה' רק לעת הזאת שעל ידך תהיה תשועתם היום, ואם תמתיני עד למחר עבר זמנך, כי על מחר הזמין ה' סבות אחרות, כמשל בית החורף שאינו צריך בזמן הקיץ, שכבר הוכנו סבות אחרות לגידול הצמחים, ותאבדי אחר שפסים מציאותך בגדולה לבטלה:

(טז) לך כנוס, אחר שהבטיחה מרדכי שבין כך יבך ישראל יושע בה', ולא ירויתו מתנה רק שעל ידה תוקדם התשועה, נתרצית ללכת אחר שבטה לבה שגם. אם תהרג לא תאבד תקוה ויושעו ע"י סבות אחרות, ע"ז בקשה שעכ"פ יצומו עליה ויבקשו עליה רחמים, ובזה תבא אל המלך גם נגד דת המלך, וכאשר אבדתי ויהרגני המלך ע"י שאעבור מצותו, הלא לא יהיה חק כולל רק אבדתי אני לבדי ורוח והצלה יעמוד ליהודים ממקום אחר:

ויעבר

אָבַדְתִּי אָבָדְתִּי: יז וַיַּעֲבֹר מָרְדֳּכָי וַיַּעַשׂ כְּכֹל אֲשֶׁר־
צִוְּתָה עָלָיו אֶסְתֵּר:
ה א וַיְהִי ׀ בַּיּוֹם הַשְּׁלִישִׁי וַתִּלְבַּשׁ אֶסְתֵּר מַלְכוּת
וַתַּעֲמֹד בַּחֲצַר בֵּית־הַמֶּלֶךְ הַפְּנִימִית נֹכַח
בֵּית הַמֶּלֶךְ וְהַמֶּלֶךְ יוֹשֵׁב עַל־כִּסֵּא מַלְכוּתוֹ בְּבֵית
הַמַּלְכוּת נֹכַח פֶּתַח הַבָּיִת: ב וַיְהִי כִרְאוֹת הַמֶּלֶךְ אֶת־
אֶסְתֵּר הַמַּלְכָּה עֹמֶדֶת בֶּחָצֵר נָשְׂאָה חֵן בְּעֵינָיו וַיּוֹשֶׁט
הַמֶּלֶךְ לְאֶסְתֵּר אֶת־שַׁרְבִיט הַזָּהָב אֲשֶׁר בְּיָדוֹ וַתִּקְרַב
אֶסְתֵּר וַתִּגַּע בְּרֹאשׁ הַשַּׁרְבִיט: ג וַיֹּאמֶר לָהּ הַמֶּלֶךְ מַה־
לָּךְ אֶסְתֵּר הַמַּלְכָּה וּמַה־בַּקָּשָׁתֵךְ עַד־חֲצִי הַמַּלְכוּת

וינתן

שפתי חכמים

עד עכשיו נבעלתי באונס ועכשיו אלך מדעתי: י דק"ל ויעש מרדכי כל אשר צותה מהו ויעבור לכ"פ שעבר על דת: כ דאל"כ בגדי מלכות מבע"ל. פ"ק דמגילה: דק"ל

רש"י

(יז) ויעבר מרדכי. על דת להתענות י יום טוב ראשון של פסח שהתענה י"ד בניסן וט"ו וט"ז שהרי ביום י"ג נכתבו הספרים: (א) מלכות. בגדי מלכות, ורבותינו אמרו שלבשתה כ רוח הקדש כמה דאת אמר (דברי הימים א יב יח) ורוח לבשה את עמשי: (ג) עד חצי המלכות. דבר שהוא באמצע ובאי המלכות הוא בית המקדש שהתחילו לבנותו בימי כורש וחזר בו וצוה לבטל המלאכה ואחשורוש שעמד אחריו גם הוא ביטל המלאכה, ופשוטו של מקרא אף אם תשאלי ממני חצי המלכות אתן לך:

יבוא

פירוש

(יז) ויעבור בכל רחובות היהודים וגזר תענית כציווי אסתר:

(א) ותלבש אסתר מלכות, המלכות לבשתה ויהי כמדה, עד שכל רואיה הכירו כי לה יאות המלוכה ע"ד (איוב כט) צדק לבשתי וילבשני: ותעמוד והמלך יושב, בית המלכות היה קרוב אל החצר ששם ישב על כסאו לשפוט את העם ולפנים ממנו היה בית המלך, שהם החדרים המזומנים לצרכו לשבת שם, ושם היה יושב תמיד בעת שלא היה עוסק בצרכי הנהגת העם, ולכן עמדה אסתר נוכח בית המלך המיוחד לו. אבל בהשגחת ה' הזדמן שהמלך ישב עתה בבית המלכות שהוא קרוב אל החצר, וגם הזדמן שהעמיד את הכסא נכח פתח הבית, באופן שראה אותה תיכף ומיד:

(ב) ויהי מספר כי באהבת המלך את אסתר לא עלה בלבו מעולם שהגזירה הזאת שלא יכנס איש לחצר המלך הפנימית בלא רשות יכלול גם את אסתר, כי ביאתה אצלו אף לבית מלכותו היה חביב ויקר ע ולא חשב עליה כלל שתצטרך לעמוד בחצר ולהמתין עד שיושיטו לה השרביט, וע"כ כראות המלך את אסתר, הגם שהיא אסתר המלכה ולא עליה תחול הגזירה זאת, מ"מ בטעותה עומדת בחצר ואינה נכנסת לפנים, מצד זה נשאה חן בעיניו, כי ראה שזה אך מענות וצדק אשר בלבה. עתה רצונה ויושט לה את שרביט הזהב, ומספר כי הזדמן שהשרביט היה בידו בעת ההיא שזה ג"כ דבר שאין רגיל, ובהשגחת האל המשגיח:

(ג) מה לך, אחר שהבין כי ודאי איזה דבר גדול הניעה לבא אל המלך ובהחלט שדבר ההוא, הוא, או להסיר ממנו איזה היזק, או בעבור שתשיג איזה תועלת. ולכן אמר מה לך אסתר המלכה, היינו מה הגיע לך מן ההיזק שבעבורו באת, או מה בקשתך להשיג איזה ריוח ותועלת. והנה תחלה לא אמר ותעש, כי לא רצה לתת לה רק אם תבקש דבר לצרכה, לז"א וינתן לך, לא אם תבקש שיעשה דבר לערך אחרים בעניני המלוכה, שזה נכלל בלשון ותעש:

יבא

השאלות

א הילו"ל בגדי מלכות. מהו ההבדל בין בית המלך ובית המלכות:

ג הכפל מה לך ומה בקשתך, פה אמר וינתן לך, ובכ"מ אמר אצל הבקשה ותעש:

וְיִנָּתֶן לָךְ׃ ד וַתֹּאמֶר אֶסְתֵּר אִם־עַל־הַמֶּלֶךְ טוֹב יָבוֹא
הַמֶּלֶךְ וְהָמָן הַיּוֹם אֶל־הַמִּשְׁתֶּה אֲשֶׁר־עָשִׂיתִי לוֹ׃
ה וַיֹּאמֶר הַמֶּלֶךְ מַהֲרוּ אֶת־הָמָן לַעֲשׂוֹת אֶת־דְּבַר
אֶסְתֵּר וַיָּבֹא הַמֶּלֶךְ וְהָמָן אֶל־הַמִּשְׁתֶּה אֲשֶׁר־עָשְׂתָה
אֶסְתֵּר׃ ו וַיֹּאמֶר הַמֶּלֶךְ לְאֶסְתֵּר בְּמִשְׁתֵּה הַיַּיִן מַה־
שְּׁאֵלָתֵךְ וְיִנָּתֵן לָךְ וּמַה־בַּקָּשָׁתֵךְ עַד־חֲצִי הַמַּלְכוּת
וְתֵעָשׂ׃ ז וַתַּעַן אֶסְתֵּר וַתֹּאמַר שְׁאֵלָתִי וּבַקָּשָׁתִי׃

אם

רש"י

(ד) יבוא המלך והמן. רבותינו אמרו טעמים הרבה בדבר מה ראתה אסתר שזימנה את המן כדי לקנאו במלך ובשרים שהמלך יחשוב שהוא חושק אליה ויהרגנו, ועוד טעמים רבים: אל המשתה, כל סעודה

השאלות

ד פה אמרה אם על המלך טוב ולקמן (פסוק ח' וסי' ז' ג') אם מצאתי חן · מה היה כוונתה שזמנה את המן לבית המשתה:

ה מהו לעשות את דבר אסתר:

ו מה רצה בכפל שאלתך ובקשתך ואצל שאלתך אמר וינתן לך ואצל בקשתך אמר ותעש, וכן דייק (בפסוק ח') לתת את שאלתי ולעשות את בקשתי וכן בסימן ז' (פסוק ב'):

פירוש

(ד) יבא המלך. הטעמים שזמנה את המן רבים במפר', והיותר קרובים אלי, הם שלשה, א) בל יחשוב האויב כי משנאה עצמיית שיש לה עליו מבקשת את נפשו, לכן הראית כי היא אין לה עליו שום משטמה רק הצלת נפשה ועמה מבקשת, ב) כדי שתעמיד טענותיה נגדו פתאום שלא יהיה לו פנאי לסדר טענותיו, ולעת מצוא שתוכל להעלות בקל חמת המלך עליו במשתה היין, שבעת ההיא יהיה המלך בכעסו עת לכעוס ולעשות משפט חרוץ, ג) כי הצלחת המזל כשעולה עד תכלית נקודת הרום, שוב מתחיל לירד כידוע, ואחר שראתה מזל הרשע מצליח עד, קצה המעלה ולא חסר לו אך המלוכה העלתה אותו גם בזה שיהיה בעיניו תכלית הצלחתו כמו שיתבאר בפסוק י"ב, שמעתה תתחיל המסבה להתהפך בהכרח להורידו אל עמקי בור. והנה פה לא אמרה אם מצאתי חן, כי לדבר כזה שיבא אליה לשתות א"צ למציאת חן, רק אם על המלך טוב לבוא ולאכול, ואמרה אשר עשיתי. לאמר שהכל נכון באופן שימהר ביאתו ולא ידחנו ליום מחר:

(ה) לעשות את דבר אסתר, ר"ל בל יחשוב כי אסתר תתכבד בביאת המן, רק המן יבא מצד צווי אסתר ופקודתה, כעבד המחוייב לעשות רצון אדוניו:

(ו) מה שאלתך, המפרשים הבדילו בין שאלה ובקשה, כי בכל מבוקש מה שישאל תקרא שאלה, והתכלית הנרצה אל השואל תקרא בקשה, כמשל המבקש אלף זהובים כדי לקנות בעדם נחלת שדה וכרם, יהיה האלף זהובים השאלה, והשדה והכרם הבקשה. וע"ז השיבה כי שאלתה ובקשתה אינם שני דברים רק דבר אחד, שיבא המלך והמן אל המשתה, כי זה תשאל וזה תכלית המבוקש שלה. ולדעתי, שאלה הקטנה אשר ישיגה השואל בקל תקרא שאלה, והדבר הגדול שצריך לבקשו ע"י תחנונים נקרא בקשה, וכבר בארתי זה במק"א. ועפ"ז כל שתשאל המלכה לצרכה נקרא שאלה, כי ע"ז אינה צריכה להתחנן ולבקש כי ודאי לא ישיב את פניה, ואשר תבקש לצורך אחרים נקרא בקשה, כי ע"ז צריכה לבקש ולהתחנן. ואחר שאמר ומה בקשתך עד חצי המלכות ויתן לך, שקרא גם הדבר שתבקש לצרכה, שיתן לה בשם בקשה יען שיהיה דבר גדול הנוגע עד חצי המלכות, אבל עתה אחר שעל מה שתבקש לצרכה כבר הובטחה מן המלך וע"ז אין צריכה להתחנן, קרא כל מה שתבקש לצרכה בשם שאלה ואשר תבקש לצורך אחרים כמ"ש ועם קרא בשם בקשה, כי ע"ז לא הובטחה עדיין וצריכה להתחנן:

(ז) שאלתי ובקשתי. אסתר השיבה לו בהשכל ודעת, שהלא אמרה כי אין לה לשאול מן המלך שום דבר רק שתמצא חן בעיניו לעשות שאלתה, כי מציאת חן ונדיבת רוחו למלאות שאלתה זאת היקר בעיניה מן השאלה עצמה אשר תשיג, וזה שאמרה שאלתי ובקשתי העקרית היא אם מצאתי חן בעיני המלך לתת את שאלתי:

אם

ח אִם־מָצָאתִי חֵן בְּעֵינֵי הַמֶּלֶךְ וְאִם־עַל־הַמֶּלֶךְ טוֹב
לָתֵת אֶת־שְׁאֵלָתִי וְלַעֲשׂוֹת אֶת־בַּקָּשָׁתִי יָבוֹא הַמֶּלֶךְ
וְהָמָן אֶל־הַמִּשְׁתֶּה אֲשֶׁר אֶעֱשֶׂה לָהֶם וּמָחָר אֶעֱשֶׂה
כִּדְבַר הַמֶּלֶךְ׃ ט וַיֵּצֵא הָמָן בַּיּוֹם הַהוּא שָׂמֵחַ וְטוֹב לֵב
וְכִרְאוֹת הָמָן אֶת־מָרְדֳּכַי בְּשַׁעַר הַמֶּלֶךְ וְלֹא־קָם וְלֹא־
זָע מִמֶּנּוּ וַיִּמָּלֵא הָמָן עַל־מָרְדֳּכַי חֵמָה׃ י וַיִּתְאַפַּק הָמָן
וַיָּבוֹא אֶל־בֵּיתוֹ וַיִּשְׁלַח וַיָּבֵא אֶת־אֹהֲבָיו וְאֶת־זֶרֶשׁ
אִשְׁתּוֹ׃ יא וַיְסַפֵּר לָהֶם הָמָן אֶת־כְּבוֹד עָשְׁרוֹ וְרֹב בָּנָיו
וְאֵת כָּל־אֲשֶׁר גִּדְּלוֹ הַמֶּלֶךְ וְאֵת אֲשֶׁר נִשְּׂאוֹ עַל־הַשָּׂרִים

ועבדי

רש"י

סעודה נקראת על שם היין שהוא עיקר: (ח) ומחר אעשה כדבר המלך. מה שבקשת ממני כל הימים לגלות לך את עמי ואת מולדתי: (י) ויתאפק. נתחזק לעמוד על כעסו כי היה ירא להנקם בלא רשות

השאלות

ח מהו הכפל מצאתי חן ואם על המלך טוב, ולמה התחיל שנית שאלתי ובקשתי, מה תעשה מחר כדבר המלך שהמפרשים מחולקים בבאורו:

ט ביום ההוא מיותר, ולא קם ולא זע כפל ענין. פה אמר על מרדכי חמה ולמעלה (ג' ה') וימלא המן חמה:

י מ"ש ויתאפק ויבא אל ביתו, המשמעות שהיתה בדעתו ללכת אל מקום אחר:

יא למה ספר עתה כבוד עשרו:

פירוש

(ח) **אם מצאתי חן**, ר"ל התחילה בזה שני תנאים, א] שתהיה רצוי אליו לתת שאלתה מצד חן השואל, ב] שיהיה המבוקש עצמו דבר שטוב לפני המלך ואינו נגד רצונו, כי מה שנגד רצונו אינה מבקשת שיתן לה, כי מבטלת רצונה מפני רצונו, ואז **יבא המלך והמן אל המשתה** שתעשה למחר, **ומחר אעשה כדבר המלך** לאמר את הבקשה שאני מבקשת, וגם בזאת השכילה לאמר כי היא איננה כדאי לבקש דבר מן המלך אבל אחר שהמלך פקד עליה שתבקש ממנו דבר הנה תבקש בקשתה כדי לקיים דבר המלך ופקודתו שרוצה בזה שתבקש:

(ט) **ויצא המן**, מספר גנות הרשע הזה ורוע תכונתו, שעד עתה בכל המעלות אשר עלה לא שמח מימיו, כי כל מעלה שהשיג היה מבקש מה שאחריה, והיתה המעלה הקודמת קטנה בעיניו, רק היום ההוא שהגיע לקצה הגדולה והכבוד להיות שוה עם המלך אז היה היום הראשון שיצא שמח וטוב לב, אולם גם זאת לא נמשך הרבה, כי אך כאשר ראה מרדכי שהתהפכו מחשבותיו ליגון ואנחה, **ולא זע**, ראה שחוץ מה שלא קם מלפניו, אין לו שום יראה ופחד במה שיודע כי בנפשו הוא, שאם נמנע להשתחוות לו מצד דתו, עכ"פ ראוי שיפחד ביודעו כי עמו יענש ולכן עתה התמלא על מרדכי עצמו חמה, (כי בראשונה היה החמה כוללת כל עם מרדכי ודתם, וע"ז למעלה כתב סתם וימלא המן חמה:

(י) **ויתאפק**, מבואר שעלה על לבו לשוב אל המלך ולהלשין את מרדכי להמיתו, אבל שוב התאפק ולא שב אל המלך, רק **ויבא אל ביתו** וישלח אחר אהביו להתיעץ על הדבר:

(יא) **ויספר**, הנה מה שנמנע המן עד הנה לשלוח יד במרדכי לבדו, היה מפני שנחשב לו להעדר כבוד שיהיה לו ריב ומשפט נגד איש יהודי השפל בעיניו על שבלתי משתחוה לו, שלפי גדולת המן ראוי שלא ישקיף כלל על כבוד איש כמוהו או בזיונו, לפ"ז גדולת המן היה סבה שיגדל חטא מרדכי על שמקל בכבודו, והוא עצמו היה סבה שלא יכול לשלוח בו יד כי בזה יופחת כבודו, ולכן הקדים לספר גדולתו הרב כי הוא היסוד שבעבורו נמנע מלהתיעץ. ויען שגדולת האדם יהיה בשלשה ענינים, ריבוי הקנינים והבנים והמעלה, לכן השתבח בשלשת אלה כי בכולן הצליח, וע"ז **כבוד עשרו ורוב בניו** ואשר גדלו המלך:

ויאמר

וְעַבְדֵ֥י הַמֶּֽלֶךְ׃ יב וַיֹּאמֶר֮ הָמָן֒ אַ֣ף לֹא־הֵבִיאָה֩ אֶסְתֵּ֨ר
הַמַּלְכָּ֧ה עִם־הַמֶּ֛לֶךְ אֶל־הַמִּשְׁתֶּ֥ה אֲשֶׁר־עָשָׂ֖תָה כִּ֣י אִם־
אוֹתִ֑י וְגַם־לְמָחָ֛ר אֲנִ֥י קָֽרוּא־לָ֖הּ עִם־הַמֶּֽלֶךְ׃ יג וְכָל־זֶ֕ה
אֵינֶ֥נּוּ שֹׁוֶ֖ה לִ֑י בְּכָל־עֵ֗ת אֲשֶׁ֨ר אֲנִ֤י רֹאֶה֙ אֶת־מָרְדֳּכַ֣י
הַיְּהוּדִ֔י יוֹשֵׁ֖ב בְּשַׁ֥עַר הַמֶּֽלֶךְ׃ יד וַתֹּ֣אמֶר לוֹ֩ זֶ֨רֶשׁ אִשְׁתּ֜וֹ
וְכָל־אֹהֲבָ֗יו יַֽעֲשׂוּ־עֵץ֮ גָּבֹ֣הַּ חֲמִשִּׁ֣ים אַמָּה֒ וּבַבֹּ֣קֶר ׀ אֱמֹ֣ר
לַמֶּ֗לֶךְ וְיִתְל֤וּ אֶֽת־מָרְדֳּכַי֙ עָלָ֔יו וּבֹֽא־עִם־הַמֶּ֥לֶךְ אֶל־
הַמִּשְׁתֶּ֖ה שָׂמֵ֑חַ וַיִּיטַ֧ב הַדָּבָ֛ר לִפְנֵ֥י הָמָ֖ן וַיַּ֥עַשׂ הָעֵֽץ׃ ס
ו א בַּלַּ֣יְלָה הַה֔וּא נָדְדָ֖ה שְׁנַ֣ת הַמֶּ֑לֶךְ וַיֹּ֗אמֶר לְהָבִ֞יא
אֶת־סֵ֤פֶר הַזִּכְרֹנוֹת֙ דִּבְרֵ֣י הַיָּמִ֔ים וַיִּהְי֥וּ

נקראים

רש"י

רשות. ויתאפק איספורצי"ר בלעז: (יג) איננו שוה לי. איני חש לכל הכבוד אשר לי: בכל עת וגו'. אמרו רבותינו שהיה מראה לו שטר שמכר עצמו לעבד על הוסר מזונות כשנתמנו ראשי גייסות מרדכי והמן במלחמה אחת: (א) נדדה שנת המלך. ל נס היה

שפתי חכמים

ל דק"ל למה זה נדדה שנת המלך בלילה הזאת ולא היה יכול לישן בהיותו שמח וטוב לב בשמחה במשתה אסתר וכדכך הטבע

השאלה

יב מ"ש לא הביאה כי אם אותי, וכי היה מן ההכרח שתביאה עוד אחרים והלא עקר הרבותא שהביאה אותו, והיל"ל ואף הביאה אסתר אותי אל המשתה בהיוב ולא בשלילה:

יד מה חכמתם בעצה זאת שיעשה העץ, ולמה יהיה גבות חמשים אמה ולמה יבא בבוקר דוקא:

א מה היא סבת נדידת השינה, מדוע כפל ספר הזכרונות דברי הימים:

פירוש

(יב) ויאמר הוסיף לאמר כי הגיע לקצה האחרון מן המעלה, כי המשתה שעשה המלכה ראוי שתקרא אליה כל שרי המלך, שלא נשמע מעולם לעשות משתה לאיש אחד או שנים, כמו שנאמר ויעש המלך משתה גדול לכל שריו ועבדיו, אבל אני גדול כ"כ בעיני המלכה עד שאני שקול בעיניה ככל שרי המלך בכלל, ובמה שזמנה אותי נחשב כאילו היתה משתה כוללת לכל שרי המלך, ועז"א לא קראה כי אם אותי, והוסיף עוד וגם למחר אני קרוא לה, ר"ל ראו גדולתי, המלכה יש לה לבקש דבר מן המלך, ויראה שלא ימלא בקשתה וקראה אותי ג"כ שאני אבקש בעדה למלאות שאלתה, שזה מבואר שאני גדול יותר מן המלכה והיא צריכה אלי:

(יג) וכל זה איננו שוה לי, ר"ל שלא יוכל להשוות הגדולה הזאת נגד הבוז שמשיג מן מרדכי, כי בעבור גדולתו זאת חטא מרדכי גדול מאד, ונגד זה בעבור זאת בעצמו אינו יכול להתבזות לשלוח בו יד, וע"ז שאל עצה איך יהרוג את מרדכי ולא יחשב לו לבוז וקלון:

(יד) יעשו עץ. הנה יעצוהו בחכמה, שיוכל לנקום במרדכי ובכ"ז לא יוחשב לו להעדר כבוד, כי אם יתלה את מרדכי רק מצד חטאו בעצמו שלא השתחוה לו, הוא לו פחיתות כבוד שהיה לו ריב עם איש יהודי בעבור שהקל בכבודו, אבל לפעמים יצוה המלך לתלות איש אחד מן המורדים בו להפיל מורא על העם, לאמר כל מי שיעשה כזה כן יהיה משפטו להתלות, ובזה בוחרים תמיד היותר שפל מן העם, ותולים אותו על עץ גבוה שיראוהו כל העם למען יראו וייראו, ואם יתלה מרדכי על אופן הזה לא יהיה זה לו להעדר כבוד, במה שתלה איש שפל ונבזה, כי לא בעבור חטאו נגד המן שלא השתחוה לו נתלה רק להיות לנס עמים, ובזה יעצוהו בערמה, שיעשה העץ גבוה חמשים אמה, שזה הסימן שנתלה למען יהיה לאות ומופת אשר הנשארים ישמעו וייראו, ב] שיתלה בבקר השכם כי כן היה הדרך לתלות הנתלים על הכוונה הזאת, כדי שמיד בצאת העם מביתם יראו ולא יזידון עוד, לא כן הנתלה עבור חטאו שהיה נתלה אחר עבור עת המשפט בנמשך עד הצהרים, ונתלה על עץ נמוך, ובזה הבא אל המשתה שמח:

(א) בלילה, אין ספק כי המלך בראותו את כל החרדה שחרדה אסתר לבא אליו, ידע כי בקשה גדולה יש

נִקְרָאִים לִפְנֵי הַמֶּלֶךְ׃ ב וַיִּמָּצֵא כָתוּב אֲשֶׁר הִגִּיד מָרְדֳּכַי
עַל־בִּגְתָנָא וָתֶרֶשׁ שְׁנֵי סָרִיסֵי הַמֶּלֶךְ מִשֹּׁמְרֵי הַסַּף אֲשֶׁר
בִּקְשׁוּ לִשְׁלֹחַ יָד בַּמֶּלֶךְ אֲחַשְׁוֵרוֹשׁ׃ ג וַיֹּאמֶר הַמֶּלֶךְ
מַה־נַּעֲשָׂה יְקָר וּגְדוּלָּה לְמָרְדֳּכַי עַל־זֶה וַיֹּאמְרוּ נַעֲרֵי
הַמֶּלֶךְ מְשָׁרְתָיו לֹא־נַעֲשָׂה עִמּוֹ דָּבָר׃ ד וַיֹּאמֶר הַמֶּלֶךְ
מִי בֶחָצֵר וְהָמָן בָּא לַחֲצַר בֵּית־הַמֶּלֶךְ הַחִיצוֹנָה לֵאמֹר
לַמֶּלֶךְ לִתְלוֹת אֶת־מָרְדֳּכַי עַל־הָעֵץ אֲשֶׁר־הֵכִין לוֹ׃
ה וַיֹּאמְרוּ נַעֲרֵי הַמֶּלֶךְ אֵלָיו הִנֵּה הָמָן עֹמֵד בֶּחָצֵר

°פתח באתנח °רגש אחר מלאפ"ם — ויאמר

רש"י

היה. ויש אומרים שם את לבו על שזמנה אסתר את המן שמא נתנה עיניה בו ויהרגהו: להביא את ספר הזכרונות. דרך המלכים כששינתן נודדת אומרים לפניהם משלים ושיחות עד ששינתם חוזרת עליהם.

ורבותינו אמרו מתוך שנתן לבו על המן ואסתר אמר אפשר שלא ידע אדם שהוא אוהבי עצתם ויגלה לי וחזר ואמר שמא עשה לי אדם טובה ולא גמלתיו ואין חוששין עוד לי לפיכך ויאמר להביא את ספר הזכרונות

פירוש

ם לא לבקש, כי בעבור זה אמר עד חצי המלכות, ויען שכפלה בדבריה אם מצאתי חן, ואם על המלך טוב, הבין שהשאלה שמבקשת הוא דבר הטוב לפני המלך בעצמו, והרהורי אליו מלך ישרו באשר הוא פועל עמים והוכן בחסד כסאו, ובזה עלה בלבו כי אין ספק מחוייב לשלם איזה גמול למטיב עמו, ולא שלם פעלו, ועל"כ צוה להביא ספר הזכרונות. והנה המפרשים כתבו כי דברי הימים היה הד"ה הגדול שבו כתוב הכל בארוך, והיה עוד לוח המפתחות שהיה כתוב בו ראשי דברים ועל"י היו מחפשים בד"ה הגדול. ולי נראה כי היו שני דברי הימים, א) דברי הימים שנכתב לזכרון לדור אחרון קורות המלך ומעשיו ופעולותיו הן טוב והן רע, וד"ה הזה לא היה ביד המלך רק ביד המשנה, ב) דברי הימים שנכתב לפני המלך שיהיה לזכרון אל המלך עצמו, וזה נקרא ספר הזכרונות דברי הימים שהיה תכליתו למזכרת דברים, וכבר כתבתי כי מן המלך נשכח מי היה המגיד על בגתנא ותרש, ועל"כ גדל את המן, כי לא ידע למי ישלם גמול בעד הטובה הגדולה הזאת, אם לא למי שסבב ביאת אסתר שעל ידה ניצל ממות, וגם שאח"כ השתדל המן שידמה להמלך שהוא היה המגיד, ועל"כ גדלו ורוממו, ובודאי מספר דברי הימים שהיה ביד המן נמחק שם מרדכי ונכתב שם המן במקומו שהמן היה המגיד, אבל בספר הזכרונות שהוא הדברי הימים אשר היה תחת יד המלך שם היה כתוב האמת, שמרדכי היה המגיד, ועז"א,

(ב) **וימצא כתוב**, כי משם לא נמחק שם מרדכי רק נמצא כתוב כי לא המן היה המגיד רק **אשר הגיד** מרדכי, ומזה נודע למלך כי כל מה שגדל את המן בחשבו שהוא היה סבה להצלתו היה בטעות, ועקר הגדולה הזאת מגיע למרדכי. ובזה ספר השגחת ה', איך באותו הרגע שהשב המן לבקש נפש הצדיק להלותו, נהפך הדבר כי נתודע למלך שגדולת המן מגיע למרדכי:

(ג) **מה נעשה יקר וגדולה**, המלך שאל שלא מגיע לו ע"ז שני דברים, א) יקר בטעתו להודיע אשר פעל ועשה שהציל את המלך ממות, ב) גדולה לעתיד לגדלו על כל השרים, והגם שידע שנעשה גדולה למרדכי שישב בשער המלך, שאל מה נעשה לו גדולה על זה, כי מה שישב בשער המלך היה בעבור שהיה אומן את אסתר לא בעבור זה:

(ד) **מי בחצר**, מודיע תוקף הנס שלא היה טבעי רק השגחיי, כי באותו הרגע בא המן לתלות את מרדכי ומשכב הכבוד כבר הכין לו כלי מות:

השאלות

ב מלשון וימצא כתוב משמע שהיה חידוש שנמצא כתוב ולא נמחק:

ג מהו הכפל יקר וגדולה, ולהמן לא אמר רק אשר המלך חפץ ביקרו, מלות על זה מיותר:

וַיֹּאמֶר הַמֶּלֶךְ יָבוֹא׃ ו וַיָּבוֹא הָמָן וַיֹּאמֶר לוֹ הַמֶּלֶךְ מַה
לַּעֲשׂוֹת בָּאִישׁ אֲשֶׁר הַמֶּלֶךְ חָפֵץ בִּיקָרוֹ וַיֹּאמֶר הָמָן
בְּלִבּוֹ לְמִי יַחְפֹּץ הַמֶּלֶךְ לַעֲשׂוֹת יְקָר יוֹתֵר מִמֶּנִּי׃
ז וַיֹּאמֶר הָמָן אֶל־הַמֶּלֶךְ אִישׁ אֲשֶׁר הַמֶּלֶךְ חָפֵץ בִּיקָרוֹ׃
ח יָבִיאוּ לְבוּשׁ מַלְכוּת אֲשֶׁר לָבַשׁ־בּוֹ הַמֶּלֶךְ וְסוּס אֲשֶׁר
רָכַב עָלָיו הַמֶּלֶךְ וַאֲשֶׁר נִתַּן כֶּתֶר מַלְכוּת בְּרֹאשׁוֹ׃
ט וְנָתוֹן הַלְּבוּשׁ וְהַסּוּס עַל־יַד־אִישׁ מִשָּׂרֵי הַמֶּלֶךְ
הַפַּרְתְּמִים וְהִלְבִּישׁוּ אֶת־הָאִישׁ אֲשֶׁר הַמֶּלֶךְ חָפֵץ בִּיקָרוֹ
וְהִרְכִּיבֻהוּ עַל־הַסּוּס בִּרְחוֹב הָעִיר וְקָרְאוּ לְפָנָיו כָּכָה
יֵעָשֶׂה לָאִישׁ אֲשֶׁר הַמֶּלֶךְ חָפֵץ בִּיקָרוֹ׃ י וַיֹּאמֶר הַמֶּלֶךְ
לְהָמָן מַהֵר קַח אֶת־הַלְּבוּשׁ וְאֶת־הַסּוּס כַּאֲשֶׁר דִּבַּרְתָּ
וַעֲשֵׂה־כֵן לְמָרְדֳּכַי הַיְּהוּדִי הַיּוֹשֵׁב בְּשַׁעַר הַמֶּלֶךְ אַל־

תפל

רש"י

הזכרונות: (ט) ונתון הלבוש והסוס על יד איש. ואת הכתר לא הזכיר שראה עינו של מלך רעה על

השאלות

ו מדוע מהר לשלם למרדכי תיכף בבקר השכם:

ז מדוע חזר המן איש אשר המלך חפץ ביקרו:

י המן אמר והלבישו והרכיבהו, והמלך צוה שיעשה הכל בעצמו:

פירוש

(ו) מה לעשות, אחשורוש ידע שהמן יעשה שאליו הדברים נוגעים, ורצה בזה כדי שהיקר שיבקש המן לעצמו יעשה למרדכי אחר שבאמת אין היקר מגיע להמן רק למרדכי, ומטעם זה לא שאל לו מה לעשות באיש אשר המלך חפץ ביקרו וגדולתו, כי אז יבין המן שלא עליו חושב המלך, כי הוא כבר הגיע להכלית הגדולה שהגדילו מכל השרים, ולכן לא אמר רק ביקרו שבזה יטעה המן שאליו רוצה לעשות יקר ויכריז על המדה, ויעשה כן למרדכי, ובל"ז על הגדולה לא הוצרך לשאול, כי כבר חשב לתת גדולת המן למרדכי אחר שאליו מגיע עיקר הגדולה:

(ז) איש, השיב לו במועצות ודעת, לאמר איך יתכן לשאול מה לעשות באיש אשר המלך חפץ ביקרו, הלא זה עצמו מה שהמלך חפץ ביקרו, זה הוא הכבוד והיקר היותר גדול, עד שאין יקר יותר ממנו, ונ"ש על מה שאתה שואל מה לעשות, אני משיב לך זאת עצמו יעשה לו שיודיעו שהוא איש אשר המלך חפץ ביקרו, כי הוא היקר היותר גדול, רק יביאו לבוש מלכות לפרסם הדבר:

(ח) ואשר נתן, י"מ שהיו נותנים כתר מלכות בראש הסוס, וי"מ אשר רכב עליו המלך בעת שניתן כתר מלכות בראשו, היינו ביום שנכתר למלוכה:

(ט) והלבישו והרכיבהו, המן רצה להרבות כבודו ע"י שרים רבים ומכריזים כבירים כדי שיתפרסם הדבר, ע"כ אמר בלשון רבים שיעשה הדבר ע"י רבים ונכבדים:

(י) מהר קח, המלך בראה שגדולת המן הוא שלא במשפט, ובאמת למרדכי יאות הכבוד הזה, וראה עד היכן הגיע גאותו עד שרוצה להשתמש בשרביטו של מלך. ועוד לו אך המלוכה, כמו שאמר שנמה בדבר אדוניהו ששאל שרביטו של מלך שדע כמורד במלך, לכן אמר בחמתו שימהר לעשות כן למרדכי, כי אליו מגיע הכבוד הזה, וגם מגיע לו שיעשה לו זאת ע"י המן עצמו אחר שהוא לקח גדולתו בערמה ראוי שירוץ לפניו כעבד, ואל תפל דבר, כי הכל ביושר ובצדק, וע"כ צוה שהוא עצמו יעשה הכל בלי עזר להלבשה והרכבה משרים אחרים, ועז"א מכל אשר דברת, שגם ההלבשה תעשה בעצמך:

וישב

תַּפֵּל דָּבָר מִכֹּל אֲשֶׁר דִּבַּרְתָּ׃ יא וַיִּקַּח הָמָן אֶת־הַלְּבוּשׁ
וְאֶת־הַסּוּס וַיַּלְבֵּשׁ אֶת־מָרְדֳּכָי וַיַּרְכִּיבֵהוּ בִּרְחוֹב הָעִיר
וַיִּקְרָא לְפָנָיו כָּכָה יֵעָשֶׂה לָאִישׁ אֲשֶׁר הַמֶּלֶךְ חָפֵץ
בִּיקָרוֹ׃ יב וַיָּשָׁב מָרְדֳּכַי אֶל־שַׁעַר הַמֶּלֶךְ וְהָמָן נִדְחַף
אֶל־בֵּיתוֹ אָבֵל וַחֲפוּי רֹאשׁ׃ יג וַיְסַפֵּר הָמָן לְזֶרֶשׁ אִשְׁתּוֹ
וּלְכָל־אֹהֲבָיו אֵת כָּל־אֲשֶׁר קָרָהוּ וַיֹּאמְרוּ לוֹ חֲכָמָיו וְזֶרֶשׁ
אִשְׁתּוֹ אִם מִזֶּרַע הַיְּהוּדִים מָרְדֳּכַי אֲשֶׁר הַחִלּוֹתָ לִנְפֹּל
לְפָנָיו לֹא־תוּכַל לוֹ כִּי־נָפוֹל תִּפּוֹל לְפָנָיו׃ יד עוֹדָם
מְדַבְּרִים עִמּוֹ וְסָרִיסֵי הַמֶּלֶךְ הִגִּיעוּ וַיַּבְהִלוּ לְהָבִיא אֶת־
הָמָן אֶל־הַמִּשְׁתֶּה אֲשֶׁר־עָשְׂתָה אֶסְתֵּר׃

°הל׳ דגושה

ריבא

שפתי חכמים

בשנת שהמיס במשתה ביום ששם ישנים שינה שקועה בלילה המשכת אחר המשתה. לכ״פ גם סיה: ם דק״ל לנ״ל דשב מרדכי שלא כל עלמו של הכתוב אינו אלא לספר במפלתו של המן. לכ״פ לשקו ולתעניתו ויום ג׳ לתעניתו היה שהתחיל להתענות ביום י״ד בניסן ומה שקרא המקרא ליום אתמול שלישי ויהי ביום השלישי והלבש אסתר מלכות יום שלישי לשילות הרגיס היה: ג דק״ל מה אבילות שייך כזה לגם אמר ר״פ וכו׳ דדרשו בפ״ק דמגילה ע״ז: ם בגמרא בפ״ק דמגילה דייק מסיפיה דקרא כי נפול תפול לפניו שתי נפילות

רש״י

על שאמר שיתפו הכהר ברשא אדם: (יב) וישב מרדכי. לשקו ם ולתעניתו: אבל וחפוי ראש. רבותינו ב פירשו הדבר במסכת מגילה: (יג) אשר החלות לנפל וגו׳. אמרה אומה זו נמשלו לכוכבים ם ולעפר כשהם יורדים יורדים עד לעפר וכשהם עולים

פירוש

(יב) וישב, מספר איך מרדכי שב לגדולתו, והמן נרדף לבאר שחת, כאומר ראו מעשה ה׳ כי פלא הוא, מהשבות אדם הבל, ועלת מסבב הסבות לעולם תעמוד:

(יג) ויספר, פי׳ מהרא״ה שהמן השב שבני ביתו בשמעם את הנעשה, יחרדו ויפחדו פן בקש המן מן המלך לתלות את מרדכי, וע״י הויכוח והבירור נודע למלך כי שקר דבר עליו, ומתוך כך יצא הפסק הזה, ובזה אין תרופה למכתו, ועי״ז בא לבשרם בשורה טובה, כי זה היה רק מקרה בעלמא ושעדן לא בקש שאלתו ועוד יש תקוה שאח״כ יבקש לתלותו וימלא המלך בקשתו אחר שכבר קבל מרדכי את שכרו, אמנם הכמיו ויועציו יעצוהו לסוטו בל יתגרה עוד עם מרדכי ואל יבקש את נפשו כי לא יצליח עכ״ד. וגם ספר כי על דברת המן שחשב זאת למקרה בעלמא, הודיעוהו היועצים ההכמים ההלה, שאם מרדכי הוא מזרע היהודים, שהם העם שעליהם תהופף השגחת ה׳ הפרטיית, אז ידע כי לא היה הדבר במקרה רק בהשגחת אלהי קדושים, ואחר אשר החלות לנפול לפניו, שמורה כי ה׳ רצה בם תפש עיט עליהם לטובה לא תוכל לו עוד, ולראיה אמרו אשר החלות לנפול לפניו, טנו בזה שני פנים, א] שאתה החלות לנפול שאתה היית המתחיל בנפילה הזאת מבלי שעשה שום אדם איזה השתדלות בזה רק אתה בעצמך היית המתחיל והגורם ע״י שהסכמת לשער המלך ויעצת זאת העצה, ב] שהחלות לנפול לפניו, שהוא לא נפל עדיין רק אתה נפלת קודם לו, וזה מורה מלת לפניו, ר״ל לפני נפילתו, וזה סימן שהיה בהשגחה ע״י תפלתו ותעניתו שמתעסק בו עתה, וא״כ לא תוכל לו רק אם נפל תפול לפניו, ר״ל רק באופן הזה תוכל בו אם תפול ותכניע עצמך לפניו, עד שתתגאה דעתו ויפסיק מתפלתו ותשובתו אז תגבר ידך לעשות חיל, אבל כל עוד שתלהם בו כן ירים ידו בתפלה, והיה כאשר ירים מרדכי ידו וגבר ישראל:

(יד) עודם, גם זה היה בהשגחה שהסריסים באו באמצע הויכוח ושמעו את הנדבר ביניהם שהמן אמר שרוגז

השאלות

יג צ״ל למה ספר זאת לאנשי ביתו והלא בשורת רעה כזאת טוב להעלימה לא לפרסמה, ולשון אשר קרהו כאילו מקרה היה אינו מובן, ויפלא מה זאת הנאמר במ״ש כי נפל תפול וקראם חכמיו, ומה כסילות להפיל מורך ופחד בלבבו:

יד למה מספר כי סריסי המלך הגיעו בעודם מדברים:

ז א וַיָּבֹא הַמֶּלֶךְ וְהָמָן לִשְׁתּוֹת עִם־אֶסְתֵּר הַמַּלְכָּה׃
ב וַיֹּאמֶר הַמֶּלֶךְ לְאֶסְתֵּר גַּם בַּיּוֹם הַשֵּׁנִי
בְּמִשְׁתֵּה הַיַּיִן מַה־שְּׁאֵלָתֵךְ אֶסְתֵּר הַמַּלְכָּה וְתִנָּתֵן לָךְ
וּמַה־בַּקָּשָׁתֵךְ עַד־חֲצִי הַמַּלְכוּת וְתֵעָשׂ׃ ג וַתַּעַן אֶסְתֵּר
הַמַּלְכָּה וַתֹּאמַר אִם־מָצָאתִי חֵן בְּעֵינֶיךָ הַמֶּלֶךְ וְאִם־
עַל־הַמֶּלֶךְ טוֹב תִּנָּתֶן־לִי נַפְשִׁי בִּשְׁאֵלָתִי וְעַמִּי
בְּבַקָּשָׁתִי׃ ד כִּי נִמְכַּרְנוּ אֲנִי וְעַמִּי לְהַשְׁמִיד לַהֲרוֹג
וּלְאַבֵּד וְאִלּוּ לַעֲבָדִים וְלִשְׁפָחוֹת נִמְכַּרְנוּ הֶחֱרַשְׁתִּי כִּי

אין

רש"י

עולים עולים עד לרקיע ועד הכוכבים: (ג) תנתן לי נפשי. שלא אהרג בשלשה עשר באדר שנגזרת גזירת הריגה על עמי ומולדתי: ועמי. ינתן לי בבקשתי שלא יהרגו, וא"ת מה איכפת לך כי איככה אוכל וראיתי וגו': (ד) כי אין הצר שוה בנזק המלך, אינו חושש בנזק המלך שאילו רדף אחר הנזק

היה

השאלות

ב מדוע קראת פה אסתר המלכה:

ג למה יחסה השאלה אל נפשה והבקשה על עמה:

ד מדוע היתה מחרשת אם לעבדים היו נמכרים, ומהו כי אין הצר שוה, שנדחקו המפ' בבאורו:

פירוש

טוב להשתדל אצל המלך לתאותו, והם יעשו כל ילחם עמו, ומזה ידע חרבונה שהיה אחד מן הסריסים האלה ששפה המן את העץ, (מהרש"א)·

(ב) מה שאלתך אסתר המלכה, עתה הוסיף לה באהבתו שגם אם תשאל בשאלה דבר גדול הראוי לה מצד שהיא מלכה יתן לה, וע"ז הוסיף אסתר המלכה:

(ג) נפשי, למה שבארתי למעלה כי השאלה היא מה שמבקש לצורך עצמו, והבקשה היא מה שמבקש לצורך אחרים, אמרה אני מבקש לצורך עצמי איש דבר זולתי, רק את נפשי, וכן בבקשה לצורך עמי אינו דבר זולתם מהעושר והכבוד רק הצלת נפשם ממות, ולדעת המפרשים שזכרתי למעלה, שהשאלה היא גוף השאלה והבקשה היא התכלית הנרצה אצלו מן השאלה, והנה המבקש להציל נפש חבירו ממות, השאלה יהיה הצלת נפש חבירו אבל התכלית הנרצה אצלו הוא מפני שאינו יכול לראות ברעת חבירו, וא"כ הבקשה היא, הוא בעבור עצמו, והיה יכול להקורים לטעות כי אסתר בקשה על עמה ואמרה כי איככה אוכל וראיתי ברעה אשר ימצא את עמי, שמילא עקר הבקשה היא בעבור עצמה שאינה יכולה לראות האבדן עמה ומולדתה, לז"א כי לא כן הוא רק כ"כ יקר בעיניה הצלת עמה עד שהיתה מסכמת שתאבד היא בלבד שעמה ינצלו, באופן שהשאלה אל המלך היה בעבור עצמה כמ"ש כי איככה אוכל וראיתי, אבל עקר הבקשה ותכליתה הוא עמה:

(ד) כי נמכרנו טענה שני טענות, א) שעיקר המכירה היתה בעבורה שעיקר מחשבת המן היה לאבד אותה ועי' מלא עלילה על עמה כדי שאח"כ יוכל להתגולל עליה לאמר שהיא מבני אומתה ויהרוג גם אותה, וז"ש כי נמכרנו אני ועמי, ר"ל אני הייתי העקרית והסבה אל המכירה ועל ידי נמכרו גם עמי, ב) גוף המכירה שלא נמכרו לעבדות רק להשמיד ולאבד [ולכן כפלה תמיד בדבריה אם מצאתי חן ואם על המלך טוב, כי המציאות חן מגביל נגד השאלה שהיא בעבור עצמה וצריכה מציאות חן שתנצל, ואם על המלך טוב מגביל נגד הבקשה עבור עמה, כי למלאות הבקשה הזאת אין צריך למציאות חן רק הדבר טוב מצד עצמו כי לא לתפארת יהיה אל המלך לאבד הגוי כולו בלי פשע], וגם בררה בדבריה איך המן רמה את המלך בשני דברים, א) במה שאמר אליו ישנו עם אחד, שהם עם בלתי מפורסם, והלא זה אני ועמי, זה העם אשר אנכי בקרבו, והיה צריך להודיע זאת להמלך, ב) במ"ש יכתב לאבדם שהיה כוונת המלך לאבד צורת האומה ודתה לא להשמידם כנ"ל, והוא תכסס להשמיד להרוג ולאבד, ושז"א ואלו לעבדים ולשפחות נמכרנו וכו', ר"ל אם עכ"פ לא היה מרמה את המלך רק בדבר אחד במה שלא גלה את אמו מי הוא העם, אז החרשתי, ולא הייתי מגלה המרמה והמאנס אחר שסבר יצא הדבר בשוגג מאת המלך, לא כן עתה שהדבר כולו מוטעה וכדי בזיון וקצף למלך, שהראוי שהמלכה נמרמה אותו יקבל את עונו,

וגם

אֵין הַצָּר שֹׁוֶה בְּנֵזֶק הַמֶּלֶךְ׃ ס ה וַיֹּאמֶר הַמֶּלֶךְ אֲחַשְׁוֵרוֹשׁ
וַיֹּאמֶר לְאֶסְתֵּר הַמַּלְכָּה מִי הוּא זֶה וְאֵי־זֶה הוּא אֲשֶׁר־
מְלָאוֹ לִבּוֹ לַעֲשׂוֹת כֵּן׃ ו וַתֹּאמֶר אֶסְתֵּר אִישׁ צַר
וְאוֹיֵב הָמָן הָרָע הַזֶּה וְהָמָן נִבְעַת מִלִּפְנֵי הַמֶּלֶךְ וְהַמַּלְכָּה׃
ז וְהַמֶּלֶךְ קָם בַּחֲמָתוֹ מִמִּשְׁתֵּה הַיַּיִן אֶל־גִּנַּת הַבִּיתָן
וְהָמָן עָמַד לְבַקֵּשׁ עַל־נַפְשׁוֹ מֵאֶסְתֵּר הַמַּלְכָּה כִּי רָאָה
כִּי־כָלְתָה אֵלָיו הָרָעָה מֵאֵת הַמֶּלֶךְ׃ ח וְהַמֶּלֶךְ שָׁב
מִגִּנַּת הַבִּיתָן אֶל־בֵּית ׀ מִשְׁתֵּה הַיַּיִן וְהָמָן נֹפֵל עַל־

המטה

שפתי חכמים

כשלות אלו לפי מלמד שאמרה לו אומה זו נמשלת לעפר ולכוכבים וכו', גם רש"י עיקר דיוקו מכיסיה דקרא לכן כתב וגו' להורות שדיוקו ממה שכתב אח"כ: ע פירוש של כלתה גמרה ואח"כ ק"ל מה רעה עשו לו שאומר כלתה הרעה ועוד במה ידע שנגמרה הרעה דלמא ירע לו עוד כאשר אידע באמת לכ"ש השנאה והנקמה כלומר נגמר השנאה שישנאהו ונעשה בו נקמה: פ והמן נופל נפל מבע"ל לכ"ש המלאך דוחפו. והכי איתא בפ"ק דמגילה ופירש"י נופל משמע לשון עושה והולך נפל פתיד רוצה לזקוף ומלאך מפילו:

דקסה

רש"י

היה לו לומר מכור אותם לעבדים ולשפחות וקבל הממון או ההיה אותם להיות לך לעבדים הם וזרעם: (ה) ויאמר המלך אחשורוש ויאמר לאסתר המלכה. כל מקום שנאמר ויאמר ויאמר שני פעמים אינו אלא למדרש, ומדרשו של זה בתחלה היה מדבר עמה ע"י שליח עכשיו שידע שממשפחת מלכים היא דבר עמה הוא בעצמו: (ז) כי כלתה. נגמרה הרעה ע והשנאה והנקמה: (ח) והמן נפל. פ המלאך דחפו: על

המטה

פירוש

זנם עד מ"ש המן במלשינותו ולמלך אין שוה להניחם, שהעם יהיו מזיקים את המלך, השיבה שדרכה אין הצר שוה בנזק המלך, המן אינו שוה ביחה המלך אותו בחיים מפני ההיזק שהמלך מוצא ממנו שמהרס את מלכותו:

השאלות

ה מהו ויאמר ויאמר. כפל מי הוא זה ואי זה הוא, כבר העירותי הלא אחשורוש עצמו הסכים ע"ז ומה שאל עתה:

ו כפל צר ואויב:

ז מדוע לא בקש מאת המלך והמלכה ביחד:

(ה) ויאמר, תחלה שאל המלך לכל אנשי הבית והמן בכללם כמתמיה מי הוא זה, ואחר שאין משיבו שאל לאסתר המלכה, מי הוא זה, שאל שני דברים, א) מי הוא האיש הזה שעשה נבלה כזאת, ב) ואי זה הוא, הסבה אשר עררתו לזה, ועז"א אשר מלאו מוסב על הסבה אם היא הסבה אשר מלאה את לב האיש ההוא לעשות כן:

(ו) איש צר, נגד מה ששאל מה היא הסבה שמלאה לב האיש אל הנבלה הזאת, אמרה הסבה היא יען שהוא איש צר ואויב, וכפלה צר ואויב, כי צר הוא המציר לחברו בפועל ואויב המבקש רעת חבירו ומ"מ אינו מציר לו בפועל. והנה מי שאינו אכזרי כ"כ לא יהיה אויב רק טרם היותו צר, אבל אחר שיהיה צר לא יהיה אויב, רצוי, שאחר שיצר לחבירו ויכנקום ממנו תסתלק האיבה, אבל המן באכזריותו, הגם שהציר והרע עדיין הוא אויב, והסבה זאת, הניעה לבו להציר לישראל באיבתו, ונגד השאלה מי הוא זה השיבה המן הרע הזה. והמן נבעת, פי' מהרא"ח כי אל המלך עצמו היה יכול להתאל להחזיק דבריו, כי מה שהלשין על עם היהודים כולו אמת ולא מאיבה עשה זאת, אבל הלא אז תגדל יותר חמת אסתר, ולפני אסתר בפני עצמה היה יכול להתחנן, שעשה זאת טרם שידע שהיהודים עמה ומולדתה, ועתה מבטיחה שיוסיף לדבר טוב על היהודים להשיב את הספרים, אבל אז תגדל חמת המלך, כי יאמר הלא בזה נגלה כי לא מאהבת האמת רצית להשמידם, כי אם אמת כדבריך שהם ראוים להשמידם, איך תהפך עליהם עתה מיראת המלכה, וע"כ נבעת מלפני המלך והמלכה בהיותם ביחד:

(ז) וע"כ בעת צאת המלך אל גנת הביתן מצא עת רצון לבקש על נפשו מאסתר בפ"ע:

(ח) הגם, אחר שכבר היה בדעתו כי המן חשב להרוג את אסתר עם אבדן כללות היהודים, ועתה גם עתה נדמה לו ג"כ שרוצה להרגה, אמר וכי גם תכבוש את המלכה, אם את עמה מכרת להרוג,

הגם

המטה אשר אסתר עליה ויאמר המלך הגם לכבוש
את־המלכה עמי בבית הדבר יצא מפי המלך ופני
המן חפו: ט ויאמר חרבונה אחד מן־הסריסים לפני
המלך גם הנה־העץ אשר־עשה המן למרדכי אשר
דבר־טוב על־המלך עמד בבית המן גבה חמשים
אמה ויאמר המלך תלהו עליו: י ויתלו את־המן על־
העץ אשר־הכין למרדכי וחמת המלך שככה: ס
ח א ביום ההוא נתן המלך אחשורוש לאסתר המלכה
את־בית המן צרר היהודיים ומרדכי בא
לפני המלך כי־הגידה אסתר מה הוא־לה: ב ויסר המלך
את־טבעתו אשר העביר מהמן ויתנה למרדכי ותשם

°יתיר י'ד אסתר

רש"י

המטה אשר אסתר עליה. דרכן היה לישב בסעודה על לדן על גבי המטות כמו שנאמר בראש הספר מטות זהב וכסף לבני המשתה: הגם לכבוש. לשון תימה הוא, לכבוש לאנוס בחזקה כמו (במדבר לב כב) ונכבשה הארץ: (ט) גם הנה העץ. גם רעה אחרת עשה שהכין העץ לתלות אוהבו של מלך שהציל את המלך ממות: (א) מה הוא לה. איך הוא קרוב לה:
להעביר

השאלות

ט מאין ידע הסריס מענין העץ, מדוע הזכיר אשר דבר טוב על המלך, ומה נ"מ אם עומד בבית המן או אינו עומד עתה, ואם גבוה חמשים אמה או לא:

א למה נתן בית המן לאסתר, ומהו הרבותא שמרדכי בא לפני המלך שאין בזה גדולה כ"כ כי כל אדם היה יכול לבא בעת הצורך ולמה קראו להמן פה צורר היהודים:

ב אשר העביר מהמן מיותר, ולמה מספר מה ששמה אסתר את מרדכי על בית המן:

פירוש

כנס המלכה בכללם, זאת שנית הכי **גם עמי בבית**, והלא גם החייב מיתה וברח לבית המלך לא יהרג, ואף כי להרוג המלכה בבית. **ופני המן חפו**, היה דרך הפרסיים לחפות פני מי שהמלך כועס עליו, למען ישוכך קצף המלך (ראב"ע):
(ט) **אחד מן הסריסים**, שהלכו לקרוא את המן אל המשתה ועי"כ ידעו מן העץ כנ"ל. **גם הנה העץ** ר"ל הנה יש עוד ראיות ברורות, שזה האיש המן אך רעת המלך הוא מבקש, כי הלא עשה עץ לתלות את מרדכי, ולא מצא בו שום עון רק **אשר דבר טוב על המלך**, שבעבור שמרדכי הציל נפש המלך ממות, זאת חרה להמן ורצה לתלותו, כי גם המן היה בקושרים על המלך, זאת שנית **עומד בבית המן גבוה וכו'**, הלא העץ עומד עדיין וגבוה חמשים אמה, למען יתראה לעיני הכל, וזה חרפה גדולה להמלך, שבעת שלבש מרדכי לבוש מלכות וקראו לפניו שהמלך חפץ ביקרו, בכל זאת העץ המוכן לו לתלותו עליו עומד בגלוי לעיני כל, לאמר שהאיש אשר המלך חפץ ביקרו מזומן להתלות, ואין לך מרד גדול מזה, ועפ"ז כדין פסק המלך וחרץ משפטו לתלותו. כן יאבדו כל אויבי ה':

(א) **ביום ההוא**, כבר היה החק מימי קדם, כי הרוגי מלך נכסיהם למלך, ואם היה המן נהרג בשביל שמרד במלך היה ביתו ונכסיו מגיעים אל המלך, אבל המלך רצה להראות שלא עבור מרדו במלך נתלה רק עבור מה שמרד בהמלכה ובעמה היהודים, לכן נתן בית המן לאסתר, כי אחר שנהרג בשבילה נכסיו מגיעים אל המלכה, ולכן קראו פה צורר היהודים לגלות הטעם שלכן נתן בית המן לאסתר יען והריגתו היה על שהיה צורר היהודים, **ומרדכי** נראה שתיכף גדלו המלך ונתן לו רשות לבא לפני המלך כל עת שירצה ובל יצטרך להמתין עד שיקרא לו ויושיט לו השרביט:

(ב) **ויסר**. המשנה היה נושא טבעת המלך מעת שנתן המלך הטבעת להמן, ומספר כי תיכף נתן הטבעת
למרדכי

אֶסְתֵּר אֶת־מָרְדֳּכַי עַל־בֵּית הָמָן׃ ס ג וַתּוֹסֶף אֶסְתֵּר
וַתְּדַבֵּר לִפְנֵי הַמֶּלֶךְ וַתִּפֹּל לִפְנֵי רַגְלָיו וַתֵּבְךְּ וַתִּתְחַנֶּן
לוֹ לְהַעֲבִיר אֶת־רָעַת הָמָן הָאֲגָגִי וְאֵת מַחֲשַׁבְתּוֹ אֲשֶׁר
חָשַׁב עַל־הַיְּהוּדִים׃ ד וַיּוֹשֶׁט הַמֶּלֶךְ לְאֶסְתֵּר אֵת שַׁרְבִט
הַזָּהָב וַתָּקָם אֶסְתֵּר וַתַּעֲמֹד לִפְנֵי הַמֶּלֶךְ׃ ה וַתֹּאמֶר אִם־
עַל־הַמֶּלֶךְ טוֹב וְאִם־מָצָאתִי חֵן לְפָנָיו וְכָשֵׁר הַדָּבָר לִפְנֵי
הַמֶּלֶךְ

רש"י

(ג) להעביר את רעת המן. שלא תתקיים עצתו הרעה:

כנס

השאלות

ג למה הוסיפה עתה לחנן יותר מאשר חננה קודם, ומה הכפל שכפל במלות שונות, ומה הכפל רעת המן ומחשבתו:

ה הכפל בדברי אסתר מבואר, מלות מחשבות המן מיותר:

פירוש

למרדכי מבלי ספק, ולא נתנה על ידו, רק מיד המן ליד מרדכי, ותשם אומר הנה שני דברים שבהם התהלל אותו רשע כבוד עשרו ואת אשר גדלו המלך, עתה כרגע השבו למרדכי הצדיק יכין רשע וצדיק ילבש עד גדולתו ויסר את טבעתו אשר העביר מהמן, ונגד עשרו ותשם את מרדכי על בית המן:

(ג) ותוסף אסתר, פי' המפרשים כי אסתר אחרי ראותה שנתן לה המלך ענינים אחרים ועל גוף הבקשה לא ענה לה מאומה, אז עלה מורא על ראשה, כי כבר התיאש המלך מאת לה שאלתה זאת, וע"כ רוצה לדחותה במתנות אחרות, כדרך מי שאינו רוצה למלאות שאלת אוהבו שמבטיח לו ענינים אחרים, כי אם היה רוצה למלאות שאלתה הלא היה צריך להבטיח לה תחלה על גוף בקשתה שזאת העיקר אולם שרצה יתן לה דברים אחרים, ולכן עתה דוקא שהר ורהב לבבה להפציר בתחנונים, והנה לא נמנעה מלעשות כל הפעולות אשר יסבבו שימלא המבקש את בקשתו, כי לפעמים ימלא את בקשתו ע"י שירבה דברים ומליצות להראות כי המבוקש ראוי להעשות מצד היושר והצדק, וע"ז ותדבר לפני המלך בדברי טעם ודעת, ולפעמים ימלאו שאלת השואל מצד שיעורר בכי ותחנונים וירחמו על השואל, וע"ז ותפול לפני רגליו ותבך ותתחנן לו להעביר את רעת המן. הנה הסגר בקשה שהמלך ישלח רצים לקחת את הספרים בחזרה ולבטל את הגזרה, כי אם ימתין עד זמן המוגבל, והמלך ירצה לשלוח ספרים אחרים חתומים שיונחו ג"כ עד זמן המוגבל, שיהיה כתוב בהם הפך הספרים הראשונים, כמו שעשה המלך אח"כ באמת, יראה מצד שני דברים, א) כי עד בוא הזמן המוגבל שיפתחו הספרים ויראו שבטל את הגזרה, בתוך כך יעברו על היהודים צרות רבות, וכל אותו הזמן יתעוללו בם מוניהם באשר כבר נתפרסם כי נמכרו להשמיד. וע"ז א' להעביר את רעת המן, הוא הרע שהוא בהווה עתה. ב) כי גם בבוא הזמן הלא בהספרים שלח המן הרבה להבאים ביד היהודים וגם בבוא ספרים אחרים, לא יאמינו לקול האות האחרון רק לקול האות הראשון, ועז"א ואת מחשבתו אשר חשב, גם כללה בדבריה שני טענות לעומת שידעה כי חק מלכי פרס שכתב אשר נכתב בשם המלך אין להשיב, עז"א פיה פתחה בחכמה, שאין להמלך לשים לבו על זאת, אם מצד המלך, אם מצד השרים, אם שהמלך בעצמו אין לו לחוש שעובר על דת המלוכה להשיב פקודתו, אחר שבאמת לא מאתו יצאו הדברים האלה, והמלך יודע האמת כי לא חשב כזאת על עם ה', רק זאת היתה מחשבת המן לא מחשבת המלך, ואם מצד השרים שאין להמלך להתירא שימרדו בו בני מלכותו אם יראה שמשנה דת המדינה להשיב את פקודת המלך, ע"ז טענה הלא הספרים עדיין חתומים ולא נפתחו, כמו שבארתי למעלה שהיו ספרים חתומים שלא נפתחו, ובהם היה כתוב מחשבת המן בפרטות להשמיד את כל היהודים, אבל בפתשגן שהיה גלוי לכל העמים לא נכתב תוכן מחשבתו רק שיהיו עתידים ולא נתבאר על מה ולמה, ולכן יעצה שישיב רק הספרים שבהם כתוב מחשבת המן שהם הספרים החתומים, שמצד הספרים האלה אין לו לשמירה אחר שהם רק מחשבת המן, שנשארו במחשבה ולא נתפרסמו עדיין לבני אדם, ואם ישיבם וישלח אחרים תמורתם לא יודע לאיש כי השיב פקודתו·

(ד) ויושט, הוא רשות שתקום ותדבר דבריה בפרטות:

(ה) אם על המלך טוב, ר"ל כי הממלא בקשת חבירו, יהיה או מפני המבקש או מפני המבוקש וכל אחד יהיה בא' משני פנים, אם מפני שהמבקש או המבוקש מצא חן בעיניו, או מפני שמצד להשיב

הַמֶּלֶךְ וְטוֹבָה אֲנִי בְּעֵינָיו יִכָּתֵב לְהָשִׁיב אֶת־הַסְּפָרִים
מַחֲשֶׁבֶת הָמָן בֶּן־הַמְּדָתָא הָאֲגָגִי אֲשֶׁר כָּתַב לְאַבֵּד
אֶת־הַיְּהוּדִים אֲשֶׁר בְּכָל־מְדִינוֹת הַמֶּלֶךְ׃ ו כִּי אֵיכָכָה
אוּכַל וְרָאִיתִי בָּרָעָה אֲשֶׁר־יִמְצָא אֶת־עַמִּי וְאֵיכָכָה אוּכַל
וְרָאִיתִי בְּאָבְדַן מוֹלַדְתִּי׃ ס ז וַיֹּאמֶר הַמֶּלֶךְ אֲחַשְׁוֵרֹשׁ
לְאֶסְתֵּר הַמַּלְכָּה וּלְמָרְדֳּכַי הַיְּהוּדִי הִנֵּה בֵית־הָמָן נָתַתִּי
לְאֶסְתֵּר וְאֹתוֹ תָּלוּ עַל־הָעֵץ עַל אֲשֶׁר־שָׁלַח יָדוֹ
בַּיְּהוּדִיִּים׃ ח וְאַתֶּם כִּתְבוּ עַל־הַיְּהוּדִים כַּטּוֹב בְּעֵינֵיכֶם
בְּשֵׁם הַמֶּלֶךְ וְחִתְמוּ בְּטַבַּעַת הַמֶּלֶךְ כִּי־כְתָב אֲשֶׁר־
נִכְתָּב בְּשֵׁם־הַמֶּלֶךְ וְנַחְתּוֹם בְּטַבַּעַת הַמֶּלֶךְ אֵין לְהָשִׁיב׃

°יתיר יו״ד

ויקראו

רש״י

(ז) הנה בית המן וגו'. ומעתה צ הכל רואים שאני חפץ בכם וכל מה שתאמרו יאמינו הכל שמאתי הוא לפיכך אין צריכין אתם להשיבם אלא כתבו ספרים אחרים כטוב בעיניכם: (ח) אין להשיב. אין נאה להשיבו ולעשות כזב

שפתי חכמים

צ דקשה ליה היא בקשה להפר מחשבות המן והוא השיב הנה

השאלות

י הכפל מבואר:
ז תשובת המלך הנה בית המן וכו' אין לו טעם ולא בזה יניח לבה הדואג מאבדן עמה:
ח בעצה הזאת נבוכו כל המפרשים ולא מצאו כל אנשי חיל ידיהם, אחר שכתב אשר נכתב בשם המלך אין להשיב, איך אמר כתבו כטוב בעיניכם, איך ישיבו את הספרים הראשונים הלא אין להשיב ואם לא ישיבו הלא כפשע בינם ובין המות:

פירוש

להשיג איזה תועלת או הנאה מן המבקש בשאלת שאלתו, או מן המבוקש עצמו בשיעשהו, והתחלה אמרה אם רצה למלאות שאלתה מצד שהיא או המבוקש עצמו מצא חן בעיניו, וז"ש אם על המלך טוב הוא שהמבוקש טוב ויפה בעיניו, ואם מצאתי חן לפניו הוא שהמבקש נושא חן, והוסיפה אופן השני אם רוצה למלאות שאלתה מצד שישיג הנאה ותועלת מן המבקש או המבוקש, ועז"א וכשר הדבר לפני המלך היינו שישיג תועלת מן הדבר בעצמו כי היושב על כסא עמים ימצא תועלת בשיעשה צדק ויושר, וטובה אני בעיניו הוא שמוצא תועלת ממנו, ובזה ימצא שאלתי מצדי לבל אמות בראותי צרת עמי, וכוונה בזה שצריך הוא למלאות שאלתה מצד ארבעת הפנים האלה יחד שכולם כאן נמצאו וכאן היו, יכתב להשיב, שפה פרטה עתה הנ"ל בפרטות שישלח המלך רצים לקחת את הספרים החתומים שבהם כתוב מחשבת המן בחזרה, כי השרים אין יודעים עדיין מה כתוב בהן, ולא יהיה בזה בזיון אל המלך:

(ו) כי איככה, נתנה טעם על שא"א לכתוב ספרים אחרים חתומים שיוגשו ג"כ ביד השרים עד בוא מועד, ויהיו כתוב בהן הפך הראשונים, כי בזה יש שני רעותות: א) כי איככה אוכל וראיתי ברעה אשר ימצא את עמי תיכף עד שיגיע הזמן המוגבל, כי בתוך הזמן הזה יהיו נכונים למשסה ולחרפות, ב) עקר הדבר כי בהגיע הזמן לא ישמעו לקול הספרים האחרונים, ואיככה אוכל וראיתי באבדן מולדתי, והם ממש הדברים שדברה בפסוק ג':

(ז-ח) הנה בית המן, ואתם כתבו. הנה המלך לא הסכים לעצה להשיב את הספרים החתומים בחזרה, כי כתב אשר נכתב בשם המלך אין להשיב, אולם יעץ להם עצה נכונה בהשכל ודעת, שישארו הספרים הראשונים ביד השרים, ובכל זאת ינוח לבם מכל פחד. והנה היה בענין זה שתי עצות: א) כי בכתבים הראשונים היה כתוב להשמיד להרוג ולאבד את כל היהודים, ובזה יש לבאר מלת היהודים לנושא המאמר להשמיד להרוג ולאבד את כל, ומי יהיה המשמיד, היהודים, הם יהיו המשמידים, ובזה חסר הפעול, כי לא פורש באגרת הראשונים את מי ישמידו, ואם יבארו האגרות האחרונות

שהוסיף

ט ויקראו ספרי־המלך בעת־ההיא בחדש השלישי
הוא־חדש סיון בשלושה ועשרים בו ויכתב ככל־אשר־
צוה מרדכי אל־היהודים ואל האחשדרפנים והפחות
ושרי המדינות אשר ׀ מהדו ועד־כוש שבע ועשרים
ומאה מדינה ומדינה ככתבה ועם ועם כלשנו
ואל

רש"י

כתב המלך בזיוף: (ט) ככתבה. באותיות שלה:
כלשונו

פירוש

שהוסיף בהם מלת עם ומדינה הצרים אותם להשמיד להרוג את כל חיל עם ומדינה הצרים, ומי ישמיד, היהודים ישמידו את כל חיל עם ומדינה, ומעתה שהאגרות האחרונות לא יבינו ויבטלו את הראשונות רק יאמרו אותם, וכל שהכתב השני איננו מגרע מן הראשון רק מוסיף בו דברים לבארו אין זה נקרא משיב דברי המלך, וזאת כוונה אסתר בעצת המלך, ועז"א ואתם כתבו על היהודים כטוב בעיניכם, ר"ל על מות היהודים תוכלו לכתוב הבאור כטוב בעיניכם, לבארו שהיהודים יהיו המשמידים לא הנשמדים:

השאלות

ט למה המתין עד כ"ג סיון:

ואת שנית כי הגם שזה רק באור רחוק, ובפרט אחר שהאגרות הראשונות נכתבו בכתב לשונות הלא ימלאו הרבה לשונות שלא יסבלו הבאור הזה, ומ"מ השיב עצתו להסיר כל התשובות, כי זאת מבואר שאם יאמר האומר ראובן יתן מעות לשמעון, ראובן לא יתן מעות לשמעון, ראובן יכה את שמעון, ראובן לא יכה את שמעון, הם משפטים סותרים אחד את חבירו, אבל אם יאמר ראובן יתן מעות לשמעון ושמעון יתן מעות לראובן, ראובן יכה את שמעון ושמעון יכה את ראובן, אין זה בגדר הסתירה, כי שניהם יוכלו להתקיים, וכן אם היה האחשורוש חוזר וכתב שהעמים לא ישמידו את היהודים היו האגרות האחרונים סותרים את הראשונות, אבל אחר שכתב שנית שהיהודים ישמידו את הצרים אותם, אין זה סתירה כי שניהם יוכלו להתקיים, שנתן לשתי הכתות רשות להלחם זה בזה, אולם הלא בזה עדיין היהודים בסכנה, דאחר שיש גם לצורריהם רשות להרוג בם, ומי יודע מי מהם תגבר ידו, ע"ז הקדים לאמר הנה בית המן נתתי לאסתר וכו', ר"ל הנה בזאת האגרות האחרונות יש שני תשובות: א) מן העמים שקבלו כתב הפתשגן הגלוי להיות עתידים ליום הזה, ושמעו קול השמועה בעל פה, כי הגזרה היא על היהודים, ואף שיגיעו אגרות להפך הלא ילחמו עם היהודים וירעו להם, אך זה תקן בקל דאחר שהפתשגן הגלוי לכל העמים לא נכתב בו רק להיות עתידים ליום הזה ולא נכתב לא מי יהיה עתיד, ולא על מה יהיו עתידים, ועתה בפתשגן השני נכתב בבאור, (א) מי יהיו עתידים, להיות היהודים עתידים, ב) על מה יהיו עתידים, להנקם מאויביהם, ממילא הפתשגן השני הוא רק באור להראשון, ואין להם להרים ידם ורגלם לעשות רע ליהודים, כי גם הפקודה הראשונה מפורשת ע"י השניה, שאדרבה היהודים ינקמו מאויביהם, ובזה תקן השטות אסתר שיראה שעד שיגיע יום המוגבל יעשו רע עם יהודים, כמ"ש איככה אוכל וראיתי ברעה אשר ימצא את עמי, והתשובה השני שיש להם לירוא מן הסכנה שיעבור עליהם בהגיע היום המוגבל שאז יפתחו האגרות הראשונות והאחרונות החתומים, ויראו מבואר בהאגרות הראשונות שניתן דת לאבד היהודים, ואף שבאחרונות נכתב שרשות גם ליהודים להנקם מאויביהם, הלא יש חשש, אם מצד הצוררים, שיגבר ידם על היהודים, אם מצד השרים פן יעזרו להצוררים, אחר שרשות בידם לעשות כאחד משתי האגרות, ע"ז הקדים לאמר, הנה מה שבית המן נתתי לאסתר ומה שתלו אותו על העץ היה מפני ששלח ידו ביהודים, וזה דבר ידוע ומפורסם, כי מטעם זה נתתי ביתו לאסתר על שמרד במה שרצה לאבד עמה ומולדתה, וממילא ככל ידעו השרים כי האגרות הראשונות נכתבו נגד רצון המלך, ובודאי בבוא יום המוגבל ויפתחו שתי האגרות יסתירו את האגרות הראשונות מפני האחרונות, כי יראו לנפשם בל יגיע להם כמו שהגיע להמן, ובודאי יעזרו אל היהודים, והעמים לא ידעו כלל מה היה כתוב באגרות הראשונות, כי השרים יסתירו אותם, ובזה אין שום חשש וסכנה:

(ט) **ויקראו**, פי' מהרא"ל שהמתין עד כ"ג סיון מפני שרצה שהרצים בעצמם שהובילו אגרות המן יובילו גם אגרות האלה ובזה יאמינו את דבריהם, והם לא שבו עד כ"ג סיון, ובעם נכון הוא. והנה מרדכי הוסיף לכתוב גם אל היהודים, ובזה נתן תוקף אל האגרות האחרונות כי השרים אשר הגיעו אליהם שני הספרים, ממילא נתן להם רשות לעשות כמו שירצו, כי שתי הפקודות תלוין בהקפס, אבל אחר שהגיעו

הספרים

וְאֶל־הַיְּהוּדִים כִּכְתָבָם וְכִלְשׁוֹנָם׃ י וַיִּכְתֹּב בְּשֵׁם הַמֶּלֶךְ
אֲחַשְׁוֵרֹשׁ וַיַּחְתֹּם בְּטַבַּעַת הַמֶּלֶךְ וַיִּשְׁלַח סְפָרִים בְּיַד
הָרָצִים בַּסּוּסִים רֹכְבֵי הָרֶכֶשׁ הָאֲחַשְׁתְּרָנִים בְּנֵי הָרַמָּכִים׃
יא אֲשֶׁר נָתַן הַמֶּלֶךְ לַיְּהוּדִים ׀ אֲשֶׁר בְּכָל־עִיר־וָעִיר
לְהִקָּהֵל וְלַעֲמֹד עַל־נַפְשָׁם לְהַשְׁמִיד לַהֲרֹג וּלְאַבֵּד אֶת־
כָּל־חֵיל עַם וּמְדִינָה הַצָּרִים אֹתָם טַף וְנָשִׁים וּשְׁלָלָם
לָבוֹז׃ יב בְּיוֹם אֶחָד בְּכָל־מְדִינוֹת הַמֶּלֶךְ אֲחַשְׁוֵרוֹשׁ
בִּשְׁלוֹשָׁה עָשָׂר לְחֹדֶשׁ שְׁנֵים־עָשָׂר הוּא־חֹדֶשׁ אֲדָר׃
יג פַּתְשֶׁגֶן הַכְּתָב לְהִנָּתֵן דָּת בְּכָל־מְדִינָה וּמְדִינָה גָּלוּי
לְכָל־הָעַמִּים וְלִהְיוֹת הַיְּהוּדִיִּים עֲתִידִים לַיּוֹם הַזֶּה לְהִנָּקֵם
מֵאֹיְבֵיהֶם׃ יד הָרָצִים רֹכְבֵי הָרֶכֶשׁ הָאֲחַשְׁתְּרָנִים יָצְאוּ
מְבֹהָלִים וּדְחוּפִים בִּדְבַר הַמֶּלֶךְ וְהַדָּת נִתְּנָה בְּשׁוּשַׁן

הבירה

°בס״ס כ״י ולהרג בוי״ו : °יתיר י״ד °עתודים כתיב

רש"י

כלשונו. הוא הדבור : (י) ביד הרצים. רוכבי סוסים שנוה להם לרוץ : האחשתרנים. מין גמלים הממהרים לרוץ : (יא) ושללם לבוז. כאשר נכתב בראשונות, והם בבזה לא שלחו את ידם שהראו לכל שלא נעשה לשם ממון : (יג) פתשגן. אגרת מפורש : (יד) מבהלים. ממהרים אותם לעשות מהרה לפי שלא

השאלות

י למה שלח רצים בסוסים, והמן שלח רגלים :

יא המן אמר להשמיד ביום אחד ושללם לבוז, משמע הבזה תהיה אח"כ, ומרדכי אמר ושללם לבוז ביום אחד שגם הבזה תהיה בו ביום :

יב מרדכי אמר בכל מדינות, והמן לא הזכיר זה :

יד למה הוסיף פה מבוהלים :

פירוש

הספרים האחרונים אל אנשים אשר לא הגיעו אליהם הספרים הראשונים, גלה דעתו שלא נתן ברירה לעשות כמו שירצו, כי האנשים שלא הגיעו הספרים הראשונים אין בידם רק הפקודה השנית ובזה ממילא הפקודה השנית קיימת ומבטלת הראשונה :

(י) והנה שלחם בסוסים, או מפני שהיו עיפים מן הדרך, או מפני כי בתוך כך היו היהודים בצרה גדולה ומהר לעשות מצר ומציר :

(יא) והנה מה שהמן אמר בפקודתו להשמיד להרוג ביום אחד ושללם לבוז, ומרדכי אמר ושללם לבוז ביום אחד, כי באמת מרדכי רצה שהיהודים לא יקחו מן השלל, כי לא לתפארת יהיו להם שיראו כאלו עקר מגמתם היה לשלול שלל ולבוז בז, אבל אחר שהאגרות האחרונות נכתבו באופן שיהיו באור והוספה אל מה שחסר בראשונות, בהכרח לא יכלו לגרוע דבר ממה שכתוב בראשונות רק להוסיף עליהם, כי כתב המלך אין להשיב, וע"כ הוכרח לכתוב באגרותיו ושללם לבוז בל יהו מגרעת בפקודת המלך, והתחכם בזה ששנה לכתוב שההשמדה והבזה תהיה ביום אחד, וזאת ידע שאחר שלא נתן להם רשות לשלול רק ביום אחד יום י"ג שהוא יום המיוחד אל הנקמה בשונאיהם, בודאי לא יעזבו ישראל את העקר לעשות נקמה באויבי ה' בשביל השלל, ובזה יבינו שהוזהרו מקחת מן השלל מאומה, אבל המן אם היה פוקד שהשלל יהיה רק ביום אחד ידע שיעטו כולם אל השלל ולא ישמידו, ולכן עשה שביום י"ג לא יבוזו רק יהרגו והשלל יהיה אח"כ :

(יב) וגם מרדכי, הודיע שההשמדה והבזה תהיה בכללות מדינות המלך, והמן העלים זה, כי המן חשש בהודע להשרים שהיא גזרה כוללת תחוס עינם מלאבד אומה שלימה, ולכן רצה שכ"א יסבור שרק במדינתו היא הגזרה. ומרדכי רצה בהפך שידעו כי נהפך הפור ליהודים לששון ושמחה בכל המדינות :

(יג) פתשגן כבר מבואר למעלה :

(יד) הרצים רוכבי הרכש האחשתרנים יצאו מבוהלים, כי לא ידעו מדוע נבהלים פעם שנית, וגם

מרדכי

הַבִּירָה׃ ס טו וּמָרְדֳּכַי יָצָא ׀ מִלִּפְנֵי הַמֶּלֶךְ בִּלְבוּשׁ
מַלְכוּת תְּכֵלֶת וָחוּר וַעֲטֶרֶת זָהָב גְּדוֹלָה וְתַכְרִיךְ בּוּץ
וְאַרְגָּמָן וְהָעִיר שׁוּשָׁן צָהֲלָה וְשָׂמֵחָה׃ טז לַיְּהוּדִים הָיְתָה
אוֹרָה וְשִׂמְחָה וְשָׂשֹׂן וִיקָר׃ יז וּבְכָל־מְדִינָה וּמְדִינָה
וּבְכָל־עִיר וָעִיר מְקוֹם אֲשֶׁר דְּבַר־הַמֶּלֶךְ וְדָתוֹ מַגִּיעַ
שִׂמְחָה וְשָׂשׂוֹן לַיְּהוּדִים מִשְׁתֶּה וְיוֹם טוֹב וְרַבִּים מֵעַמֵּי
הָאָרֶץ מִתְיַהֲדִים כִּי־נָפַל פַּחַד־הַיְּהוּדִים עֲלֵיהֶם׃
ט א וּבִשְׁנֵים עָשָׂר חֹדֶשׁ הוּא־חֹדֶשׁ אֲדָר בִּשְׁלוֹשָׁה
עָשָׂר יוֹם בּוֹ אֲשֶׁר הִגִּיעַ דְּבַר־הַמֶּלֶךְ
וְדָתוֹ לְהֵעָשׂוֹת בַּיּוֹם אֲשֶׁר שִׂבְּרוּ אֹיְבֵי הַיְּהוּדִים לִשְׁלוֹט
בָּהֶם וְנַהֲפוֹךְ הוּא אֲשֶׁר יִשְׁלְטוּ הַיְּהוּדִים הֵמָּה בְּשֹׂנְאֵיהֶם׃

נקהלו

רש"י

שלא היה להם פנאי שהיה להם להקדים רצים בהסונים להעבירם: (טו) ותכריך בוץ. מעטפה בוץ טלית העשוי להתעטף: (יז) מתיהדים. מתגיירים:

ועמי

פירוש

מרדכי התהכם שלא לתת הדת בשושן עד לאחר הרצים, שאותו הפעם שהשמש גם המן פן בהודע זאת לאויבי היהודים יעמידו מליצים אל המלך לשנות את הדת:
(טו) וספר שמרדכי יצא להודיע לדקת מרדכי שלא קבל על עצמו שום גדולה עד שנכון לבו במוה שהיתה אורה ותשועה לאחיו האומללים שאז יצא בלבוש מלכות לא קודם, וספר שהעיר שושן שמחה, לקיים דברי החכם (משלי כט) ברבות צדיקים ישמח העם, שגם העמים כולם שמחו ברבות מרדכי הצדיק:
(טז) וביחוד ליהודים היתה שמחה כפולה וששון בגלוי וכבוד גדול:
(יז) ואמר פה ובכל עיר ועיר, כי פתשגן הכתב היו מבואר על מה יהיו עתידים, משא"כ אצל המן לא נודע מהו, רק מפי השמועה ולא נודע בערים הפרסיים כנ"ל:
ט (א) ובשנים, עד עתה ספר איך ניצלו ישראל מן הרעה עד בוא זמן המוגבל שלא האגרות האחרונות היו נכונים למשסה וע"י האגרות האחרונות נפל פחדם על כל העמים, כי עד בוא יום המוגבל לא היה שום פקודה מהעדת אליהם, כי פתשגן הגלוי שנכתב על ידי המן לא אמר בו שום דבר, ופתשגן הגלוי של מרדכי אמר בבאור שיד היהודים רמה, ועתה מספר איך היו ענינים בעת הגיע תור המוגבל שאז נפתחו שני ספרים החתומים, ועז"א אשר הגיע דבר המלך ודתו להעשות, שאז נגלה גם הדת שהוא הכתוב בהספרים החתומים, וזאת שנית שהיה הזמן להעשות, שלא היה אפשר להיות באותו היום בשב ואל תעשה, שיתפשרו שני הצדדים ולא יתרונו לא זה בזה ולא זה בזה, כי דבר המלך היה מוכרח להעשות ללחום ולהלחם. אבל כבר אמה מזל אותו יום לתשועת ישראל ונראה בו ההשגחה הנפלאה הדבקה בעם קדושו, כי ע"פ המזל היה כוכב ישראל אז בתכלית השפלות, ונגד זה כוכב עמלק בתכלית המעלה, ולכן בחר המן באותו יום, ועז"א ביום אשר שברו אויבי היהודים לשלוט בהם שהיום היה גורם אשר שבר לתפוס ממשלה על ישראל ועתה הראה ה' מה יד ההשגחה עשה, כי לא לבד שלא התגברו הצוררים עליהם, נהפך הדבר מהפך אל הפך שירדו הצוררים מתכלית גדולתם אל עמקי בור, וישראל עלו משאול התחית אל רום ההצלחה, וזה גם האחד הכולל שעז"א ונהפוך הוא שנתהפך הדבר מהפך אל הפך, וגם השני, שלא היה הדבר בדרך הטבע, שכבר יקרה שמי שמושל בתכלית השפלות

השאלות

טו והעיר שושן משמע ת"ץ היהודים:
יז אצל המן לא כתיב בכל עיר ועיר ופה הוסיף בכל עיר ועיר:
א מלת המה מיותר:

בשפלות

ב נִקְהֲלוּ הַיְּהוּדִים בְּעָרֵיהֶם בְּכָל־מְדִינוֹת הַמֶּלֶךְ
אֲחַשְׁוֵרוֹשׁ לִשְׁלֹחַ יָד בִּמְבַקְשֵׁי רָעָתָם וְאִישׁ לֹא־עָמַד
בִּפְנֵיהֶם כִּי־נָפַל פַּחְדָּם עַל־כָּל־הָעַמִּים׃ ג וְכָל־שָׂרֵי
הַמְּדִינוֹת וְהָאֲחַשְׁדַּרְפְּנִים וְהַפַּחוֹת וְעֹשֵׂי הַמְּלָאכָה אֲשֶׁר
לַמֶּלֶךְ מְנַשְּׂאִים אֶת־הַיְּהוּדִים כִּי־נָפַל פַּחַד־מָרְדֳּכַי
עֲלֵיהֶם׃ ד כִּי־גָדוֹל מָרְדֳּכַי בְּבֵית הַמֶּלֶךְ וְשָׁמְעוֹ הוֹלֵךְ
בְּכָל־הַמְּדִינוֹת כִּי־הָאִישׁ מָרְדֳּכַי הוֹלֵךְ וְגָדוֹל׃ ה וַיַּכּוּ
הַיְּהוּדִים בְּכָל־אֹיְבֵיהֶם מַכַּת־חֶרֶב וְהֶרֶג וְאַבְדָן וַיַּעֲשׂוּ
בְשֹׂנְאֵיהֶם כִּרְצוֹנָם׃ ו וּבְשׁוּשַׁן הַבִּירָה הָרְגוּ הַיְּהוּדִים
וְאַבֵּד חֲמֵשׁ מֵאוֹת °אִישׁ׃ ז וְאֵת ׀ פַּרְשַׁנְדָּתָא וְאֵת ׀

°איש בראש דף ועשרת בניו ואין לכותבם כעין שירת האזינו וכדף אחד לבדו. °ת׳ זעירא   דלפון

רש"י

(ג) ועושי המלאכה. אותם שהיו ממונים ק לעשות צרכי

שפתי חכמים

כנה בית המן ואין זה תשובה לשאלתם. לכך פירש ומפרש בכל רואים וכו': ק דק"ל וכי עושי מלאכה לבד הם למלך בכתב ועושי המלאכה אשר למלך והלא כל העמים כולם הם למלך. לכ"פ אותם שהם ממונים לעשות צרכי המלך כלומר אשר

השאלות

ב אשר יל"ד בפסוקים אלה תמצא בפסוק ט"ז, מדוע אצל העמים אומר שנפל פחד היהודים עליהם ואצל השרים אומר שנפל פחד מרדכי עליהם:

ד מהו כי האיש מרדכי הולך וגדול:

ה מה ההבדל בין אויביהם לשונאיהם, ועיין לקמן פט"ז:

פירוש

השפלות יתגבר אם יעזרהו ויתחבר עמו איש שמזלו מצליח והצלחה בותפו מכריע רוע מזלו לטוב על ידי שהוא מתוסף עמו, אבל פה לא היה זה רק אשר ישלטו היהודים המה בעצמם בלי שום עזר וסיוע:

(ב) נקהלו, פה דבר איך היו ענינם בהערים הגדולות בצורות שבם נמצאו השרים והסגנים וחיל צבא המלך והם היו למגן בעדם ועוזרים בפועל באופן שצורריהם בתוכן מקרוב אליהם או לעמוד כנגדם, כי נעזרו משרי המלך וחיל הצבא, ח"ש שנקהלו בעריהם שהם הערים הגדולות אשר במדינות המלך אבל איש לא עמד בפניהם, והנה היה הבדל בין העמים ובין השרים, כי העמים שלא ידעו מן הספרים החתומים לא נודע להם כלל אם יש רשות מן המלך ללחום ביהודים ולהרגם ג"כ ושגם האגרות הראשונות לא נבטלו, והם פחדו מן היהודים בעצמם אחר שידם רמה מצד פקודת המלך, אבל,

(ג) וכל שרי המדינות, שהם ידעו מן הספרים החתומים, והם לא פחדו מן היהודים כלל כי ידעו שגם הם נתונים ליהרג ויכולים לשלוח יד גם מצד הפקודה הראשונה, היו יכולים לעמוד לעזרת צוררי היהודים ולאחוז הספרים הראשונים, או עכ"פ לעמוד מנגד ולא לעזור לשום אחד מן הכתות, אבל הם לא כן עשו רק היו מנשאים את היהודים לעזרם נגד צורריהם והעלימו האגרות הראשונות, וזה לא היה מפחד היהודים, רק כי נפל פחד מרדכי עליהם, וירא שמרדכי ינקום בם:

(ד) כי גדול, יש שרים המיוחדים להנהגת בית המלך, ויש המיוחדים להנהגת המדינה, ויש המיוחדים ללחום עם אויבי המלך מבחוץ ולכבוש מדינות, והשרים האלה אם מצליחים הם הולכים וגדולים תמיד כל עוד שירבו לכבוש מדינות ולעשות חיל, אומר כי מרדכי היה כולל שלשה המשרות האלה. א) כי היה גדול בבית המלך עצמו ורב ביתו, ב) ושמעו הולך בכל המדינות. כי היה משנה למלך להנהיג המדינות, ג) כי האיש מרדכי הולך וגדול, ע"י שהכניע מדינות רבות תחת מלכות אחשורוש כמ"ש (בסימן י' פסוק א'):

(ה) ויכו, הנה ודאי לא היה הרשות נתונה ליהודים להרוג את כל מי שירצו, כי לא היה כתוב בהספרים רק להנקם מצורריהם, ולזה כי עתה איש לא עמד בפניהם בהכרכים הגדולים, לא היו הורגים רק האויבים

דלפון ואת | אספתא: ח ואת | פורתא ואת | אדליא
ואת | ארידתא: ט ואת | פרמשתא ואת ארסי ואת |
ארידי ואת | ויזתא: י עשרת בני המן בן־המדתא
צרר היהודים הרגו ובבזה לא שלחו את־ידם: יא ביום
ההוא בא מספר ההרוגים בשושן הבירה לפני המלך:
יב ויאמר המלך לאסתר המלכה בשושן הבירה הרגו
היהודים ואבד חמש מאות איש ואת עשרת בני־המן
בשאר מדינות המלך מה עשו ומה־שאלתך וינתן לך
ומה־בקשתך עוד ותעש: יג ותאמר אסתר אם־על־
המלך טוב ינתן גם־מחר ליהודים אשר בשושן לעשות
כדת היום ואת עשרת בני־המן יתלו על־העץ:

ש"ן זעירא ת' רבתי ז' זעירא

ויאמר

רש"י

צררי המלך: (י) עשרת בני המן. ראיתי בסדר עולם אלו עשרה שכתבו שטנה על יהודה וירושלים כמש"כ בספר עזרא (עזרא ד) ובמלכות אחשורוש בתחלת מלכותו כתבו שטנה על יושבי יהודה וירושלים ומה היא השטנה לבטל העולים מן הגולה בימי כורש שהתחילו לבנות את הבית והלשינו עליהם הכותים והחדילום וכשמת כורש ומלך אחשורוש והתנשא המן דאג שלא יעסקו אותן שבירושלים בבנין ושלחו בשם אחשורוש לשרי עבר הנהר לבטלן: ובבזה לא שלחו את ידם. שלא יתן המלך עין צרה בממון: (יג) ואת.

עשרת

פירוש

האויבים שאיבתם אל היהודים היה מפורסם שהיו מזימים להרע להם, אבל לא את השונאים (כי ההבדל בין אויב ושונא שהאויב איבתו גלויה, והשונא אין שנאתו גלויה) רק ויעשו בשונאיהם כרצונם, שהיו יכולים לענות אותם ולהשפילם:

(יא) ביום ההוא, אחר שלא היה להם רשות להרוג רק את אויביהם אשר היה איבתם גלוי להרע עמהם, כנ"ל, ממילא לפי רוב ההרוגים שהרגו נדע כי רבו צורריהם הקמים עליהם, וע"כ הביאו תיכף מספר ההרוגים לפני המלך, להראות איך רבו הצוררים הקמים עליהם עד שגם שאחר פקודת המלך מ"מ נמצא עדיין חמש מאות איש שהרימו ראש נגד ישראל והרגנו:

(יב) ויאמר המלך, מזה ראה אחשורוש איך רבו צוררי היהודים ואיך צריך הוא להרבות השתדלות להצילם, וז"ש אל אסתר אם בשושן הבירה שהיא עיר המלוכה ואימת המלכות עליהם מ"מ רבו צוררי היהודים כ"כ עד שהרגו ת"ק איש, מי יודע בשאר מדינות המלך מה עשו, ואם גם שם הגליתו נגד הצוררים הרבים האלה, כי שם בודאי קמו עליהם ביותר שאת אחר שאין פחד המלך עליהם, ומה שאלתך לעשות עוד להצלת היהודים להצילם מן הסכנה המרחפת על ראשם וינתן לך:

(יג) ותאמר אסתר, עפ"ז מצאה אסתר מקום לבקש מהמלך, והיתה עצתה שיהרגו בשושן גם מחר, כי בזה תפול אימה ופחד על צוררי היהודים, אם יראו שעדיין יד המלך נטויה עליהם. אמנם לפי דעתי היה בקשתה על שושן העיר לא שושן הבירה, כי שושן נחלקת לשני חלקים, מקום הבירה ששם ישב המלך והשרים, והיא היתה נקראת שושן הבירה, והעיר בפ"ע היתה נקראת שושן סתם, וביום י"ג הרגו בשושן

הבירה

השאלות

יב אם המלך התרעם על שהרבו מספר ההרוגים, מדוע אמר לאסתר שתבקש עוד, הלנצח תאכל חרב, וגם גזרתו זאת ליתן רשות ליהודים להרוג באנשי מדינתו סכלות מבוארת ולא נשמע כזאת:

יג ואיך מלאה אסתר את לבבה אחרי הרגישה תלונת המלך לבקש לעשות גם יום מחר יום הרג רב. מדוע בכל המגלה קראה שושן הבירה ופה בספור מה שהרגו ביום ט"ו קראה שושן סתם:

יד וַיֹּאמֶר הַמֶּלֶךְ לְהֵעָשׂוֹת כֵּן וַתִּנָּתֵן דָּת בְּשׁוּשָׁן וְאֵת
עֲשֶׂרֶת בְּנֵי־הָמָן תָּלוּ׃ טו וַיִּקָּהֲלוּ הַיְּהוּדִיִּים אֲשֶׁר־בְּשׁוּשָׁן
גַּם בְּיוֹם אַרְבָּעָה עָשָׂר לְחֹדֶשׁ אֲדָר וַיַּהַרְגוּ בְשׁוּשָׁן
שְׁלֹשׁ מֵאוֹת אִישׁ וּבַבִּזָּה לֹא שָׁלְחוּ אֶת־יָדָם׃ טז וּשְׁאָר
הַיְּהוּדִים אֲשֶׁר בִּמְדִינוֹת הַמֶּלֶךְ נִקְהֲלוּ ׀ וְעָמֹד עַל־נַפְשָׁם
וְנוֹחַ מֵאֹיְבֵיהֶם וְהָרוֹג בְּשֹׂנְאֵיהֶם חֲמִשָּׁה וְשִׁבְעִים אָלֶף
וּבַבִּזָּה לֹא שָׁלְחוּ אֶת־יָדָם׃ יז בְּיוֹם־שְׁלוֹשָׁה עָשָׂר לְחֹדֶשׁ
אֲדָר וְנוֹחַ בְּאַרְבָּעָה עָשָׂר בּוֹ וְעָשֹׂה אֹתוֹ יוֹם מִשְׁתֶּה
וְשִׂמְחָה׃ יח וְהַיְּהוּדִיִּים אֲשֶׁר־בְּשׁוּשָׁן נִקְהֲלוּ בִּשְׁלוֹשָׁה
עָשָׂר בּוֹ וּבְאַרְבָּעָה עָשָׂר בּוֹ וְנוֹחַ בַּחֲמִשָּׁה עָשָׂר בּוֹ
וְעָשֹׂה אֹתוֹ יוֹם מִשְׁתֶּה וְשִׂמְחָה׃ יט עַל־כֵּן הַיְּהוּדִים
הַפְּרָזִים הַיֹּשְׁבִים בְּעָרֵי הַפְּרָזוֹת עֹשִׂים אֵת יוֹם אַרְבָּעָה
עָשָׂר לְחֹדֶשׁ אֲדָר שִׂמְחָה וּמִשְׁתֶּה וְיוֹם טוֹב וּמִשְׁלוֹחַ

מנות

ʼיתיר יו"ד °הפרוזים כתיב

רש"י

עשרת בני המן יתלו על העץ. אותן שנהרגו:
(יד) ותנתן דת. נגזר חוק מאת המלך:
(יט) הפרזים. שאינם יושבים בערי חומה בארבעה עשר ומוקפין חומה בט"ו כשושן והיקף ר זה צריך

שפתי חכמים

אשר למלך שב על המלאכה לא על עושי המלאכה: ר פי' מדקאמר פרזים בי"ד ש"מ מוקפין אינם בי"ד ומדלא רמז לך בכתוב אימת הוה ואשכחן דשושן עשו בט"ו מסתברא שאותו היום שייך למוקפים וזהו שאמר כשושן, וכדי שלא הבין במה שכתוב כשושן

השאלות

טז פסוק זה כולו מיותר אחר שכבר הזכיר בפסוק ב' ג' ה' איך הרגו היהודים ואבדו צורריהם, גם סותר לפסוק ב' ששם אמר כי איש לא עמד בפניהם, ופה אמר שנקהלו ועמוד על נפשם משמע שלחמו. מדוע פה אמר ונוח מאויביהם והרוג בשונאיהם, ולמעלה פ"ה אמר שהכו באויביהם ועשו בשונאיהם כרצונם:
יט בפסוק הזה נראה שרק הפרזים קבלו עליהם לעשות משתה ושמחה ולא המוקפים ולמה, ולמה תחלה לא קבלו עליהם רק יום י"ד ומרדכי שלח שיעשו י"ד וט"ו. הם קבלו עליהם יו"ט ומרדכי לא גזר שיעשו יו"ט:

פירוש

הבירה, ובקשה אסתר שיתן רשות להרוג ביום י"ד האויבים שנשארו בשושן העיר, גם לתלות עשרת בני המן להפיל אימה ופחד, כדי שלא יוסיפו להזיד על ישראל:
(טז) והנה בפסוק ג' דבר מן הערים המוקפים חומה, ששם היה מושב השרים ושם עמדו חיל המלך והיו למגן בעד היהודים, ושם איש לא עמד בפניהם, ולא הוצרכו לעמוד על נפשם ולהלחם, אבל פה מספר איך היו ענינם בהפרזים, כי בערים הפרזות הקטנים ובהכפרים ששם לא היו לא השרים אשר נשאו את היהודים ולא חיל המלך, ושם באמת הרימו אויביהם יד נלחם בם, ולכן ספר כי שאר היהודים אשר במדינות המלך, שהם אותם שאינם יושבים בערים המוקפים נקהלו ועמוד על נפשם ולחמו בחרבם וכלי מלחמה עד שנחו מאויביהם, ונגבר ידם עליהם, וע"כ ספר כי הם הרגו בשונאיהם כי הם כללו ההריגה לכל זרע עמלק אחר שכלתה המלחמה, משא"כ בהמוקפים ספר שעשו בשונאיהם כרצונם ולא הרגום, אחר שלא היה מלחמה ביניהם:
(יט) על כן היהודים הפרזים, מבואר כי בשנה הראשונה לא קבלו עליהם לעשות משתה ושמחה רק הפרזים, לא המוקפים, והטעם בזה כי הספרים החתומים שנשלחו מאת המן להשמיד את היהודים
לא

מְנ֖וֹת אִ֥ישׁ לְרֵעֵֽהוּ׃ כ וַיִּכְתֹּ֣ב מָרְדֳּכַ֔י אֶת־הַדְּבָרִ֖ים הָאֵ֑לֶּה
וַיִּשְׁלַ֨ח סְפָרִ֜ים אֶל־כָּל־הַיְּהוּדִ֗ים אֲשֶׁר֙ בְּכָל־מְדִינוֹת֙
הַמֶּ֣לֶךְ אֲחַשְׁוֵר֔וֹשׁ הַקְּרוֹבִ֖ים וְהָרְחוֹקִֽים׃ כא לְקַיֵּם֙ עֲלֵיהֶ֔ם
לִהְי֣וֹת עֹשִׂ֗ים אֵ֣ת י֤וֹם אַרְבָּעָה֙ עָשָׂר֙ לְחֹ֣דֶשׁ אֲדָ֔ר וְאֵ֛ת

יום

רש"י

שהיה מימות יהושע בן נון כך דרשו ולמדו רבותינו: ומשלוח. שם דבר כמו מִשְׁמַר מִשְׁמָע לפיכך השי"ן נקודה רפי: (כ) ויכתב מרדכי. היא המגילה הזאת כמות

פירוש

לא נתפרסמו כי השרים העלימו אותם כנ"ל, ולא נודע לאיש כלל כי היה רשות גם לאויבי היהודים להרוג ביהודים, והפשו היהודים אחת משתי אלה, או שהקול הראשון שנשמע שנתן דת להשמיד היהודים היה שקר לגמרי, ולא יצאו כלל מן המלך רק מהמן, או שהיה אמת רק שהמלך השיב את הדת הראשון ובטלו לגמרי ונתן דת אחר, עכ"פ לא היה נס מיוחד ביום י"ד אדר, אחר שמצד פקודת המלך ישלטו המה בשונאיהם, וגם לא היו בהסכנה מצד שהעמים בעצמם יפרצו בם פרץ, אחר שבערים המוקפים עמדו חיל המלך לעזרתם וע"כ לא עשו אותם לימי משתה, רק היהודים הפרזים שהם היו בסכנה מצד שפרצו אויביהם להלחם בם וחיל המלך לא היה שם והיו בסכנה, ע"כ רק הפרזים קבלו אותם לימי משתה ושמחה, וע"כ קבלו עליהם לעשותם גם יו"ט, כי באמת כלל ישראל אסור להם לקבל עליהם ימים טובים חדשים ולאסרם בעשיית מלאכה שעוברים על בל תוסיף, אבל אחר שרק הפרזים קבלוהו נדונים כיחידים, שיכולים לקבל יו"ט על עצמם:

(כ) ויכתוב, אחר שראה מרדכי שהמוקפים לא קבלו עליהם ימי הפורים יען שלא ידעו תקפו של הנס, שגם הם היו באמת באותו היום בסכנה, כי פקודת המן עדיין לא נתבטלה והיתה עדיין בתקפה רק שהיה הנס שנפל פחד מרדכי על השרים והעלימו את האגרות הראשונות, לכן הוכרח לכתוב אליהם כל הדברים באריכה, והם הדברים שיבוארו בפסוק כ"ד כ"ה, וספר להם שהאגרות הראשונות לא נתבטלו, וגם הם היו בסכנה, והודיע הדברים האלה אל כל היהודים:

(כא) לקים, וע"פ המבואר למעלה ראה מרדכי לחלק בין הפרזים להמוקפים, שהפרזים יעשו בי"ד והמוקפים בט"ו, ויש בזה טעם נכון, כי הגזרה של המן שהיה להשמיד ולאבד את כל היהודים ביום אחד, בודאי לא היתה מוגבלה לאמר שאין להם רשות להרוג רק ביום י"ג ואם יותרו יהודים אשר לא יהרגו ביום י"ג יהיו לפלטה, כי מחשבת המן היה להכחידם מגוי עד שלא יזכר שם ישראל עוד, ובודאי היה הכונה שביום י"ג יתחילו להשמידם בכל מדינות המלך, וכ"ש אם יתראה אח"כ יהודי אשר יסתר ביום י"ג יהרגוהו גם אח"כ, וכן אם עיר אחת ישגבו בה היהודים ביום י"ג ולא יוכלו להאבידם בו ביום שהיתה הפקודה שיהרגום אח"כ. עפ"ז אחר שבאו האגרות האחרונות אשר כתוב בם שיש רשות לישראל להרוג את צורריהם ביום י"ג, והרשות הזה היה נגבל רק על יום י"ג, כי לא היתה הפקודה שישמידו את כולם, והראיה שלא אסתר ברצותה שהיהודים אשר בשושן יהרגו גם ביום י"ד, הוצרך המלך ליתן ע"ז דת חדש כמ"ש ותנתן דת בשושן, כי הדת הראשון לא היה רק על יום אחד, וממילא כשהגיע יום י"ד היו היהודים בסכנה גדולה, כי אחר שהפקודה הראשונה של המן לא נבטלה, ובה ניתן הרשות להרוג את היהודים גם אחר יום י"ג, ואם היו האויבים קמים עליהם להרגם, לא היו השרים יכולים להצילם וליתן להם תוקף ללחום באויביהם כי התוקף שלהם נשלם ביום י"ד ומעתה פקודת המלך מצוה רק שאויבי היהודים ישלטו בם, לא המה בשונאיהם. ורק אחר שעבר יום י"ד וראו כי השרים העלימו הפקידה הראשונה לגמרי ואויביהם לא הרימו יד אז נודע עיקר הנס, מעתה אחר שעשו הפורים ביום שנחו מאויביהם הנה כל המוקפים לא נחו עד יום ט"ו, ולכן צוה שיעשו פורים ביום ט"ו, אבל הפרזים ששם לא היו השרים ולא צבא כלל, והם בעצמם גברה ידם על שונאיהם היה נודע להם שעבר הסכנה מאתם תיכף ביום י"ד, כי אחר שהתגברו בי"ג לא היו מפחדים עוד, ולכן תקן להם הפורים ביום י"ד:

השאלות

כ מהו ויכתוב את הדברים, מה היו הדברים:
כא ולמה צוה לעשות יום י"ד וט"ו, וביחוד זה נפלא מאד, וכי מפני שבשושן לא נחו עד יום ט"ו, צוה שבכל הערים המוקפות חומה יעשה פורים בט"ו, ומה טעם יש בזה מה להן ולשושן, ואם עשה זאת לכבוד עיר המלוכה היה לו לתקן שיהיה פורים בט"ו, וגם לא נודע מה כבוד יהיה בזה לשושן:

בימים

יוֹם־חֲמִשָּׁה עָשָׂר בּוֹ בְּכָל־שָׁנָה וְשָׁנָה׃ כב כַּיָּמִים אֲשֶׁר־
נָחוּ בָהֶם הַיְּהוּדִים מֵאֹיְבֵיהֶם וְהַחֹדֶשׁ אֲשֶׁר נֶהְפַּךְ לָהֶם
מִיָּגוֹן לְשִׂמְחָה וּמֵאֵבֶל לְיוֹם טוֹב לַעֲשׂוֹת אוֹתָם יְמֵי
מִשְׁתֶּה וְשִׂמְחָה וּמִשְׁלֹחַ מָנוֹת אִישׁ לְרֵעֵהוּ וּמַתָּנוֹת
לָאֶבְיֹנִים׃ כג וְקִבֵּל הַיְּהוּדִים אֵת אֲשֶׁר־הֵחֵלּוּ לַעֲשׂוֹת
וְאֵת אֲשֶׁר־כָּתַב מָרְדֳּכַי אֲלֵיהֶם׃ כד כִּי הָמָן בֶּן־הַמְּדָתָא
הָאֲגָגִי צֹרֵר כָּל־הַיְּהוּדִים חָשַׁב עַל־הַיְּהוּדִים לְאַבְּדָם
וְהִפִּל פּוּר הוּא הַגּוֹרָל לְהֻמָּם וּלְאַבְּדָם׃ כה וּבְבֹאָהּ לִפְנֵי
הַמֶּלֶךְ אָמַר עִם־הַסֵּפֶר יָשׁוּב מַחֲשַׁבְתּוֹ הָרָעָה אֲשֶׁר־
חָשַׁב עַל־הַיְּהוּדִים עַל־רֹאשׁוֹ וְתָלוּ אֹתוֹ וְאֶת־בָּנָיו עַל־

העץ

רש"י

כמות שהיא: (כד) כי המן בן המדתא. חשב להומם ולאבדם: (כה) ובבאה. אסתר אל המלך להתחנן לו: אמר עם הספר. אמר המלך בפיו וצוה לכתוב ספרים שתשוב מחשבתו הרעה בראשו:

על

השאלות

כב משמע שקבלו שני דברים מה שהחלו לעשות ומה שכתב מרדכי והלא שניהם היו דבר אחד שיעשו ימי משתה ושמחה:

כד מדוע ספר פה כי המן בן המדתא כו' וזה כבר נודע וידוע, ולמה אמר חשב לאבדם. והפיל פור להומם ולאבדם מוסיף להומם, ולמה הזכיר הפור:

כה המפ' נדחקו על מלת ובבאה שחסר מי הבא ומהו עם הספר שאין לו ביאור:

פירוש

(כב) **כימים אשר נחו**, ר"ל כ"א יעשה הפורים ביום שנח מאויביו, הפרזים בי"ד והמוקפים בט"ו, כנ"ל. ועתה מבאר למה צוה לעשות משתה ומשלוח מנות, אומר **והחדש אשר נהפך להם**, כי שני דברים נהפך להם בחדש הזה, א' מיגון לשמחה, וב' מאבל ליום טוב, ונגד השמחה יעשו ימי משתה ושמחה, ונגד היו"ט, שעתה לא יכול מרדכי לתקן שיעשו יו"ט, כי אסור לגזור על כלל ישראל יו"ט חדשים, תקן מתנות לאביונים, שזאת לא קבלו הפרזים מעצמם, כי תכלית היו"ט היה לפרוש בו מהבלי העולם לעבודת ה' ותורתו, וצוה נגד זה שיתנו לדקה שהוא ג"כ מצוה:

(כג) **וקבל**, עפ"ז מספר כל ישראל **קבלו** בין **מה שהחלו לעשות**, דהיינו הפרזים קבלו עליהם יום י"ד שהחלו לעשות בעצמם. ובין **מה שכתב מרדכי אליהם** שהמוקפים יעשו בט"ו שהם לא עשו בעצמם:

(כד) **כי המן**, עתה ספר מה שכתב מרדכי ומוסב עמ"ש בפסוק כ' ויכתוב מרדכי, הודיע להם תוקף הנס וענינו, א) בל ידמו שהיה השנאה רק עבור שמרדכי לא השתחוה להמן ולא היתה מגעת לכלל האומה, לז"א **כי המן** מגיד שהוא **אגגי** מזרע עמלק נטר איבת אבותיו, ומצד זה היה **צורר כל היהודים**, ורצה להכריתם בכלל, ב) **כי** גם המערכה היתה אז מתנגדת אל היהודים ועוזרת לרעתם, כי הוא לא **חשב** תחלה רק **לאבדם** שהוא לאבד עדת האומה ודתה כנ"ל, אבל בעת **שהפיל פור יצא** הגורל מצד המזל והמערכה של אותו החדש והיום להומם ג"כ ולהכחידם בהרג ואבדן:

(כה) **ובבאה**, עתה ספר איך מלבד שכבר היה הנס גדול מצד עצמו שהיה נגד המערכה והמזל, היה גדול נס ביום ההוא, כי **בבואה** מוסב על המחשבה שהזכיר בפסוק הקודם עת באה מחשבת המן לפני המלך, היינו עת שנודע להמלך מחשבתו כי יעץ רעה, ולא השיב את הספרים הראשונים, רק **אמר עם הספר** שעם הספר בעצמו **ישוב מחשבתו על ראשו**, שע"י שהמלך לא יכול להשיב הספר הקודם, רק השאיר הספרים הראשונים וכתב ספרים אחרים, וע"י כ"ז היה מוכרח לתלות את המן למען יבינו השרים פן יענשו גם המה, ולא יחושו להספרים הראשונים רק להאחרונים, ועפ"ז נודע להם כי הספרים הראשונים לא נבטלו, וממילא היה הנס בתקפו גם ביום י"ג אדר, כנ"ל:

על

הָעֵץ׃ כו עַל־כֵּן קָרְאוּ לַיָּמִים הָאֵלֶּה פוּרִים עַל־שֵׁם
הַפּוּר עַל־כֵּן עַל־כָּל־דִּבְרֵי הָאִגֶּרֶת הַזֹּאת וּמָה־רָאוּ עַל־
כָּכָה וּמָה הִגִּיעַ אֲלֵיהֶם׃ כז קִיְּמוּ וְקִבְּלוּ הַיְּהוּדִים עֲלֵיהֶם ׀
וְעַל־זַרְעָם וְעַל כָּל־הַנִּלְוִים עֲלֵיהֶם וְלֹא יַעֲבוֹר לִהְיוֹת
עֹשִׂים אֶת־שְׁנֵי הַיָּמִים הָאֵלֶּה כִּכְתָבָם וְכִזְמַנָּם בְּכָל־
שָׁנָה וְשָׁנָה׃ כח וְהַיָּמִים הָאֵלֶּה נִזְכָּרִים וְנַעֲשִׂים בְּכָל־
דּוֹר וָדוֹר מִשְׁפָּחָה וּמִשְׁפָּחָה מְדִינָה וּמְדִינָה וְעִיר וָעִיר
וִימֵי הַפּוּרִים הָאֵלֶּה לֹא יַעַבְרוּ מִתּוֹךְ הַיְּהוּדִים וְזִכְרָם
לֹא־יָסוּף מִזַּרְעָם׃ ס כט וַתִּכְתֹּב אֶסְתֵּר הַמַּלְכָּה בַת־
אֲבִיחַיִל וּמָרְדֳּכַי הַיְּהוּדִי אֶת־כָּל־תֹּקֶף לְקַיֵּם אֵת אִגֶּרֶת

°וקבל כתיב °ת׳ רבתי

הפרים

שפתי חכמים

כשושן קאי ג״כ אמוקפין חומה דהיינו שיהיו מוקפין חומה מימות אחשורוש כשושן לכ״פ והיקף זה צריך שיהיה מימות יהושע בן נון כך דרשו ולמדו רז״ל כנ״ש בפ״ק דמגילה ע״ש: ש וקשה הרי תרגומו לא ישתיצי וטעות הוא ברש״י, וה״ג לא יסוף תרגום עד סוף ודברי רש״י הוא שמפרש לא יסוף לא יתום וכ״ה בספרים מדוייקים, ויותר נראה לגרום לא יסוף לא יתום דמתרגם עד תום עד דסף: ת דק״ל את תוקף מבע״ל מאי כל תוקף תקפו של טולם:

חסלת מגלת אסתר

רש״י

(כו) על כן על כל דברי האגרת הזאת. מקנש הימים האלה ולכך נכתבה לדעת דורות הבאים: ומה ראו. עושי המעשים האלה שעשאום: ומה הגיע אליהם. מה ראה אחשורוש שנשתמש בכלי הקודש ומה הגיע אליהם שבא שטן ורקד ביניהם והרג את ושתי. מה ראה המן שנתקנא במרדכי ומה הגיע אליו שתלו אותו ואת בניו. מה ראה מרדכי שלא יכרע ולא ישתחוה ומה ראתה אסתר שזימנה להמן: (כז) הנלוים עליהם. גרים העתידים להתגייר: ככתבם. שתהא המגילה כתובה כתב אשורית: (כח) נזכרים. בקריאת מגילה: ונעשים. משתה ושמחה ויום טוב לתת מנות ומתנות: משפחה ומשפחה. מתאספין יחד ואוכלים ושותין יחד וכך קבלו עליהם שימי הפורים לא יעברו: וזכרם. קריאת מגילה: לא יסוף. תרגום שלא ש יתום דמתרגם עד תום עד דסף, וא״א לומר להיות מגזרת (בראשית יט) פן תספה ומגזרת (ש״א כז) עתה אספה יום אחד שא״כ הי״ל לכתוב לא יִסָּפֶה מזרעם: (כט) את כל תקף. תקפו של ת נס של אחשורוש ושל

פירוש

(כו) על כן באר שהשם שקראו לימים האלה פורים, היה על שם הפור להיות לזכר לתקפו של נס שהשם פורים מורה עליו שפור המן נהפך לפורע כי המזל היה אז נגד ישראל ונהפך בהשגחת ה׳ המסדר המערכות: על כן מוסב למטה ור״ל ועל כל דברי האגרת הזאת שהודיע להם הכל בפרטות איך היה הנס בתקפו גם באותו יום כי ע״י האגרת נודע להם מה ראו על ככה וכל הענין בפרטות:

(כז) קימו, לכן קימו וקבלו, א) שיהיה קבלת הפורים כולל גם לדורות הבאים אחריהם, ועז״א עליהם ועל זרעם, ב) ולא יעבור שלא ידמה לשאר גזרות שגזרו חכמים שב״ד אחר הגדול בחכמה ובמנין יכול לבטל דברי ב״ד חברו, אבל בזה התנו שלא יעבור ויתבטל בשום אופן, ג) להיות עושין שני הימים פרזים בי״ד ומוקפים בט״ו, ד) וככתבם בקריאת המגילה:

(כח) והימים נזכרים ע״י קריאת המגילה, ונעשים ע״י משתה ושמחה ומשלוח מנות בכל דור ודור:

(כט) ותכתוב, המבואר מזה כי אסתר רצתה שהמגלה הזאת תשלך בין הכתובים ועמדה ע״ז מחלוקה

השאלות

כו ומה הכונה בקריאת השם, וכפל ע״כ על כל דברי האגרת וכו׳ שאין לו באור:

כז מהו ולא יעבור, ומהו ככתבם וכזמנם:

כט למה כתבה אסתר שנית, ומהו כל תוקף, ומה היתה האגרת השנית מה הוסיף בשנית על הראשונה:

כן

הַפֻּרִים הַזֹּאת הַשֵּׁנִית׃ ל וַיִּשְׁלַח סְפָרִים אֶל־כָּל־הַיְּהוּדִים
אֶל־שֶׁבַע וְעֶשְׂרִים וּמֵאָה מְדִינָה מַלְכוּת אֲחַשְׁוֵרוֹשׁ
דִּבְרֵי שָׁלוֹם וֶאֱמֶת׃ לא לְקַיֵּם אֶת־יְמֵי הַפֻּרִים הָאֵלֶּה
בִּזְמַנֵּיהֶם כַּאֲשֶׁר קִיַּם עֲלֵיהֶם מָרְדֳּכַי הַיְּהוּדִי וְאֶסְתֵּר
הַמַּלְכָּה וְכַאֲשֶׁר קִיְּמוּ עַל־נַפְשָׁם וְעַל־זַרְעָם דִּבְרֵי
הַצּוֹמוֹת וְזַעֲקָתָם׃ לב וּמַאֲמַר אֶסְתֵּר קִיַּם דִּבְרֵי הַפֻּרִים
הָאֵלֶּה וְנִכְתָּב בַּסֵּפֶר׃ ס
א וַיָּשֶׂם הַמֶּלֶךְ אֲחַשְׁוֵרוֹשׁ° מַס עַל־הָאָרֶץ וְאִיֵּי הַיָּם׃
ב וְכָל־מַעֲשֵׂה תָקְפּוֹ וּגְבוּרָתוֹ וּפָרָשַׁת גְּדֻלַּת

°אחשרש כתיב

מרדכי

רש"י

של המן ושל מרדכי ושל אסתר: הפרים. לשנה הבאה חזרו ושלחו ספרים שיעשו פורים: (לב) ומאמר אסתר קיים וגו'. אסתר בקשה מאת חכמי הדור לקבעה ולכתוב ספר זה עם שאר הכתובים. וזהו ונכתב

השאלות

ל מהו דברי שלום ואמת:

לא מהו דברי הצומות וזעקתם לא נודע מה הם הצומות האלה, וביחוד הלא כבר נזכר שקיימו וקבלו ומה היה צריך עוד בזירוז הזה:

לב מהו ומאמר אסתר קיים שאין לו באור:

א למה שם מס, ולמה מספרו פה: ומה ענין להמגלת תקפו וגבורותו של אחשורוש:

פירוש

בין ההכמים כי אסור להוסיף על כתבי הקודש. וכמ"ש חז"ל במגלה ששלחה אסתר להחכמים קבעוני לדורות והחכמים לא רצו בתחלה, וכן נפל תלונה על קבלת הימים האלה לחק קבוע, שעוברים על בל תוסיף, ומצד זה הוצרכה אסתר להשתתף עם מרדכי וכתבה בתוקף המלכות אשר בידה **לקיים את אגרת הפורים הזאת השנית**, הוא קיום האגרת בעצמו, כי אז שלחה את המגלה כמו שהיא עתה בידינו, מן ויהי בימי אחשורוש עד סופו, וכתבה אל החכמים שיקיימו את אגרת הזאת להיות דינו ככתבי הקדש:

(ל) **וישלח ספרים דברי שלום ואמת**, שלעומת שעמדה ע"ז מחלוקת כתבה דברים לעשות שלום בין ההכמים ולבקש את האמת לפי ההלכה שדבריה נכונים:

(לא) **לקיים**, ונגד מה שהתלוננו על ימי הפורים שא"א להוסיף מועד מדעתו ולקבעו להק עולם על ישראל, השיבה שאינו עובר על בל תוסיף רק אם מקבלו מצד דין תורה ורוצה להשוותם בכל עניניו כדין תורה, לא אם מקבלו מצד הנדר וכדומה (כמ"ש הרמב"ם (הלכות ממרים), ולכן אמרה שלא יקבלום מצד דין תורה רק **כאשר קים עליהם מרדכי ואסתר** מצד הנדר לא זולת. והביאו ראיה לזה ממה **שקיימו וקבלו תחלה הארבעה צומות**, שהם מדברי קבלה, כמ"ש צום הרביעי וצום החמישי וצום העשירי (זכריה ח') והלא גם זה היא הוספה על דברי תורה, וקבלום עליהם כל ישראל, מבואר שיש רשות להוסיף גזרות כאלה מצד נדר לבד:

(לב) **ומאמר** ע"פ מאמרי אסתר אלה וטענותיה שכתבה אל חכמי הדור ההוא, **נתקיים דברי הפורים האלה**, הסכימו אליה להחזיק בהפורים ולעשותו חק עולם, וזאת שנית **ונכתב בספר**. שהסכימו שיכתב בספר ותהיה המגלה הזאת בכלל כתבי הקדש, שע"ז היה מחלוקת תחלה בין החכמים ועתה נתקיים והסכימו לדברי אסתר:

י (א) **וישם**, מספר איך הצליח מרדכי בהנהגתו בעניני המלוכה שכבש מדינות רבות בחיל המלך עד ששם המלך מס על כל הארצות הסמוכים אל מלכותו, וגם על איי הים הרחוקים. וייחסו להמלך מצד כבודו כי באמת היה מרדכי העושה זאת:

(ב) **וכל מעשה תקפו**, שעשה ע"י הנהגת מרדכי ואיך ע"כ גדלו המלך מבואר בספר דברי הימים:

[אברבר] עד

מָרְדֳּכַי אֲשֶׁר גִּדְּלוֹ הַמֶּלֶךְ הֲלוֹא־הֵם כְּתוּבִים עַל־סֵפֶר
דִּבְרֵי הַיָּמִים לְמַלְכֵי מָדַי וּפָרָס׃ ג כִּי ׀ מָרְדֳּכַי הַיְּהוּדִי
מִשְׁנֶה לַמֶּלֶךְ אֲחַשְׁוֵרוֹשׁ וְגָדוֹל לַיְּהוּדִים וְרָצוּי לְרֹב אֶחָיו
דֹּרֵשׁ טוֹב לְעַמּוֹ וְדֹבֵר שָׁלוֹם לְכָל־זַרְעוֹ׃

סכום פסוקי מגלת אסתר מאה ושסים ושבעה. וסימן על כן קראו לימים האלה פורים. וסדריו עשרה. והסימן בא גד. וחציו ותען אסתר ותאמר:

רש"י

תכתב בספר: (ג) **לרב אחיו.** ולא לכל אחיו מלמד שפירשו ממנו מקצת סנהדרין לפי שנעשה קרוב למלכות והיה בטל מתלמודו: **לכל זרעו.** טובת כל עמו לכל זרע עמו:

חסלת מגלת אסתר

פירוש

(ג) עד שמרדכי נשאר בתקפו ולא נשכחה הצלחתו, צדיקים יירשו ארץ וישכנו לעד עליה (תהלים לז), והגם שהיה משנה על כל המדינה וממונה על היהודים בפרסות, מ"מ היה רצוי לרוב אחיו, **כי** היה בכל ענייניו **דורש אך טוב לעמו.** ולא התנהג עמם בתוקף וחזקה רק בשלום ובמישור: